MIDLAND GENEI

with

Notts & Derby

by
Alan Oxley

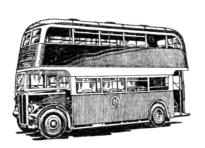

Robin Hood Publishing

**Attenborough Notts
NG9 6AP**

Other transport titles by the Publisher

Barton 100
Barton (part two and three)
East from Huddersfield by Bus
Huddersfield Corporation Buses
Hulley's
South Notts
Trent (part one, two and three)
West Bridgford

Front Cover

Guy Arab II 5LW No.415 (GRR 62) with Weymann lowbridge bodywork, rebuilt by Bond in 1953. For some unknown reason this former MDT bus was visiting the East Midland, Chesterfield, New Street garage on the 1st June 1957, at the time of their livery change. In the background can be seen AEC Regal III/Weymann B31R (KAL 130) No.A10 in the original chrome yellow and chocolate colours and to the left are the rear of buses repainted in red and ivory.

Opposite

An evocative WW2 view of Cotmanhay Road, Cotmanhay featuring both forms of transportation; No.182 a 1938 AEC Regent/Weymann and No. 318 AEC661T/MCCW trolleybus. The white cottage in the background was demolished c1946 for the provision of a roundabout and access to a new housing estate.

ISBN 978 0 948854 19 4
© April 2009 Alan Oxley
Softback edition of ISBN 0 948854 19 7
first published 1999

Designed and published by

ROBIN HOOD PUBLISHING

MIDLAND GENERAL

with

NOTTS. & DERBY TRACTION Co.

CONTENTS

In presenting this reprint of the book first published in 1999 I decided to keep everything as the original, taking the opportunity to correct a few typos and modernise the preamble layout. Also it has now been possible to amend JT Boam's fleet details and thanks to David Fletcher to identify the location of the tram on page 18. To bring everything up-to-date with the story Ilkeston depot did indeed close in 2000, as foreseen in Mr Brian King's foreword to the book, and is now lost beneath the Tesco supermarket in the town. Alfreton was subsequently sold to become a social enterprise business and leisure centre with café and crèche all contained within the outer skin of the bus depot as rebuilt in 1976.

And in conclusion Mr King has provided an updated version of the

'Postscript' on page 64: Both companies still survive under the Wellglade umbrella, and in April 1998 NDT became operational again, originally trading as 'Blue Apple', with a low cost operation using vehicles cascaded down from the main fleet. Initially providing transport for students at the University of Derby more work has been obtained with various authorities. Schools, contract and local bus work was transferred from Barton Buses Ltd (Barton Transport operations and vehicles being acquired in July 1989). So NDT lives on, and during 2005 the MGO name was introduced on some vehicles working out of Hucknall on low cost operation. In July 2008 MGO also acquired the assets and trading name of Derby Community Transport operating from Meadow Road, Derby.

Within a few years The Midland General Omnibus Co Ltd, (MGO) had firmly established its own territory, which basically served the heavily industrialised Erewash Valley, and in fact drove a wedge between the Trent Motor Traction area on the Nottinghamshire and Derbyshire borders. Most of this was achieved by acquiring many small independent bus companies, who were only too glad to sell up when the 1930 Road Traffic Act was implemented. However, the earliest developments were provided by Nottinghamshire and Derbyshire Tramways Company (NDT) which became a part of the Balfour Beatty group in 1912, who had interests in other tramway systems and electricity supplies. When the tramway became unviable, Balfour Beatty introduced

the trolleybus, which continued to give them a customer for their own electricity, provided at a significantly reduced price.

The nationalisation of the electricity supply companies, also saw the Balfour Beatty bus companies being sold out, although not surrendered readily, the East Midlands companies eventually became a part of the Tilling Group within the British Transport Commission.

I have derived a lot pleasure from writing this book and trust it gives an insight into not only MGO and NDT but the locality also.

Alan Oxley   April 2009

The overhead turning circle at the Ilkeston, Rutland Hotel junction of Manor Road, Granby Street and Heanor Road. The short lived waiting room, for the interchange facility between bus and tram, was in the single storey shop on Granby Street to the right of the picture. No.89 TSM B39A7 with Beadle body had worked in along Heanor Road, possibly from Mansfield, and No.315 an AEC-EEC with EEC body turns into Granby Street. Note the rear destination display and large fleet numbers, whilst at the front they had been replaced by metal plate numbers .

Chapter One: Revolution

The border area of Nottinghamshire and Derbyshire which are divided by the River Erewash, was a part of the largest coal field in Britain. Unfortunately in the 18th and 19th Centuries some delightful scenery was ravaged by the spoil heaps, pit heads and smoke filled towns, although by the nineteen nineties most of the area had returned to its original state.

It was this mineral rich area which attracted the industrialists, and entrepreneurs, but more interestingly the imaginative engineers. The first rail tracks in England were at Wollaton and Strelley. In Richard Smith's 'England's first rails; A reconsideration' from 'Renaissance and modern studies Vol. IV Item VI,1960, (University of Nottingham) he dates these being laid at Wollaton between October 1603 and October 1604. They were wooden rails which horses dragged carts along from the Wollaton and Strelley coal workings through Wollaton to Wollaton Lane. It is thought, but not proven, that it was extended to the river Trent? Ordnance Survey Sheet 71 top quarter published on 1st July 1839 shows two tram roads in existence, serving pits in Strelley.

It is often believed that the Outrams, a local family with strong engineering connections, gave their name, by omitting the first two letters, to become 'tram' road or tramway. However, as Neil Cossons states in 'The BP Book of Industrial Archaeology', the word is possibly derived from the old German or Scandinavian word for a beam of wood, a 'traam'.

However, the Alfreton and Belper Journal of 22nd February 1901 gives an interesting, if not correct, account of the family from which the following has been abstracted; James (Joseph?) Outram born in 1733, was an engineer, surveyor and iron master who resided in Alfreton. He was largely employed by the Duke of Norfolk surveying his various properties. It was he who advised the Duke to pull up the whole of the wooden way at the Sheffield colliery and lay his own design of cast iron plates. Cast in the shape of the letter L, these were spiked down to cross wooden sleepers to maintain the gauge of five feet on the outside of the rail. They were made in his foundry at Ripley in 1775 and laid the following year. Almost immediately it was found that fewer horses and drivers were needed and a riot ensued: the plates were torn up and the sleepers burnt. Outram then designed hollow cast iron boxes one foot square and six inches deep, upon which the plates were laid. This worked for a short time until rioters again smashed the boxes. Benjamin Outram, who had now joined his father as an engineer, decided to substitute solid stone for the boxes, which could not be damaged or easily stolen.

Outram-ways were so successful they were installed widely, and within the East Midlands examples remained in use at the Little Eaton Gangway linking the Derby Canal with Denby Colliery, from 1795 until 1908 and the Ashby-de-la-Zouch to Ticknall plateway (having flanged wheels rather than the rails). This was in use from 1802, with a section remaining open until 1916 and parts are still visible today.

Benjamin Outram formed Benjamin Outram & Co in 1790. One of his three partners was William Jessop a canal and rail engineer of some considerable repute. (This business eventually became the Butterley Company.) A little known Outram-way was also built from the Butterley Works at Ripley

William Brunton's Mechanical Traveller

following the main road through Kilburn to Derby. It was at these ironworks that a later engineer William Brunton patented the mechanical traveller in 1813. This locomotive had a pair of legs and claw like feet working alternately like a horse which pushed the engine and boiler which were mounted on four wheels. A second engine was sold to the Newcastle Colliery working successfully until the boiler burst killing thirteen onlookers, during a demonstration.

In the Erewash Valley over forty horse plateways were laid between pits and the local canals. The first steam railways in the area were built with the prime intention of moving coal. The first line in the area was opened by the Midland Railway and worked through the Erewash Valley to Leicester and London. Branch lines were later built between Basford and Bennerley Junction to link two main lines and from Butterley to Langley Mill. The Great Northern Railway later built a Basford to Eggington Junction line with a branch from Awsworth Junction to Pinxton. The competing lines ran very closely to each other and had rather chequered lives.

After the Light Railway Act of 1896 various prospectuses were introduced by tram companies, who had in mind the potential passenger traffic in a highly populated area.

Eventually the Notts & Derby Tramways Co built what was claimed to be the longest through tramway line in the British Isles, except parts of the Glasgow system, when the Ripley to Nottingham route opened in 1913, serving a population of 48.000. However, this was achieved after considerable delays and when a substantial amount of capital had been injected into the company. It is of interest to go back to the early days and follow to see how the system came into being.

1901

The Erewash Valley Light Railway Company prepared details of a tramway which had one main route from Alfreton to Nottingham via Ripley and Cinderhill, with a Heanor to Ilkeston link. This would have been built to standard gauge, with a third rail on the part covering the existing 3ft. 6in gauge of the Ilkeston Corporation's system. The overall length was almost 18 miles.

A proposal which appeared in the press on the 11th October for a light railway between Nottingham, Long Eaton and Derby, with a line to Alfreton from Long Eaton, Ilkeston, Heanor and Ripley may have been the original Nottinghamshire & Derbyshire tramways 1902 scheme.

The Derby & Nottingham Light Railways Company proposed three routes all based on Long Eaton: (1) Chilwell, Beeston,and Lenton to join the Nottingham Corporation tracks. (2) Draycott, Borrowash, and to Chaddesden to join the Derby Corporation system (3) Sandiacre, and Stapleford joining the Ikeston system near the boundary. It was to be built built in standard gauge except for the Ilkeston route which was to be 3ft. 6in with mixed gauge in Long Eaton.

Mansfield and District Light Railways Company was authorised in 1889 to construct the town system in 3ft.6in gauge (actually built by Notts & Derbyshire Tramways in 1905 to standard gauge), and applied in 1901 for extensions. These were from Huthwaite, one of the five authorised routes radiating from Mansfield, to Ripley, Heage and Belper, plus a Ripley to Heanor and Ilkeston extension.

During November the Nottingham Suburban Light Railway proposed the extension of the existing Nottingham Corporation tracks from Sherwood to Arnold, from Thorneywood to Carlton, from Bulwell to Hucknall and from Nottingham to Trowell (Church).

1902

The influential Midland Railway opposed at least two of the above schemes and they were refused the go-ahead by the Light Railway Commissioners.

It may have been from this that the Nottinghamshire and Derbyshire Tramways Bill decided to promote 79 miles of standard gauge track again linking with or passing through the three local authorities of Nottingham, Derby and Ilkeston. This covered all the Mansfield, Erewash Valley and Derby & Nottingham proposals, plus an extension to Derby and Duffield from Belper, Stapleford and Bramcote to Beeston, Trowell and Wollaton to Nottingham, and Cinderhill to Radford. There were

three extensions to existing Nottingham Corporation routes- Bulwell to Hucknall, Sherwood to Arnold, Sneinton to Carlton, of which the last two were extended by Nottingham Corporation at a later date.

1903

Revisions to the act saw the abandonment of sections and reduction of the mileage to just over 37. The remaining parts were; Huthwaite (linking into the Mansfield system) to Heanor and Alfreton Road/Bentinck Road Nottingham, with a Ripley to Belper extension, and two connecting Pye Bridge lines. Around Nottingham were three extensions to existing Nottingham Corporation (NCT) lines:- Beeston to Lenton, Sherwood to Arnold and Sneinton to Carlton.

On the 16th May the Ilkeston Corporation Tramways opened their system.

The Nottinghamshire & Derbyshire Tramways Company (NDT) was incorporated by an Act of Parliament on the 11th August. An application for Debenture Stock was issued offering £30.000 in stock (in part of the company's borrowing powers) bearing interest at 5% per annum.

1904

The first board meeting of NDT was held at the offices of the Engineers-Braithwaite & Harris, 5 Great Central Street, Westminster, London, on Monday 1st February. Walter McLaren was appointed Chairman, A T C.Worsley Secretary and amongst those in attendance was Alfred R Holland who was appointed a director. Six hundred and twenty £10 shares were allotted of which The British Power Co Ltd, took up 300. Local offices of the company were established at Queens Chambers, King Street, Nottingham. A draft agreement between NDT and the Nottinghamshire & Derbyshire Tramways Development Co Ltd, provided payment by NDT to the Development Co, for expenses incurred in respect of the Mansfield undertaking, the Tramways Act and payment of remuneration. An advance of £4.000 was deposited before commencing construction of the Mansfield section, against the borrowing power of £30.000. On the 2nd November George D Prince was appointed Secretary to replace A T C Worsley.

1905

A new bill was approved by the Board, to extend the time limit for the purchase of lands and for the construction and completion of the tramways, street widenings and works authorised in the N&DT Act of 1903.

1906

The new bill was approved on the 9th February and was passed unopposed in both Houses of Parliament on the 10th July.

At the board meeting on the 30th October, it was decided to close the Nottingham office (the terminus of the later trolleybus system was to be very close to this building), at the soonest possible time. It was also agreed that the Development Co, accounts would be settled once the new Mansfield company had been floated. Alfred Holland took over the chairmanship.

The Newark & District Light Railway Co, a subsidiary of the Derbyshire and Nottinghamshire Electric Power Co, was authorised to build 3.5 miles of tramway. The proposed three legs in the township were to serve the GNR station, Balderton and Farndon. The rights were eventually owned by Balfour Beatty & Co Ltd, who allowed the powers on this system to lapse.

1907

The office was transferred to 53 Temple Chambers, Temple Avenue, London EC for both NDT and the Development Co. This was the base of G Prince who provided both secretarial services and office accommodation.

The following month it was decided to apply to Parliament in the coming session for an extension Act to keep the company alive. It was agreed a Short Bill be presented after conferring with Nottingham Corporation .

1908

An agreement was reached with Nottingham Corporation on the 22nd May. This saw the transfer of the extension routes around the City in the NDT Bill of 1903 to Nottingham. The biggest change was the abandonment of all other routes except the Ripley, Heanor to Nottingham route, which instead of travelling directly via Nuthall Road to Alfreton

Road/Bentinck Road was now diverted through Dark Lane (private right of way), Stockhill Lane, Percy Street, Alpine Street, High Street (now Basford Road) and Church Street, to join NCT tracks at Radford Road. This relieved the Company of an obligation under the 1903 Act when it was then intended to construct tramways inside the City and leased them to NCT at the equivalent of only 2.25% return on the capital invested. This proved to be quite onerous and prevented the Company from raising any capital. However, this later agreement saw the NCT take over powers to construct the lines within the City and the direct neighbourhood. When constructed the City would lease to NDT at a rent of 5% on the cost for a period of 42 years. NDT were to pay the cost of maintaining the line and would be given running powers into Nottingham, via Radford Road, Bentinck Road, Alfreton Road, Derby Road, to Upper Parliament Street. At the same time the NCT had an option to take similar running powers for a similar distance on the Company's lines outside the City (which was never exercised).

1909

Little progress was made except for agreements on road widenings, one being Rock House, Stockhill Lane, Basford.

Balfour Beatty & Co Ltd, was formed during the year by A H Beatty and George Balfour with offices at 22A College Hill, Cannon St, London EC, shared with J G White & Co Ltd. Beatty had been a director of Cavehill and Mansfield tramways and also Secretary to J G White, a British subsidiary of an American firm, with interests in engineering, and as civil engineers constructing tramways. They leased the Dartford and Luton tram systems, which Balfour Beatty took over in 1909. Balfour had been a director of tramway companies at Broughty Ferry, Dumbarton, Fife and Mansfield. Later they were to have a considerable affect on the future of NDT. At this time they formed the Halesowen Lighting & Traction Co Ltd, to take over the powers of the local Rural District Council who had the authorisation for 10.75 miles of track. However, nothing was constructed and British Electric Traction Co, (BET) purchased the company around 1918.

The lack of a tram service encouraged the Heanor Tradesmen's Association to approach Commercial Car Hirers (CCH) requesting a bus service to encourage the folk of Langley Mill to shop at Heanor. Because of a very steep hill into the town, shoppers had preferred to walk into Eastwood. A service commenced on the 21st December between Ripley, Codnor, Heanor, Eastwood, Nuthall, Basford and Nottingham, with financial guarantees to cover the first two weeks.

1910

During early February CCH withdrew the Ripley to Nottingham service following the none too successful experiment. High fares and extreme weather conditions contributed to the failure, although CCH did offer to hire a vehicle to the association, which was not taken up. CCH who were London based, did have premises in Alfreton and were the precursors of Trent Motor Traction.

On the 22nd June the Chairman of NDT reported negotiations with a new company and on the 27th October the office was moved to 22A College Hill to share with Balfour Beatty & J G White! They also applied for powers to compulsorily purchase land required under the agreement schedule of the 1903 Act

1911

A Bill prepared to extend time on the 1908 Act, was passed through both Houses unopposed and Royal assent given on the 18th August. Following negotiations with Balfour Beatty the disposal of shares in a new company was accepted by the NDT Board. Ripley UDC opposed the Bill, as the roads were to be widened but the pavements narrowed. However, after satisfactory clauses had been inserted they withdrew their objections.

1912

Balfour Beatty formed the Tramways Light & Power Co Ltd, (TLP) who issued their prospectus on 9th December to raise £600.000 share capital to acquire the Derbyshire & Nottinghamshire Electric Power Company, Nottinghamshire and Derbyshire Tramways Company, Leicestershire and Warwickshire Electric Power Company, and Leamington & Warwick Electrical Co Ltd. The two power companies provided electric power supplies to the townships on the borders of the named counties from power stations at Ilkeston and Hinckley. It was hoped electricity for lighting would be provided during the early part of 1913. Leamington &Warwick provided electricity to its own tramway and a large number of private consumers from its own power station, which TLP would transform to a sub-station and then take the supply from Hinckley. The tramway which was purchased from BET in December, operated between Leamington and Warwick and from 1905 it was worked by electric traction. The tramway was just over three miles long, serving a population of 40.000. The prospectus also stated that contracts had been entered into with Balfour Beatty for the construction and equipping of the NDT tramway. It went on to say the tramway was to be completed to the Nottingham boundary on or before the 31st May 1913, by which date the the connecting lines to Nottingham should be constructed by the Corporation. No reference was made of the Carlisle, Llanelly, Mansfield or Newark Tramways, which came under TLP control possibly at a slightly later date.

On the 30th December the NDT Chairman reported that the Development Co, had executed on behalf of NDT documents in connection with the transfer of issued debenture scrip and shares of the company to the Tramways Light & Power Co Ltd (TLP). The TLP were to make advances for payments by NDT to contractors. It is thought the NDT Development Co, ceased as from this date.

Chapter Two:
Act 7-Curtain Rises

1913

Suddenly things were happening, Balfour Beatty recommended the ordering of 24 tram cars, half of which were to have top covers at the cost of £100 per car. On the 20th January the order was confirmed.

Two days later the Board reported W C Hawfayne had been appointed engineer. Widenings had commenced, in particular at Nuthall. The first shipment of rails had been made and land for the car shed at Langley Mill arranged with the Butterley Company. Application to build the car shed was submitted to Heanor UDC during February, and they held a special meeting to approve this as the NDT were anxious to proceed. The site being situated on the south side of Station Road, between Bailey Brook and the Midland Railway crossing, on the Derbyshire side of the county boundaries. The brick building ran parallel to the road, with side access for six tracks each for four cars with pits running the length of each with a 4 foot wide gangway between.

During February an unsuccessful petition to Parliament was produced against a Bill promoted by Nottingham Corporation which gave them powers to operate motor buses within the city boundary, trolley vehicles on certain routes, and extend the tramway

The headquarters of NDT were transferred to 66 Queen Street, London EC, which also became the new headquarters for the Balfour Beatty group.

As was to be expected Heanor UDC meetings were full of tramway business. The Council approached NDT regarding further road widenings, but the company stated they would only carry out those found necessary under the Act. A letter was received by the local authority from the Church Council of St. Andrews, Langley Mill, asking them to use their influence in persuading the NDT to lay wood blocks in front of the church, as they understood it to be an important stopping place. They felt if wood blocks were used it would not cause annoyance during divine worship. In reply the NDT secretary G D Prince stated they could not see their way to laying wood block paving, particularly as the rest of the area was not paved with wood blocks. He also pointed out that there would be very little annoyance from the granite setts, as the tramway was in the middle of the road and any additional noise that might be caused by vehicular traffic would be exceedingly little during times of worship. The Council decided to write again but nothing further was reported. At Codnor excavations had remained open a month, with rope as the only protection for the public, but Sunday working had been the biggest upset with thirty or forty carts conveying granite setts all over the district. The noise from this was such that nothing could be heard during church services. One of the councillors asked the Clerk to request Sunday work be stopped, because Sunday observance was a matter of British Statute. The Clerk reminded him that the statute applied only to certain trades. Further complaints arose from the length of time the roads were left open, and the storage of rails by the side of the road to save on wharfage. They alleged kerbstones and channels were being relaid in mud, although the councillors were assured by the Surveyor that everything would be completed to his satisfaction. Yet another incident reported stated that one Sunday twelve horse and carts passed along the roads, with the accompaniment of the usual carters language, much to the annoyance of the residents of Langley Mill.

The Heanor Tradesmen's Association was unhappy with the irregular manner that the poles were being erected and asked that the company inconvenienced the public as little as possible!

Heanor was not on its own as all the other authorities along the line listed similar complaints, which increased further when the electric company started laying power cables for domestic use.

However, NDT did take Ripley UDC to task over complaints of road reinstatements, when they complained that nothing had been done in the way of road repairs for over twelve months, and they should think more of give-and-take!

Ripley UDC questioned the position of the terminus which had been laid out by the contractors beyond Cooperative Square to halfway across Booth Street. The Chairman advised the body of the chamber that he had a little whiff of the situation and when he looked at the plans they were correct. The question was did they call the terminus the line for empty cars or where the people alighted at Cooperative Square. He suggested letting the matter rest. In fact, the single line fanned out in Cooperative Square, to form two tracks, which would have formed a passing loop if the next section of the tramway had been proceeded with.

The company were not surprisingly upset at all the comments, having spent £54.770 on widenings and improvements to the roads alone. This had involved road widenings at seventy five different points, they also widened or strengthened seventeen bridges, along the route. Four crossovers were provided at railway crossings serving collieries. Of this capital spent £24.000 was expended on road repairs under the Tramways Act of 1870. This law covered horse trams, which required that as horses wore a groove down the middle of the track, they were called upon to make good between the tracks and 18 inches on either side of the outside line. This work being carried out it in accordance with the Tramways Act, as was the general practice, in granite setts.

The Eastwood & Kimberley Advertiser was far more objective about the installations as detailed in the following abstracts of an interesting article dated the 27th June:- The road widenings consequent of the tramway scheme have caused improvements all along the route from Cinderhill, on the environs of Nottingham, to Ripley. Opposite to Heanor Church the new order has caused considerable displacement

One of the twelve covered top cars, photographed at the Preston works of United Electric, prior to despatch to Langley Mill for the final fitting out.

to ancient properties and the White Hart Inn has disappeared altogether. Next to this house has stood for over 200 years another licensed house, formerly the Admiral Rodney. A decade ago a fatal broil took place with which the name of Admiral Rodney became connected, as a result the sign was changed to that of the Crown. With the installation of the tramways the front half of the house has been demolished. The public house continued to remain open which presented a grotesque appearance. The hostess Mrs S Lomax accepts the situation with a good deal equanimity and laughingly admits she has but Half a Crown instead of a Crown, but she has less cleaning to do!

Heanor UDC contacted the Derbys & Notts Electric Power Co regarding lighting to the tram route. They were informed that in the most important parts a fifty candle power lamp suspended from each tram pole (every forty yards) would give satisfactory illumination. For less frequented parts one lamp every second pole would be sufficient. Upon hearing the price named they decided not to proceed further.

The 24 tram cars, which been delivered by rail direct, were assembled at Langley Mill. They were built by the United Electric Car Co, of Preston, with large four window saloons, and fitted with Peckham P22 Pendulum trucks of a new and improved type, having an 8ft wheel base. The 40 hp type GE 67-3T motors and type K10D controllers, two of each fitted per car, were provided by BTH of Rugby. Although the route was hilly, only normal hand operated wheel and track brakes were fitted. Of these Nos.1-12 were open top with canopies but not vestibuled. Nos.13-24 having covered tops with verandah ends. Seating was standard wooden benches in the lower saloon for 24 passengers and wooden garden seats arranged two and one on the upper deck for 32. Illuminated roller blind destination indicators were fixed to the balcony railings and wooden boards along the side, just above the waistrail, displayed the route details.

Navy blue serge double breasted uniforms were typical of the period. Peak caps were also provided with white metal badges inscribed with motorman or conductor, whilst inspector was embroidered in script. An NDT badge was placed on each epaulette For summer white cap covers were issued. Drivers who were open to the elements, were issued with oilskins as protection against the inclement weather.

The drivers, many of whom were seconded from

Workers take a rest during the completion work on the open top UEC cars at Langley Mill. Six cars are visible and it is possible to identify No. 12 on the left and Nos 11 and 10 to the right

The first tram to arrive at Co-operative Square Ripley was greeted by a gathering of townsfolk and dignitaries.

other Balfour Beatty systems, were paid 6d (2.5p) per hour and the conductors 4d per hour.

Tramcars were running between Loscoe and Kimberley from July to familiarise staff with the operation, only six months after work had started on the scheme.

On Thursday the 7th August Lieut-Col Druitt on behalf of the Board of Trade, inspected the standard gauge (4ft.8½in.)single tram track with passing loops approximately every 300 yards. It is assumed this was passed without any problem as on the 7th August the first portion of the system opened between Cinderhill and Crosshill.

One or two trial cars resplendent in their standard Balfour Beatty livery of light green, cream and gold lining, ran on the 15th August, from Crosshill to Cooperative Square, Ripley. A large crowd gathered at the terminus to see the Inspector and officials travel in two cars on the new section. A tour was then made of the whole route to Cinderhill and upon the return a halt was made at the Great Northern

Hotel, Kimberley, where the party was entertained to tea by the Chairman of Ripley Council. However, owing to the non-completion of the bridge widening the Inspector reserved his consent to run into Ripley further than the Nottingham Road Primitive Methodist Church. It was reported a deadlock had arisen as to land belonging to Midland Railway, between the booking Hall and the roadway, which NDT required to complete the widening. The railway company was constructing a luggage lift on the platform near the bridge and the opening would be on a portion of the land. They had therefore declined to sell to the promoters any of the land.

The revised terminus did not deter passengers particularly on the following Sunday and the traders in Ripley were happy with the increase in shoppers who had travelled from the area tapped by the line.

At this time no definite timetables had been issued, although it is known a 15 minute service was established Sundays to Fridays with a 12 minute service on Saturdays. Additional vehicles operated

between Loscoe and Hill Top Eastwood. The fares were set at a penny between each stage and workmen were allowed to travel any distance for a penny.

Within a fortnight a letter appeared in the Eastwood & Kimberley Advertiser complaining of the high fares and compared them with both Ilkeston and Nottingham systems which were cheaper.

Difficulties were experienced in completing the track from Cinderhill to Basford by October, due to problems with Midland Railway who were responsible for the bridge widening costs. The track was made up of 25 chains of single line and 1 mile 12 chains of double track, making a total of 1mile 37chain in length.

Within weeks there were two accidents, in the first case a car overtook a tram at Eastwood in the gloom and struck a telegraph pole which had not been moved following road widening. The second which happened in fog between Eastwood and Hill Top when two two tramcars collided. The front portions of Nos.11 and 17 were completely wrecked and other parts badly damaged, but fortunately there were no serious injuries.

The agreed rate of electricity from the Derbys & Notts Electric Power Co Ltd, was 1¼d per unit and a management fee of £1.000 per annum to TLP. The power company also agreed with Eastwood UDC to fix 27 lamps to tram poles. The AC power from Ilkeston, was converted to DC at the newly constructed substations at Kimberley and Loscoe, where it was fed into the overhead lines.

G D Prince resigned as Secretary with W C Bryden taking over the position.

The 11 mile 29 chain company line had been constructed and completed at a cost of £213.743.

1914

The Board of Trade authority was dated the 9th January, for the running of cars on the new section into Nottingham, yet the line was completed on New Years day and passengers were carried for the first time on that day.

A full Sunday service was introduced and a late through service on Wednesdays and Saturdays during the pantomime season. The company green rolling stock was distinguishable from the maroon of the Nottingham cars.

The time of one hour forty minutes for the whole journey may have been excessive, but it was in fact a shorter distance into Nottingham as the majority of the passing loops were set for the outward route, although there were seven equal angle loops between Hill Top and Cinderhill.

At Cinderhill junction on both inward and outbound journeys, fares were again collected with NCT tickets being issued for the Corporation part of the tracks. On the leased section (at a rent of £1.031 per annum) to Church Street, the fares were retained, but on the NCT metals the company had to submit each week a statement showing all tickets issued, together with the money, less 3¾d per mile for the miles run by the NDT. In the event of both the NCT and NDT cars departing at the same time, the NCT car had to proceed first, with company car maintaining a distance of of at least fifty yards between them, on the 2 miles 24 chains of track between Basford and the terminus.

Childrens fares were issued for the first time with a minimum of one penny. A collection and delivery of parcels was to be introduced with agents being appointed along the way. A comparison of the railways fares showed the trams to be much cheaper than by train. From Ripley to Nottingham by train was 1s 2½d against 11½d by tram, but it was the penny stages which raised the anomalies which locals complained of. At a Nottingham City City Council meeting during February the question of excessive charges being made by the NDT was referred to, and it was stated that the fares charged by NDT on their own line was fixed by the Act of Parliament. The fares complied with a clause of the Act which gave the company the right to demand a fare not exceeding one penny per mile.

During January Ripley UDC were still trying to resolve the problems of the Ripley terminus. It was stated that the County Surveyor had made certain suggestions, including giving up 6ins. of land by the Midland Railway and taking the measurement from the outside of the rail, which would allow the track to remain in situ. When this happened two other widenings could proceed. This was not resolved

very quickly as the Council asked in April for lighting to be provided at the temporary terminus and in May there was deadlock with NDT with regard to the reinstatements and rebuilding of a smithy. Although nothing is quoted it may be assumed that the extension was operative by the time of this latter problem as it is doubtful if they would demolish premises if all the widenings had not been completed.

All advertising was placed with the Frank Mason agency and G C Brittain & Sons secured the sole advertising rights on the back of workmens weekly tickets.

A celebratory dinner was held at the Victoria Hotel, Nottingham on Thursday the 16th January, with some 300 civic and local dignitaries and trade representatives attending. The employees were not forgotten and at about midnight on Saturday the 7th February eighty members were entertained to supper, with the usual speeches, followed by a musical programme.

During June a post box was fixed to the last car which left Ripley at 9pm and such was the popularity of this it was suggested that a larger box be fitted and also a box at the terminus which could be emptied on arrival of the tram, rather than the residents waiting for its arrival. Although only on one month's trial it was extended for further six months.

It was agreed by NDT on the 5th October to demolish the Crown Inn, Heanor and erect new premises.This was some fifteen months after the report in the local paper of the partial demolition.

Agreement was reached with Midland Railway during December for signalling arrangements at Heanor level crossing.

The Cheltenham & District Light Railway Co, operating 10.44 miles of 3ft 6in. gauge track was taken under the TLP control (thus associated with NDT) It was replaced by motor buses in 1930 and then in 1939 it passed to the Red & White group.

The first year's traffic receipts amounted to £21.803, with working expenses less sundry receipts gave a balance of £10.039

The outbreak of the First World War was to have an effect on the short life of operation, with the

enlistment of men in to the armed services, and the subsequent neglect of the system. With difficulty further staff, mainly women, were recruited and trained, as replacements.

1915

Mr C R.Walker of the Mansfield & District Tramways was also appointed manager of NDT as from the 1st June, to replace the original manager Mr Dudman who transferred to M&DT. A motor car was purchased for his use, with the costs being shared by the two companies, although it was run and based at Langley Mill.

From the 15th January up to early afternoon an half hourly headway was introduced, and then every 15 minutes, except on weekdays (Monday to Friday) when it returned to half hourly from 9pm. Obviously a wartime measure and it is not known if this changed when conductresses were introduced dur-

A fully laden car 6 passes through Loscoe Grange.

ing August owing to the depletion of staff by enlistment.

Heanor UDC were informed by the NDT that it was not advisable to install a watering car in view of the very hilly nature of the route. This had arisen from complaints received regarding the amount of

The crew of No. 16, dressed in the company issue of navy blue serge double breasted overcoats, with high necked collars. The lady conductor carries the cross strapped money pouch, bell punch, chained whistle in the top pocket, and a metal ticket rack.

dust raised by the trams.

1916

G D Prince was re-appointed this time as Assistant Secretary and Registrar. Interestingly the board decided to take a Government anti-aircraft insurance, against the possibility of an air raid. At this same time it was agreed to pay Nottingham Corporation £1.700 in settlement of repairs to both

water and gas mains.

It was reported on the 9th June that progress was being made for the acquisition of the Ilkeston tramways and lighting undertakings, on behalf of the TL&P . It was felt this to be an asset in view of the value of connecting Heanor and Ilkeston. A resolution was passed to enter into a working agreement. These were finalised and the transfer to NDT subject to consent of Parliament, as from the 30th September. The sum of £28.150 plus stock at cost price, was paid to Ilkeston Borough. Subject to certain conditions, including the following; the purchase to be completed within two years from the date of declaration of peace; to be maintained in a good state as from the date of take over. The actual transfer deed was dated the 15th November. Just prior to the sale it was stated by the Chairman of the Finance Committee that the undertaking had made a loss of £32.495 since opening, the track was in a shocking state and all the trams were cripples with four off the road!

NDT now owned a second system with a route between Cotmanhay, Ilkeston and Hallam Fields, and another which spurred off Bath Street, Ilkeston to serve Ikeston Junction. The fleet consisted of thirteen open top 48 seat trams; Nos. 1-8 Electric Railway & Tramway Works (ER&TCW) cars and Nos. 9-13 G F Milnes cars, all of which were fitted with Brill 21E trucks.

Assessment of the the leased line at Basford produced a fixed fee of £1000 per annum for two years.

Restricted street lighting saw agreements with both Heanor and Ripley UDCs to paint the poles white as a form of warning.

Two larger type GE203N motors rated at 45 hp each were purchased on trial from British Thomson Houston at £125 each, which they fitted to No. 16. A Napier motor car was also obtained at £140, for use as a tower wagon, which replaced a horse drawn model.

War bonuses were agreed with single men receiving up to 2s6d (12.5p) per week. married men 3s6d with an additional 9d for each child under fourteen. Girl conductors received an additional ¼d per hour with over 12 months service.

1917

The company were represented at four Military Tribunals by the Manager C R Walker, who was appealing against various members of staff being called up. One case in particular involved the call up of a motor inspector who was working through nights from 8pm to 9am, because they were now at rock bottom due to the shortage of labour. There had been criticism of NDT wages, which including a war bonus amounted to 35s 0d per week, and after inspection of the books the tribunal chairman was satisfied they were paying good wages. Walker also stated that they had one lady inspector (conductresses were not mentioned), but it was impossible to have women drivers because of the steep gradients!!

C R Walker received a £40 a month salary increase to include his services with the Ilkeston tramway. Authorisation was given in February to purchase a chassis from Daimler for a tower wagon, although by May the Manager was requesting a settlement of the question of a new tower for the tower wagon! He also reported on a visit with other officials including NCT to Glasgow to see women employed as tram drivers. Although not quoted it is assumed he was of the same opinion as Nottingham, who did not find it desirable!

During June the Tramway & Vehicle Workers Association were putting demands on the management and who made the following offers; the married mans bonus be increased to 6s.6d (32.5p), single men and women an additional 1shilling (5p) making 2s (10p) in all, on the understanding 54 hours per week were worked. The union demanded a 1d increase per hour but a later offer of 9s.0d per week for males and 6s.0d for females as war wage in lieu of a war bonus was accepted by other sections of the company's system. On Wednesday the 26th September the drivers and conductors came out on strike for better wages and in support of one of the drivers who had been dismissed for insubordination to a superior. The inspectors kept a skeleton service of four cars going that day with three cars on the Thursday. A meeting was held between the manager and employees, but they refused arbitration and reiterated their demand for an extra penny an hour.

Normal service resumed on Tuesday the 2nd October following a conference between the Ministry of Munitions, the management and the union. The demand for 1d per hour increase was agreed and the war bonus at present paid to remain subject to 54 hours being worked with a reduction of one-sixth for each day not worked. The sacked driver was also reinstated. The final request by the Union to make Christmas Day a holiday was left for the Manager to decide.

Eastwood UDC approached the company to provide extra cars on Saturdays, which they reluctantly deferred due to a shortage of drivers.

NDT took a passenger to the Heanor Petty Sessions charged with unlawfully interfering with the lights, ringing and signalling a car of the company. The ringing of the bell was dismissed but turning off the lights cost him 18s.3d.

Following a fire which destroyed the garage and rolling stock, Balfour Beatty surrended the lease on the Dartford tramways.

Total receipts for the Ilkeston system were £6.963, with expenses at £5.084, giving a gross profit of £1.879 for the the year, justifying their faith in purchasing the system.

1918

The Manager reported by letter (dated the 11th January) to the Board of the services rendered by motorman Parkin in promptly stopping a car which was in danger of running away. In recognition of this Mr Parkin was presented with a cheque for £5 and a further £6 being reimbursement of damage to his clothes. The facts of this case were communicated by the Chief Constable to the Carnegie Hero Trustees, who on the 28th February presented Harry Parkin with their certificate and a £5 War Bond. However, the details of the act of heroism reported in the local press stated that on the 6th January a tram was passing through Heanor Market Place at 9.40pm laden with passengers, when a wire in the controller caused a large sheet of fire. The driver jumped from the car with the intention of mounting at the rear, to cut off the current. The car, however, gained speed he failed to do this and the car sped on out of control. When Parkin saw what happened he immediately jumped on board and brought it to a standstill. The local newspaper felt that the passengers should have contributed something for saving their lives. The report also stated that the recipient was a former driver. Not quite as reported to the Board?

The Chairman of Heanor UDC protested at the monthly meeting at the reckless manner which trams were being driven. He informed them that one Saturday evening he was one of the occupants of a crowded car on Heanor Hill when it ran into another tram packed with people. He was violently shaken and covered in broken glass. It was decided that the attention of NDT be brought to the matter.

The tram letter box was withdrawn during July due to costs, but this was opposed by all the local authorities.

During July tramway employees were again looking for an increase in war wages and also the question of a Christmas day holiday was referred to the Manager.

War restraints saw a reduction of Sunday services with the first tram leaving Ripley at 1pm and the last from Nottingham to Ripley at 8.15pm from the 28th July. The following week they ran only as far as Cinderhill as Nottingham had discontinued Sunday services.

A court case of the period declared that no claims could be made by passengers if they left their seat before the car stopped.

With the cessation of hostilities, it was going to take time for things to return to some sort of normality, although life was not to be the same again. The trams and track had deteriorated very badly, due to lack of spares, and it was to be an increasing struggle to maintain any standards.

Trams did not run on Christmas Day, but on Boxing Day an half hourly service was provided until 1.45pm, and then increased to 15 minutes up to the final car at 10.45pm.

1919

It was real blow to the company when C R Walker died at the age of 48 at Torquay on the 5th January, where he had been recouperating following a bout of influenza. There was at this time a national epidemic when families had suffered similar fatalities, and it was a real irony that so many had survived the atrocities of the World War.

As a temporary measure Mr A D Phillips was appointed to sign local cheques. By the end of January Captain W Vane Morland had taken over the position. During June he was confirmed as Supervising Manager of the Ilkeston section, which was being run by a Mr Brown.

Authority was given to purchase from M&DT a half share in a motor car costing them £45, and also a tower wagon, which was bought for 350 guineas, (£367.50p).

On Sunday the 7th February the Sunday service was restored through to Nottingham.

During the May meeting the Board requested the Manager to obtain information with regard to installing a motor bus between Heanor and Ilkeston. This was to include garaging in a shed adjoining the existing car shed at Langley Mill.

Rather surprisingly the Heanor UDC were pressing the Midland Railway to reopen the Ripley to Langley Mill branch line. It re-opened on the 3rd May 1920, although it only lasted until the 4th May 1926.

The Board decided to oppose the Ministry of Ways and Communication Bill, as they felt that to attempt to concentrate the administration of railways, tramways, docks, canals and road transport into a Government department would cause confusion and inefficiency. At the same time they also opposed the Electricity (Supply) Bill 1919 as they were against the appointment of electricity commissioners to give the government powers sufficient to ensure a cheap and abundant supply, when such was not available then. The machinery of the district electricity boards would be cumbersome ineffective and expensive. The terms of compulsory purchase were inequitable and constituted a breach of existing statutory requirements upon which the industry had been built up.

The Nottingham branch of the union unanimously passed the following resolution;- "that the services of all married women whose husbands are in employment should be immediately dispensed with on the Nottingham, Mansfield, Ilkeston, and Ripley systems".

Following complaints from the Kimberley Parish Council they were advised by NDT that many of the tramcars were being repaired and they were having difficulty in obtaining spares, which was affecting the level of service.

Four cars from Ilkeston were sold for the sum of £450 each, the proceeds of which were used to reduce the company's indebtedness to Ilkeston Corporation. Two ER&TCW cars passed to City of Carlisle Tramways Co Ltd, and Nos 7-8 to Dunfermline Tramways. A little later a Milnes car was also sold to Carlisle.

Heage UDC wrote to the company asking them to consider an extension from Ripley to Belper. but it would appear that it was left in abeyance.

The Eastwood Trades Guild was unhappy with the irregular and inadequate weekend service between Underwood, Brinsley and Eastwood, (J T Boam provided a service on their behalf, which they subsidised until it was viable), and it was decided to approach Holmes Transport of Nottingham

1920

A secondhand Cubitt car was purchased for £335 and an AEC lorry-bus for £425 which it is believed came from London General. It is not known for what purpose except it may have been used as a relief vehicle, for emergencies etc.

The Manager's recommendation was approved for the removal of rails and points at the Ilkeston shed, possibly those that had accommodated the four sold trams. These were included in the additional work to the trackway which was carried out at a total cost of £3.500. The work involved the lengthening of a loop by 15yards at the bottom of Heanor Hill and an extension of 65 yards at the Langley Mill car shed. Loops at Codnor were moved 40 yards up the track and at Crosshill moved 80 yards. Cinderhill and Lodge loops were extended by 160 yards and 80 yards respectively. A suggestion of doubling the whole track was deferred. The total cost of track repairs up to date (November) was £4.085.19.7d.

It was reported to NDT that conductors refused to stop for pre-paid passengers at Cinderhill Colliery

and Broxtowe Gate, so that they could make up time. Consequently there was a scramble to get on board as the cars passed, and there was concern that there might be an accident.

Again the question of employing female labour was raised by the Union, and Capt Morland replied as follows;-"The difficulty of female labour on the cars was not a matter of finding men, but of the men securing accommodation anywhere within a reasonable distance of the depot. Much as they might sympathise with ex-service men requiring positions, if they could not live in the locality it was difficult to see how they could be employed by the company. It was with the idea of keeping everything going that the policy of gradual displacement of female labour had been followed. They had no difficulty in filling up vacancies for motormen, but they would not undertake conductors duties, stating they could not do the figuring, or were not used to handling money,

or raised other objections, all of which went to show that conducting did not seem to be increasing in popularity as a means of livelihood for male workers. In spite of these difficulties, a considerable number of female conductors had been dispensed with, while the whole of the women workers at the sheds were dismissed sometime ago". A fortnight later on the 12th June tramway men met at midnight and a resolution was moved that notices be tendered if females were not removed by the 1st July. It was decided, however, to adopt a more conciliatory course and request the manager to discharge girls at the rate of three per week commencing from the current week, and also give them a weeks holiday to which they were entitled. There were still seventeen conductresses on the pay sheet at this time. It was also reported that although NDT would accede to .75d per hour on the basic rate, the men were still 1d under the Nottingham Corporation rate and there

Open top tramcar No. 3, possibly being used for driver training, at an unknown location.

was a 3d difference between motormen and conductors, instead of the original 1d.

On the 19th of June The Midland General Omnibus Co Ltd, was incorporated. It was formed to carry on the business of owning, running, hiring, letting on hire, manufacturing, buying, selling or otherwise disposing of omnibuses, cars, cabs, carriages, lorries, wagons, tractors, etc, and other vehicles of any description for transport of passengers, mails and goods etc, common carriers etc. Sometime during this period Trent Motor Traction and Balfour Beatty had been giving serious consideration to the formation of a new jointly owned company specifically for operating in the Nottingham area. Although both had showed a willingness to join interests nothing further happened.

NDT gave notice of an amendment of their statutory powers to increase fares from 1d per mile to $1^{1/2}$d, with a minimum of 2d. Workmens tickets to be a minimum of 1d and carriage of goods increased by 100 per cent. They were granted part but not the 2d minimum and only 50% on the carriage of parcels. These came into affect from Monday the 1st November and was the first increase since the inception. This helped to cover the cost of electric current which was increased to 2d for Langley Mill and $2^{3/4}$d per unit for Ilkeston.

A new recreation and mess room was opened at Langley Mill, during December.

Complaints were still being received of overcrowding from the Eastwood Trades Guild, and the Kimberley Parish Council went further by listing several items regarding discipline of the drivers. They stated that the drivers got off cars and ran into shops to buy chips, or called into a pub for a drink and then asked for another one to be waiting for them on their return. Also when they met before a passing loop drivers would argue, swear or run full up at each other to clench the argument.

NCT also drew their attention to the practice of certain drivers who ran two cars in the same direction on both the outward and inward tracks between Church Street and Cinderhill.

They already gained a reputation for having the most dangerous tram service in England. Cars regularly left the lines and then when the next tram came along it pulled them back on to the track. Following a simple derailment, the points bar was laid on the rail and the car, allowing the current to be earthed, thus the car was able to shunt back on to the track The best remembered accident was the Alpine Street Disaster of 1917, when tram No.12 failed to take a bend and ploughed through the wall of Basford church yard depositing passengers amongst the gravestones. Fortunately there was little damage other than to the tram.

Total receipts for the year amounted to £56.463, less expenses of £38.788 which gave them a balance of almost £17.000!

1921

The Board agreed to the extension of the track from Heanor to Ilkeston and to alter the gauge of the Ilkeston section. Upon these instructions Balfour Beatty proceeded with a petition to Parliament for leave to introduce the Notts & Derbys Tramway Bill which was signed and sealed. The proposed route from Heanor was via Ilkeston Road, then on to private land, to Ella Bank Road, Breach Road Marlpool, to Shipley, and under the then mineral railway line from Woodside Colliery to Shipley Lock then over more private land to connect at the north corner of Cotmanhay Wood with the Ilkeston section. The Lenton to Beeston/Chilwell route was also resurrected by NDT, to which Nottingham responded, but the opposition of Sir Jesse Boot (Boots Cash Chemists), resulted in the Bill being thrown out of Parliament. All the proposals on this route crossed private land owned by Sir Jesse, which he presented to the city as the site for the University.

The seats on the twelve top covered cars were rearranged at an estimated cost of £133.

Between April and July a strike of coal miners affected operations of the Nottingham Corporation. Their cars ceased at the end of the evening peak on Mondays to Fridays, and at 7.30pm on Saturdays. However, NDT continued to operate. On Sunday the 24th April they ran as far as Cinderhill, but the following Sunday they were allowed to run on to Church Street. Basford. The last car from Nottingham on Saturdays was at 10.30pm and and

One of the closed top cars at an almost deserted Heanor Market Place.

7.30pm the rest of the week. By late May motor buses of NCT were taken off the Bagthorpe and Dunkirk services in the evenings to operate every half hour to Bulwell, which the NDT trams connected at Church St, Basford. The second NCT bus ran over the Sherwood route.

A cricket match was played at Langley Mill against the NCT, although the result is not known, several pounds was raised for the distressed families in the district.

NDT protested to Nottingham City Council regarding buses being licensed to compete with the trams, this followed the granting of a licence to G Edwards for a Nottingham, Cinderhill, Nuthall, Kimberley to South Normanton daily service which commenced on the 13th July. This operated within the Nottingham boundary along the original proposed tram route of Nuthall Road, and Alfreton Road, to Bentinck Road, and they applied to pick up along this section as there was no service to cater for local residents. Almost immediately t he NCT decided to operate a bus service to Bulwell to cover this section of road. When the Nottingham City Council Watch Committee issued licences they included a condition that short distance passengers could not be conveyed within the City.

By the 29th September the Underwood and Brinsley Motor Service had introduced a Thursdays only Eastwood, Brinsley, Underwood, Annesley to Mansfield service with three journeys in each direction.

Chapter Three: Rail Roaded

1922

The NDT may have been reassured when the Manager reported that the NCT new bus service would not affect the tramway traffic, but this was not the time for complacency as the Nottingham City Council were now issuing licences at an ever increasing rate;- G Edwards transferred his licence to South Normanton Motor Bus Co, and he then commenced running to Alfreton from the same stand and also to Riddings; Tansey & Severn began to run on the tram route from Eastwood to Nottingham, but with a diversion between Hill Top and Giltbrook to Moorgreen and Watnall; J T Walters was permitted to ply between Nottingham and Brinsley. All the above of course took the direct route via Bobbers Mill.

Further to the above assurances, the new NCT service was introduced between Bulwell, Cinderhill and Bobbers Mill to Nottingham, and in actual fact, did affect the leased line for which the NDT were paying £1.000 a year to the Corporation.

Ilkeston Corporation was approached regarding the granting of licences in their area, to see if they would protect the trams. This competition was instrumental in Balfour Beatty advising MCESCO (Midland Counties Electric Supply Co, a new company formed to take over the Tramways Light & Power Co.) that the Midland General Omnibus Co would provide two buses for use by NDT at a charge of £50 per month from commencement until the 30th September. All garaging and maintenance to be with NDT.

A petition was drawn up against a 'Bill to Empower the London & North Western, the Midland, the Lancashire & Yorkshire, and the Furness Railway companies to provide and use road vehicles and for other purposes'. It assumed this was successful, as the Bill never reached the statute book.

EEC balcony top covers were fitted to Nos.1-3 at a cost of £333 each and were in operation for the Easter holidays.

During May, the Manager was asked to study and report on two new single deck car bodies operated by motormen only. During November, he was also asked to report on the rebuilding of the Ilkeston cars. It was shortly afterwards this was put in hand and the new No.7 was converted to a one man operated single deck car for the Ilkeston Junction branch line. A programme of repairs and rebuilding of the Ilkeston fleet had been undertaken at Langley Mill, during this period. The fleet was also renumbered 1-8, and all remained in the original chocolate and stone livery.

The 1922 Bill was approved and during July agreements on widenings on the Heanor section had been made, and it is understood that certain parts of the route to Ilkeston were marked out.

Ripley UDC requested the provision of a shelter at the Cooperative Square terminus, but this was turned down by NDT, who also stated that they did not own the land.

Due to competition reduced fares were introduced on Wednesday and Saturday (Nottingham market day) tram services. The Eastwood Town Trades Guild had been pressing for a reduction in tram fares and W V Morland had replied; "It might interest the Guild to know that we are at present paying over 150 per cent more per hour than we did in 1914, and other costs are proportionately high. As you are doubtless aware the fares have only been increased 50 per cent and this is of comparative recent date, and we were in fact, the last people in this locality to depart from pre-war prices, which you apparently wish us to restore. Unfortunately, both my Company and the employees have to pay considerably more for their supplies than fifty per cent increase on pre-war prices, and until these come down sufficiently to

One of the the Ilkeston ER&TRCW cars (No.3) at Langley Mill, for repairs and rebuilding. The staircase and upstairs handrail have been removed suggesting this was the car selected for conversion to a single deck car which became the new No. 7. Although the reversing of the stair rail, suggests the work may have been part completed.

make both ends meet on a reduced revenue your Committee cannot reasonably expect us to take any action as suggested. Your concluding remark presumably applies to all purchasable articles and public services, all of which seem to me to show a much higher ratio of increase than tram fares. At present the difference between receipts and expenditure does not warrant my making any recommendations of this character to my directors"

An advertisement for the Nottingham Goose Fair, which was at this time held from the first Wednesday in October until the Saturday, showed trams every few minutes, waiting cars at the terminus, late journeys, and cheap return tickets. These tickets avoided re-booking at Cinderhill with no extra charge for conveyance to Parliament Street, Nottingham.

At the MGO EGM, the directors agreed to purchase two Vulcan 17 seat buses for £2.050.15s to work for the NDT. When it was announced that these buses had been delivered it stated that the company's engineers had been experimenting to evolve a pneumatic tyred vehicle to be used for either express passenger work or pleasure parties, and be driven at the full maximum speed of twenty miles an hour, instead of the twelve miles an hour limit on solid tyres. The livery was olive green with a cream roof.

Bus services were introduced over the Whitsuntide holiday. On Saturday the 27th May and the Sunday a fifteen minute service was introduced between Heanor and Ilkeston (Rutland Hotel). The Belper River Gardens were served on the Monday with a thirty minute service from Ripley where connection was made with the trams. Motor bus connections with the tram between Underwood, New Brinsley, Eastwood, Hill Top, Newthorpe, Moorgreen, Watnall, New Nuthall and Nottingham, were introduced on the following Tuesday and Wednesday. It is not known but it is assumed after this date one vehicle worked to Ilkeston, and the second on the Underwood connection also providing extras on the Ilkeston route; the Belper service being a one off or bank holiday special. Within three weeks NDT had applied to Eastwood UDC for two motor bus licences to ply for hire in the area. One

member of the Council said the capital invested in the buses could have been put to better advantage in reducing the current fares on the trams. It was observed, when granting the licences, the competition might lead to cheaper fares. This perhaps confirms the operation of the Underwood route!

W Vane Morland was appointed manager of MGO from the 1st June.

The option on a plot of land offered by Balfour Beatty at Carter Gate, Nottingham, for £200, was taken up, as a possible garage site.

During November the AEC Y lorry-bus chassis

The crews for both Vulcans pose before the camera, possibly just before the inaugural services commenced. The uniforms are NDT issue. Although both conductors have cap badges which are inscribed with their status. The driver in the centre as a MGOC badge, rather than the NDT style of motorman. To the left is Walter Basford, who is wearing the standard attire, with Inspector embroided in script. The second Vulcan is just visible in the background.

was purchased from NDT, and fitted with a bus body was obtained from M&DT for £150, and adapted to the chassis.

1923

New operators granted licences in the immediate area were; J Marson and J Williamson & Son both for Nottingham to Heanor services. Heanor UDC tried to alleviate congestion in the Market Place particularly on Saturday nights when passengers transferred from tram to bus, by allotting set parking areas.

The option on Carter Gate, Nottingham was abandoned in October.

The AEC chassis was sold back to NDT and a Guy B chassis No.3 was purchased in lieu. It received the ex M&DT body which was reconstructed the following year. A Guy BB bus (No.4) with 26 seat body was also received. Although fleet numbers are quoted it is believed they may not have been given until later.

During one foggy November morning a runaway horse hit one of the MGO buses, on the Heanor-Ilkeston route. The shafts penetrated through to the drivers seat, knocking him to the floor, sending the bus plunging through a hedge. The driver quickly regained control and was able to apply the brakes before any more damage occurred.

A notice was issued advising the public that the tram service might be suspended at any time between noon and 2pm approximately, on Saturday the 27th of January to enable the supply of electrical power to be changed over to the new Spondon power station. Intending passengers were advised to make sure their journey terminated by noon, before boarding the car. The Ilkeston supply started up at 1.27pm and the trams received current at 2.5pm. However it was not until 4.15pm that the supply was through to Langley Mill, and this section was completed at 5.45! The existing Ilkeston power station was totally inadequate producing only 25 cycles, and so it was decided the previous December to purchase an existing plant at Spondon. This had been erected during the World War being modern in every respect and of 50 cycle frequency. The link between the two sites was completed rapidly with the whole of the 25 miles of cable being laid at a rate of three miles per ten days. However, it was not all plain sailing as the power was cut off from 6am until mid-day on 27th February and of course the trams stopped running. This was due to flooding at Spondon following heavy rain and snow storms.

Although earlier references were made in 1918 to the suspension of the tram post box, it must be assumed this had been reinstated, as the Post Office were again denying they were dropping the late tram post box. Within weeks of this denial the local associations were complaining of its removal.

Yet again fares were an issue as the Heanor UDC approached W Vane Morland to reintroduce one penny fare stages. In reply he stated reductions had already been made on certain ordinary and workmens fares. Operating costs were more than double the level of 1914 and the fare increases had not exceeded 50 per cent. The general question of fare reduction was adversely affected by motor bus competition and the wear and tear of the track by the heavy motor traffic. Having reduced their fares to one penny a mile they were protected by the local authorities in the sense that no motor bus competition was permitted on tramway routes with the result that the margin of receipts over expenditure permitted the reductions being made.

Heanor UDC were also concerned with a dangerous corner at Codnor and approached NDT with a view to extending the loop to cover this point, but they could not see why they should undertake the work, suggesting that the Council provided a mirror which could fixed to one of their standards at usual nominal terms. They were not too happy with the companys reply, but the Clerk to the Council pointed out that the system had been passed by the Board of Trade. The facts were then to be placed before the County Council who were responsible for the road.

Although it was intended to sell the Star tower wagon, when it was replaced with the ex MGO AEC Y chassis, it did remain at Langley Mill for many years.

The purchase of 50 tons of track for Ilkeston was authorised and the completion of the purchase of the Ilkeston undertaking was reported, some three years

Closed top car No. 18 at the junction of Milward Road and Heanor Road, Loscoe, heading towards Crosshill with Ormonde Colliery in the background. The typical open countryside contrasted with the hustle and bustle of the industrialised townships along the route into the metropolis of Nottingham.

later than originally agreed. The Board remitted to Balfour Beatty the question of doubling a portion of the Ripley track.

Nottingham Corporation granted special permission for five NDT cars to run from Codnor to Parliament Street, then through Nottingham to the Chase Street, St Anns, Church on the 9th June. Strangely only four cars were required for the return journey.

1924

Heanor UDC informed all operators that licences would not be issued, unless emergency doors were fitted. Brewin & Hudson successfully applied for a Ripley to Nottingham licence from Eastwood UDC, during September. The Midland Motor Bus Co, commenced on the Heanor to Nottingham route

from Monday the 17th November.

W Vane Morland resigned as local manager from December, taking up duties with St.Helens for a short period. He then went on to Walsall, before joining Leeds Corporation in 1932, staying on until 1949. W W Clarke from Luton Corporation Tramways, became the replacement local manager.

Arrangements were made by NDT and D&N Electric Power Co, for the use of part of their premises at Granby Street, Ilkeston as a waiting room for the Heanor-Ilkeston service, which terminated at this point to link with the trams.

Although Vulcan buses were requested Balfour Beatty purchased a further two Guy BB buses with 32 seat dual entrances which became Nos.5-6.

Rather surprisingly the Board considered dou-

Guy BB No. 6 awaits passengers outside the short lived waiting room facilities provided on Granby Street, Ilkeston, before making the return journey to Heanor.

bling a portion of the main track, but a decision was deferred until costs were produced and to see if there was an increase in receipts.

A funeral cortege was passing over the tracks from East Nelson Street, Heanor, when a tram struck the rear end. Fortunately the coffin remained intact.

Discussions were still taking place regarding the extension of the track to Ilkeston and during July estimates were received. The cost of two and three quarter miles between Heanor and Ilkeston, excluding land and widenings was £64.000. The reconstruction of the whole of the Ilkeston system, including eight cars was £85.500. This was recommended to the MCESCO omitting the Ilkeston Junction branch line. During October this was approved by them and authority was given to acquire land and carry out embankment work with a view to proceeding in twelve months.

All this was rather surprising as the main topic of the Board meetings was combating the motor bus competition. During September applications were made for a Heanor-Nottingham bus service, via Bobbers Mill as this was the route taken by the opposition. Before the end of the year terms had been negotiated with MGO to operate on their behalf.

A peculiar accident occurred on a tram, when two hospital patients boarded on crutches. One set which was metal was deposited in the conductors quarters and came into contact with the electrical appliances.

There was an immediate bang with blue flames causing the passengers to stampede to the other end of the car. The conductor quickly reacted by disconnecting the trolley pole. Only the rescued crutches were bent and twisted.

Heanor UDC yet again referred to anomalies on the trams, pointing out that for the journey between Heanor Market Place and the GNR station, a distance of a mile the fare was 3½d.

1925

Following discussions with Ilkeston Corporation it was decided to surrender the waiting room at Granby Street, and use the common stance for buses recently introduced at Ilkeston Market Place. This would have taken further traffic from the trams which connected at that point.

A meeting of local authorities and bus operators was called to introduce scheduled timetables between Heanor and Nottingham. Objections were raised, but the proprietors agreed not to pass each other on the road unless a bus was standing to pick up passengers or going up a hill. They also agreed not to stand at the side of a loop when a tram was in the loop, but would take up a position at the rear.

Eight more Guy chassis were delivered, one was a 32 seat (No.7) and the remainder Nos.8-14 had 20 seat bodies.

Following the liquidation of the South Normanton Bus Co Ltd, the business was purchased for £3.000 which included three Leyland G7 buses (Nos.21-3) a Vulcan VSC (No.24), the service between South Normanton and Nottingham, garage and land which was taken over from the 8th July.

Just over three months later on the 29th September further opposition was taken over when the Midland Bus Co, of Kimberley was obtained along with four Leyland 20 seat buses (Nos. 17-20). This gave them further licences on the Heanor to Nottingham service and the garage lease, which was adjacent to the cinema at Kimberley, for five years. W B Wilkinson was the secretary of Midland and proprietor of The Picture House at Kimberley.

It is possible that these continued as a separate businesses until 1926, when the vehicles received fleet numbers

Following an interview with the Nottingham Town Clerk, in January, NDT gave an undertaking not to pick up within the City. During March it was agreed that both tram and bus fares on the Heanor to Nottingham service be reduced to that charged by the opposition. A loss of £30 a week was being made by July and the tram fare between Parliament St. and Cinderhill was reduced from 3½d to 2d, consequently the Corporation received less revenue. It was, however, decided to employ two additional MGO buses.

The continuing complaints about fares paid off, as one penny stages were reintroduced by NDT during June between Ripley and Hill Top.

On Thursday the 25th June a tram failed to take the points at the Station Road, Langley Mill loop. Leaving the track it crossed the road, mounted the pavement and hit the Wesleyan Chapel wall. A lady pedestrian was injured and a boy was trapped between the tram and the wall. Fortunately their injuries were not too serious and no one on the car was hurt. A lamp post was also damaged , which was reported to Heanor UDC and the Chairman suggested that India rubber lamp posts be provided!

Again the dangerous Codnor Gate loop was raised this time by a Mr. Mitton who had regularly corresponded with the Ministry of Transport and Heanor UDC. On this occasion he had informed them that tramcar No. 15 from Codnor to Ripley at 5.50pm on Thursday, the 25th of June, had stopped on the loop in front of his car. He considered whether to wait or pass on the inside, but did not attempt it as a bicycle came past followed by tram No. 20 completely blocking the road. NDT had assured the council and Mr. Mitton that drivers had been instructed not to use the loop for passing, and urged that passengers should be left, as it steadied the driver coming down hill, knowing points had to be negotiated. There had been several serious accidents at this point and he asked for assurances something would be done. A further letter in November to the Ministry informed them that the practice was continuing of cars passing on the wrong side of the loop. He also charged the department for allowing a loop which was not approved. Mr. Mitton did receive a reply in which they admitted the loop had not been laid in accordance with the plan, and they had no intention of taking any further steps to remove the danger. This seems to have settled the matter although Mitton did write again noting various items including the fact they approved of trams passing on the north west side of the loop, which was on the wrong side of the road.

1926

Sir Joseph Nall DSO MP was appointed director and chairman of both MGO and NDT boards, replacing Sir Alfred R Holland who retired owing to his advancing years. Sir Joseph represented the Hulme division of Manchester as its Member of Parliament (1918-1929 and 1931-45) and devoted much of his time to studying and solving transport problems. He was a member of the select committee who worked on the London Traffic Act 1924. It was during this time that he had criticised the operation of trams in Llandudno which resulted in George Balfour inviting him to join the board of that company and other transport associates of the Balfour Beatty group.

It was decided to dispose of the three Vulcan VSC models and three of the former Midland 20 seat Leyland buses. At the same time four South Normanton buses were fitted with pneumatic tyres (it must be assumed that these would have been the three Leyland G7s, plus the remaining Midland vehicle although it is almost certain this already had pneumatics). It would appear that the early Guys had also been converted during the year.

Early in January two 30 seat all Guy BB models (Nos.15-6) were received, but these were to be the last as a change in vehicle purchasing saw the arrival, during late December, of two (Nos.25-6) Tilling Stevens B9Bs with Strachan & Brown bodies. The latter buses, introduced the new livery of bright green (as the new tram livery), with cream above the waistrail and black mudguards.

Further competition disappeared on the Nottingham-Heanor service during March when the Marson's Enterprise business failed. Founded by J.Marson the first licences were granted in February 1923, but sadly just over a year later Mr.Marson died

leaving the concern to his wife, which included three buses. A further two were added as more licences were obtained, however this was only short term gain and no doubt the severe competition took its toll.

During February H F Pollard of Birmingham, introduced, a Nottingham-Alfreton service via the tram route to Eastwood, then to Brinsley, and Riddings. Within three weeks attention was switched to compete with MGO on the South Normanton service, albeit in the name of Viggars and Steele. Unfortunately, they failed due to financial problems arising from the Miner's Strike. J G Severn, who had made the original suggestion to work the Alfreton service, decided to work this himself.

Ernest Prince of Goldenhill, Stoke on Trent, made an unsuccessful application during October to operate between Nottingham and Ripley. He actually worked a Longton to Tunstall service, with one vehicle from April 1923 until he sold out to Tilstone in May 1928.

Kimberley Parish Council, rather naively, wrote to the bus companies asking them to stop explosions (backfiring) and reported few had replied to their request. At least one local company (Barton of Chilwell) removed baffles from exhausts to inform intending passengers they were approaching.

The Manager reported, to the NDT Board, that one set of garden seats was ready and was authorised to carry out the improvements. This may have been the time that rather surprisingly, the rolling stock received an overhaul. Nos.1-8/10 were converted from 32/24 to 30/26 seating. Nos.9/11-2 became 30/23 seating with the fitting in the lower saloon of upholstered seating. Nos. 8/9 had their destination boxes replaced with lights over the staircase, similar to the rebuilt Ilkeston cars. Some were applied with dark brighter green livery, and green rocker panels, but without the gold lining.

Estimates were accepted for the provision of a garage to house thirteen motor buses and also repairs to the car shed roof, at Langley Mill.

No doubt Sir Joseph's contact enabled the NDT to obtain 40 tons of secondhand rails from the Llandudno company, which were required for urgent repairs on various parts of the systems, particularly at Ilkeston.

It was recorded on the 6th December that the agreed charge to M&DT would be £300 for two cars (Nos.5-6 and a third again with open top was returned within a few months) loaned for one year. It is assumed that this was the time they were actually sent to Mansfield, which retained them until closure. William West & Sons of Ilkeston transported all three on a trailer, which was only available on Sundays, from John Proctor the local fairground proprietor. The tram body was raised by screw jacks

The poor condition of No. 8 can be seen in this photograph taken inside Langley Mill garage. The body had been jacked up in preparation for a complete overall. It would have been at this time that the seating was re-arranged.

at each corner connected in pairs by a cross beam, so that the trailer could be placed under the body. This action was repeated for the chassis so that the towing vehicle could reverse under it. When delivered to Mansfield the loading procedure was reversed. The lorry used was a WD Karrier with Tyler JB4 engine on solid tyres. West was the regular contractor to NDT for many years and had been responsible for the transporting of the Ilkeston fleet to Langley Mill for rebuilding in 1922-3.

Permission was obtained from NCT to allow a special hire of three tramcars to travel between North Gate and Bulwell on the 21st June.

Ripley Town & Trade Council wrote asking the motormen not to switch off car lights before passengers alighted. It might be worth considering that this may have been a company instruction to save on costs?, particularly as the Manager had been requested to re-open the question of reduction of wages! But it is probable the driver or conductor was removing the trolley at the terminus too early.

The General Strike took its toll closing the service on the 5th May until the evening of 15th May, although there was only a 50% return, giving a half hourly service. However, this aroused the Ripley miners, several of whom were summoned for stone throwing at the trams.

1927

Unlimited weekly (Monday to Saturday) tickets were introduced from September and made available through agents. This also covered the tram routes except between Cinderhill and Nottingham. Passengers had to travel by tram between Heanor and Ripley, as their buses did not cover this section.

The police were very active; checking on bus loading and most of the local operators appeared before the magistrates at regular intervals, with 25 on 14, 47 on 31 and even 56 on a 26 seat vehicle

Approval was given to MGO for the purchase of caps and dust coats for summer and greatcoats for winter wear. Prior to this it is assumed they had NDT issue, with MGO epaulette badges.

Applications were made in the name of MGO to Nottingham City Council for further licences on the Heanor route which were issued in January, June

and November. They were also granted permission to operate on two further routes; Nottingham-Alfreton via Eastwood, New Brinsley and Riddings, being in direct competition with J G Severn & Co (SMA) of Alfreton. However, Severn threatened to introduce further services in competition with the MGO, and in consequence they quickly withdrew. The Nottingham to South Normanton service was an amendment to the former South Normanton Bus Co, service which now also covered Eastwood with the deletion of Watnall and Moorgreen.

Ironically J G Severn approached MGO with a view to selling knowing he was showing a loss £850 for the eighteen months of operation. Severn was under the impression when he offered to sell, at the cost of stock and half the losses, the manager of MGO just hoped he would fade out of business.

An extension of the Heanor to Nottingham service to Rainworth was also approved. Operating via Hucknall Road, Nottingham to Hucknall, Linby, Papplewick, Newstead Abbey, Fishpool and Blidworth, it was in direct competition with Booth of Blidworth. This replaced an earlier Ilkeston, Eastwood, Sutton in Ashfield and Rainworth service, which had been introduced for the colliers transferred to the new Rainworth pit.

Mansfield Borough Council turned down a request for a Heanor to Mansfield route, possibly due to a licence already being issued to Mellows of Sutton in Ashfield, some four months earlier. Each Authority adopted different criteria when issuing licences, but it would appear Nottingham granted them so there were usually three or four concerns on each route, and the smaller authorities usually endorsed the Nottingham decision. When the authorities had the sole decision there seemed to be less thought given. This was typified when Heanor UDC publicly stated they were deferring applications for the Heanor to Ilkeston service as there were already 23 buses on the route. Much has been written about pirate operations and chasing buses which gives the impression a bus could be put into service and immediately start carrying passengers. There were controls and and only in very rare cases did buses operate without licences. However, how the

vehicles ran was a completely different story as very often timetables were never issued so that the buses could pick off passengers to suit themselves. The police did try to enforce some sort of system and regularly summoned operators for overloading.

Specials from Eastwood to the Nottingham football grounds were introduced for the first time and were to become a regular company feature.

The capital authorised was increased from £20.000 to £75.000 in £1 shares, with the Midland Counties Electric Supply Co Ltd, holding all the capital

Twenty Tilling Stevens B10B Express models were purchased in separate batches. The first ten (Nos.27-36) and six (37-42) from the second batch had Strachan & Brown bodies. Whilst the bodies on the final four (Nos.43-6) were built at the Manchester works of Davidson.

Further fare reductions were approved by NDT and the Chief Constable of Ilkeston was approached to restrict the competition from buses on the tram routes.

Part of the Ilkeston car shed floor was boarded over to give garage space for the buses.

The leasing of the illuminated sign at the Ilkeston Theatre Royal was an unusual form of advertising, but only lasted the winter months.

It was decided in the July to frame a Bill to amend powers to run trolleybus and/or (petrol) omnibuses in substitution of the 1922 powers and as an alternative on the existing routes, and to ultimately abandon Ilkeston and the Nottingham to Ripley tracks. Trading losses for the year; were £7.278 for the main line and £1.000 for Ilkeston). The revenue for the leased line fell from £3.510 in 1921 to £456 in 1927, from which they had to pay the annual rent of £1.000. There had been a dramatic slump over the previous year, as they paid £2.774 out to NCT on the 31st March 1926. NCT total receipts were £442.906. A year later this had slumped to £1.224, and even NCT total receipts dropped to £423.092, but NCT figures revived considerably the following year

Ripley UDC met and came to the conclusion that although the trams were outdated, the trolleybuses were little better. They were also concerned that the company would no longer be responsible for road maintenance. However there was some concern at the proposed monopoly NDT were asking for in the new act, but before a decision was made they were to discuss this with other authorities.

Everyone seemed agreed that trams had given good service and even been responsible for the cheap fares, but they were slow with a journey time of an hour and ten minutes against forty minutes on the bus between Heanor and Nottingham. By this time they were no longer used by through passengers. The trams and track had both deteriorated badly and M J O'Connor recalled an instance "I was in a tram from Ripley, and we came across top covered tram No.3 stranded and immobile at the foot of the hill between Codnor Gate and Codnor. The tram I was aboard pushed No.3 about four miles to the depot at Langley Mill and I remember my misgivings at having to climb the very severe gradients at Loscoe and Heanor. However, the tram was equal to the task and progress with a loaded tram and its unserviceable mate was slow but sure". On the 21st June, one of the wheels on tramcar No.10 collapsed at Alfreton Road and the NCT suffered serious losses in consequence of this, advising NDT in no uncertain terms of their annoyance. Major re-investment was obviously needed which of course would be better spent on the faster and more efficient trolley buses.

Since the inception of the mainline, it had run 7.7 million car miles and carried 49 million passengers, and at Ilkeston in the eleven years from the take over they had run 1.7 million car miles and carried 15 million passengers. Road repairs had cost £24.000.

The Ilkeston tramway was still providing a reasonable service in 1927 as shown right, but by 1929 the 13 and 14 minute headways had been changed to 15 minutes.

The tram timetables for the main route which appeared in 1927, show how competition had affected the tramway. The Monday to Friday journeys were curtailed between Kimberley and Nottingham except for peak time and evenings. Sunday timings,not shown, were half hourly until mid-afternoon when it became every twenty minutes on the whole route. By 1929, the Monday to Friday journeys were every half hour throughout the day, with the same on Sunday but not commencing until the afternoon. Saturdays were similar to 1927, except the 15 minute headway became 20 minutes.

NOTTS. AND DERBYSHIRE TRAMWAY CAR SERVICE
NOTTINGHAM & RIPLEY.   MONDAY TO FRIDAY.

KIMBERLEY AND NOTTINGHAM.   MONDAY TO FRIDAY.

Cars from Nottingham meet connections at Kimberley.

RIPLEY TO NOTTINGHAM.   SATURDAY SERVICE

† Loscoe.

NOTTS. & DERBYSHIRE TRAMWAYS CO. (Ilkeston Tramways).
Hallam Fields to Cotmanhay.   MONDAY TO FRIDAY.

‡ To Depot only.   Offices— Park Road, Ilkeston.   W. W. Clark, Engineer & Manager.   Tel. 218 Ilkeston.

Chapter Four: Transition.

1928

Discussions were held between MDT, MGO, NDT and Trent during the year regarding territorial agreements and though nothing was signed, there would appear to have been a gentlemens agreement, as there seem to have been clearly defined lines of operation. For instance G.W.Chapman of Belper and Harry Smith of Long Eaton both offered their businesses to MGO, but no decision was made. However, within a short period Chapman had sold to Trent and Smith to Barton.

It was decided to oppose the the 1928 Road Transport Bill promoted by the four railway companies (formed between 1921 and 1923 from the smaller companies). The LMS & LNER covered the Erewash Valley and the MGO territory. The Railway (Road Transport) Acts became law on 3rd August, but this was not to affect the Balfour Beatty group as was at first feared.

Negotiations opened late in 1927 with Mr Neale director of Williamson's Garage Ltd, for the business and a provisional agreement was made.

The whole of the share capital was purchased by MGO on the 19th January. The final agreement was signed and sealed on the 3rd April, and Williamson's became an associated company. Service agreements were made with William Williamson, Joseph Williamson, and Lawrence Williamson, who became directors along with Chas R Tatham and G H Neale of the associated company.

The registered office and garage was on Derby Road, Heanor and there was a branch garage on Ray Street, Heanor

Included was a fleet of forty one buses, being larger than the MGO fleet, consisting of thirty five assorted REO Speed Wagons, Sprinters and Pullmans dating from 1923 onwards, two Thornycrofts and four very new Bristol B's with Roe 32 seat front entrance bodies.

Two lorries; a Guy and a REO operated the parcels and carrier division.

Only two stage carriage services were operated by all these vehicles, which ran on the direct route between Heanor and Nottingham with certain journeys extended to Ilkeston via Shipley, plus an Ilkeston to Nottingham via Trowell and Wollaton service. There was also a works service, operated between Cotmanhay, Trowell, Strelley and the Haydn Road, Basford factories. Williamson's had very strong religous beliefs and they never allowed any buses to run on Sundays. But this changed following the takeover, when the Derbyshire inland resort of Matlock was served from Heanor, Codnor, Ripley and Ambergate on summer Sundays and Bank Holiday Mondays, from early August 1928.

There was a garage repair business which also acted as agents for REO and Bristol. Obviously their own fleet had been built up on their models, but many of the other independents in the area also purchased REOs' from them.

Tarlton & Brown of Codnor was purchased by Wiliamson's for £3.000, during September, which gave them three more REOs (one Speed Wagon and two Majors) and a Heanor-Ripley service.

The associated companies of Balfour Beatty were experiencing competition and six of the 1927 Tilling-Stevens B10Bs were loaned out, during February, to support the tram services against small bus operators. Two (Nos. 41-2) were sent to Cheltenham & District and the remaining four (Nos.43-6) went to Leamington & Warwick. These were replaced in the fleet by six Tilling-Stevens B10As with Strachan & Brown bodies, which received fleet numbers 56-61. During September, Leamington & Warwick purchased the four Tilling-Stevens for £3.780 and three brand new REOs' (UE 7085-7), no doubt from Williamson's agency, for £2.219.5s.

Permission was granted in January, for the operation of a Ilkeston, Cossall, Awsworth, Giltbrook and Maws Lane to Kimberley service, with peak and lunch time extensions to Nottingham. The terminus in Ilkeston was defined by the local authority as North Street. They were competing with Inglis & Beardsley, on the whole route, and between Ilkeston and Giltbrook with Dickson and again with Inglis & Beardsley, both working through to Eastwood. Although Dickson seemingly disappeared from the operation by 1931. F U Charlton appeared on the entire Kimberley route on Sunday afternoons and evenings.

A Ripley-Ilkeston service was introduced for a short period, but Heanor UDC were rather upset that buses were using Ray Street as a cut through, and closed it to bus traffic. This must have meant through traffic, as Williamson's had a garage on this road.

During March, negotiations opened with L Mellows (Star Saloon Services) and by the 3rd April agreement had been reached for the purchase of the business. The deal included garage premises in Russell Street, Sutton in Ashfield, six REOs and two W&G L buses plus an Ilkeston to Mansfield licence. There were also short journeys between Mansfield, Sutton in Ashfield and East Kirkby, which gave a ten minute headway on this section. This operation ran as subsidiary until October the following year

The two vehicle operation of G H Hayton, Mansfield was purchased during June. It was intended to loan both vehicles to Mansfield & District Tramways Ltd, who took over the operation of the ex Hayton service between Mansfield, Rainworth and Blidworth. However the W & G bus went to the Mellows fleet and the Guy B was sold to Cheltenham & District in July. This move of the service to M&DT may have been the fact M&DT already ran on this route and had sufficient vehicles to cover the extra, if any, requirements.

B Hatton (Hattons Motor Services) of Selston was purchased and the Ripley to Mansfield service became operational from the 1st of December. Six buses were included, of which two were Thornycroft A1s (Nos.64-5), two Dennis 30cwts (Nos.63/6) and a Karrier. The Dennis buses were loaned to M&DT, and the other three were converted to MGO lorries during 1931. A Leyland LSC1 was sold on to Truman of Shirebrook.

An agreement with M&DT for the regulation and interchange of traffic and mutual co-operation between the two companies was approved during December. The last two takeovers by MGO in this area, and those which were already in hand, and to follow, possibly led to this unusual step between two associated companies.

It was decided on the 19th April to pool receipts and mileage on the Nottingham-Heanor service on the basis of 2/3rd to Williamson's to 1/3rd to MGO. It was not agreed until the 25th July, when a timetable was drawn up which would continue until the 31st December 1928. However, it was revised yet again in September, but no details are given. Any variation on special occasions was subject to separate arrangements.

From Friday the 9th of March the first direct bus service from Ripley to Nottingham began operation. Although the local newspaper quoted this as MGO, it would have been an extension from Heanor of the statutory service, which was shared from the 19th April. The combined bus and tram service between Nottingham and Ripley.

The joint operation did not meet with the approval of the travelling public, although tickets were interchangeable, there was many complaints about the shortage of vehicles particularly at peak periods. To compound this the fares had also been increased. The local Authorities took this up with the combine. MGO wrote that they had kept a check of the times on the normal service and were assured a regular service was being maintained. In conjunction with Williamson's, they provided a regular ten minute service throughout the day and at rush periods a five minute service was run, several of the times being duplicated. Delays were, however, caused by level crossings, and often vehicles bunched due to some having more pick ups than others. They did state if more information was provided it would be investi-

One of the covered top trams in its later days, at the Ebeneezer Chapel, Nottingham Road, Ripley terminus. Repainted in the dark green, with only a small area of cream and lacking the gold lining out, it was not in pristine condition, and typified the parlous state of the system.

gated. The trams also came under attack, and a Heanor Councillor complained of their late start, with miners often waiting twenty minutes to half an hour in their wet clothes for transport home. By December extra cars were put on in the early morning, plus an extra bus, following a deputation of Heanor UDC visiting Langley Mill.

A Select Committee of the House of Lords commenced consideration on Wednesday the 25th April, of the N&DT (Trolley Vehicles) Bill. The idea of the monopoly was opposed by both Notts and Derbyshire county councils, most of the larger bus companies and urban councils. It transpired during proceedings the Company had considered various methods of speeding up the trams and came to the conclusion the best thing would be to substitute with trolley traction and buses. The buses to be used for an express service and the trolley vehicles for short stopping service. The cost of conversion being estimated at £91.000. The reason given by the company for requiring protection against competition, was that they were going to charge themselves, in return, with the entire provision of what was necessary for the convenience of the public. For that reason, they had accepted the provision of workmens fares under obligation. Local Authorities were asking the tramway companies to carry out road improvements, which was reasonable, but in return it was reasonable that other operators who had no obligations, should not be allowed to run beside them and ruin their business.

A supplement to the proof of evidence was submitted during the Parliamentary session, which listed alternatives, if it was necessary, to operate trams and trackless vehicles over the same route temporarily. They were; 1) The trams could use the same positive wire as the trackless vehicle, in which case the trackless vehicles would become virtually part of the tram service, as they would not be able to overtake a tram without the trolley pole of the tram being removed from the wire. This was considered to be inconvenient. 2) The tramway positive wire to be retained outside the trackless trolley wires in which case the two types of vehicles would be operated independently and the trolley bus would be able to overtake on the offside of the tram. 3) The tramway positive wires to be retained between the two sets of trackless wires, in which case the trackless vehicle would be able to overtake the tram, but would be compelled to do so on the near side of the tram. This being done in Nottingham along King Street, Queen Street, Upper Parliament Street, Milton Street and Mansfield Road, to its junction with Gregory Boulevard, a distance of 1.2 miles.

On 4th May it was reported the Bill had passed the House of Lords Select Committee, but was ordered to the House for the third reading. Several Clauses were adjusted, but the part that caused the most objection, the monopoly of running powers, had been allowed. This preamble of the Bill was also passed in the House of Commons, subject to a reduction of the capital of the company.

The Bill received Royal Assent and accordingly on the 19th September the company was renamed the Nottinghamshire & Derbyshire Traction Co. The Act was delivered to local authorities and they were invited to state what omnibus proprietors were, according to their records entitled to consideration as operators on sections affected by the Act.

Balfour Beatty was asked to prepare estimates for installation of trolleybus equipment for the Ilkeston Junction terminus, and Heanor Market Place, also vehicles and extensions to the two depots.

M&DT were charged £100 for rental of tram cars during the year.

1929

Heavy duty motor vehicle taxes were introduced on the 1st January, for example; a 20 to 26 seat PSV with pneumatic tyres paying £48, but with solid tyres the cost was £60. No doubt a ploy to remove the offending vehicles which caused far more damage to the highways. Furthermore, on the 1st August motor regulations were introduced to ban noisy exhausts (caused by defect in design or lack of repair), and sounding of the horn when vehicles were stationary

Route numbers appeared on timetables, not the vehicles, for the first time, receiving numbers 1 onwards.

With the new powers bestowed upon the NDT, which forbade any new competition on the new trolley routes, the obvious decision was to remove existing operators by acquisitive means. As will be seen in 1929, a positive start was made in this direction, including the formation of more associated companies. By retaining the acquired operators names, existing licences remained registered with them, thus restricting any opportunity for a competitive licence to be issued.

From the 1st January Davis & Hope became a subsidary, working jointly with M&DT on the Mansfield, Carter Lane, Berry Hill and Rainworth, to Blidworth, or Sparrow Hill and Bilsthorpe services.

The buses, three Leyland, a Tilling-Stevens and a Chevrolet, were retained to operate the routes. They were numbered into the MGO fleet as Nos.67-71, and based at a freehold garage in Southwell Road, Mansfield, obtained with the business. J H Davis

Seen in the Langley Mill coachbuilding shop, is RR 7563 former Davis & Hope Leyland PLSC with Leyland B32F body. Orginally it received fleet No. 69, and then No. 48.

was retained as Superintendent.

Dawson's Enterprise Omnibus Co Ltd, of Cotmanhay was taken over on the 1st January, and six thousand shares were transferred to the following MGO nominees; 560 W Shearer, 100 W McGill, 50 G A Thorpe, 100 G D Prince, 100 W C Bryden, 107 C R Tatham, 400 Sir Joseph Nall. The balance of 4.583 shares were in the name of MGO. Directors appointed were; Sir Joseph Nall, C R Tatham and W C Bryden. G A Thorpe was appointed Company Secretary.

The 11 Cotmanhay to Nottingham service was transferred to Williamson's on the 27th June, having been operated from takeover as a joint service, although it took effect from Friday the 12th July and the timetables still quoted this as the combined service of the two operators. However, Dawson's continued to provide vehicles for Williamson's from their base on Cotmanhay Road. The terms agreed covered interest and depreciation on vehicles, plus a sum for administration, and other charges.

On the 2nd January, the Rainworth, Blidworth and Nottingham service of Herbert Booth (Booth's Motor Services) of Blidworth, was added to the existing MGO operation. Two modern vehicles were included; No.72 a Leyland PLSC1 and 73 a Tilling-Stevens B10B, which were possibly garaged either at Mansfield or Sutton in Ashfield. This acquisition gave additional journeys on the 4 Rainworth-Nottingham service.

Negotiations opened during January/February for the purchase of Tansey & Severn Ltd, of Underwood. The final details were settled and the business became an associated company as from the 6th April, however, this was not completed until the 30th April. Directors appointed were Sir Joseph Nall, C R Tatham, W C Bryden, Archic Scvcrn, Bertie Severn and the Secretary G A Thorpe. All 2.300 shares were transferred to MGO from W H Severn (500), Wilfred Severn (500), J C Tansey (500), G D Tansey (500) and Bertie Severn (300). Archie Severn was appointed Manager and Bertie Severn Traffic Manager, for a term of three years, and thereafter subject to three months notice.

Included were the licences, thirteen Leyland

buses, an Overland lorry, garages at Underwood, and stock. The MGO 3 South Normanton-Nottingham service became a joint operation with Tansey & Severn (T&S) taking their route via Moorgreen and Watnall. It is assumed that the MGO Nottingham to Alfreton service granted in 1927 was withdrawn at this time, or possibly earlier, to be replaced by the T&S 10 service via Eastwood.

After the takeover two (Nos.64/115) Leyland bus bodied Leyland LT1s were purchased by T&S for the sum of £1395 each, less an allowance of £125 on each of the vehicles taken in exchange. Most likely being the two Leyland Z5s with 20 seat bodies, dating from 1924, which were registered NN 6696-7.

With all the activity on the acquisition side, no new vehicles were purchased except for the subsidiaries.

MDT informed MGO of a Bill being promoted for the their protection and asked for advances which were agreed; not to exceed £5.000 at 6% interest on security of £100. £2.000 was advanced for 7% debenture stock each at £15.

The Reliance Omnibus Co, was purchased by MGO from Elisha Beardsley and Arthur Bertram Inglis. Five buses (Nos.74-8; two Minerva's, two Chevrolets and a REO), and licences for a Ilkeston, Awsworth, Newthorpe and Eastwood service, were taken over on the 17th May, and became route 9.

Webster & Briggs (United Bus Service) of Sutton in Ashfield was acquired from the 8th December, with the agreement being signed on the 4th December. Only the licence for a Nottingham to Rainworth service was purchased. Although also numbered 4 it was slightly different from the existing route as it ran direct between Papplewick and Bestwood, thus avoiding the diversion into Hucknall. The Chief Constable of Nottingham was advised that MGO would run the service for the first week, after which they would submit a revised timetable embracing the two routes, for his approval.

Two Dennis (No.63/6 ex Hatton) and two Chevrolet buses (Nos.77-8 ex Inglis & Beardsley) were loaned to M&DT, with the option to purchase at an agreed sum. This was charged quarterly at the rate of 10% per annum of the capital value.

Although G H Boxall of Shipley offered his business to Balfour Beatty, which included the Cotmanhay-Derby service, via Ilkeston and Smalley. It would appear to have been rejected as a part of the gentlemens agreement of the previous year, but Trent did not acquire this as it passed to J T Haywood (Haywood Bros) of Ilkeston.

The two Tilling Stevens (Nos.41-2) loaned by MGO to Cheltenham & District were returned and operating in the Mellows fleet by the 9th February. They replaced REO Speed Wagons Nos.47/50, which had been involved in a head on collision at East Kirby on the 19th January. They were approaching each other on Low Moor Road, when one drew out to pass a coal cart, at the moment a quantity of steam from the nearby LMS locomotive depot swept down on to the road temporarily obscuring the vision of both drivers. There was a tremendous crash, which interlocked the vehicles and injured eleven passengers. By October the whole of the Mellows fleet had been transferred to MGO.

Awsworth Parish Council wrote asking for an extra bus at 6am, even though two buses were already provided, there were still sixty standing passengers.

The operation of statutory services between Nottingham and Ripley on behalf of NDT were again jointly provided as from the 27th June, with total receipts being accounted for by NDT, who paid each operator 9d (3.75p) per mile, to cover all expenses.

Traffic was held up on Nottingham Road, Eastwood during the evening of Tuesday the 29th January, for over fifteen minutes. This was the result of a Williamson's bus becoming jammed between a tram car and the causeway, at a very narrow point opposite the Post Office. The kerbing had been raised six inches to prevent the dangerous practice of buses mounting the pavement to pass tram cars at this point. The bus was so badly sandwiched, the mudguard had to be torn away to allow the release of the vehicles.

Kimberley Parish Council meeting in March received complaints that the five minute bus service was inadequate. Representatives of both companies attended the next meeting. Mr Clark refuted a statement that buses had been taken off, and said that there was a better service than formerly. The trouble arose from factories turning out at different times. It was exceedingly difficult to cope with the rush hours, particularly as people took the first bus, rather than wait five minutes for the next which was invariably half full. Mr. Williamson said there was a five minute service, and if they could make an improvement they would gladly do it. He added that it was impossible to give everyone a seat at seven o'clock (pm) out of Nottingham. They both agreed they would do all they could to remedy the situation.

The total fleet strength of the MGO group except Williamson's and Tansey & Severn stood at 58 serviceable vehicles and thirteen under repair, but by the 14th October the figure had reduced to a total of forty seven vehicles.

Mr Aubrey A Edward was appointed a Director of MGO.

Mr Atkey of A R Atkey & Co Ltd, motor engineers and motor car agents, offered a site for a central bus station and garage at Carter Gate(now Lower Parliament Street)/Pennyfoot Street, Nottingham. On the 17th January it was resolved by the Board to proceed with purchase of the 2.000 square yards of land, at a ground rent of 2s.6d (12.5p) per square yard per annum. On the 29th of April a ninety nine years lease, with an annual rent of £318.17s.6d, was signed. There was a proviso that MGO erected buildings prior to the 25th March 1932, to the value of not less than £6.000.

New directors appointed to the Williamson's board on the 27th June were; Sir J Nall, and W Bryden, with G A Thorpe as Secretary and E Bonsall as his assistant. The registered office was transferred to 66 Queen Street, as the other companies in the group.

Six Tilling-Stevens Express B10A's (Nos.7-8/11/13/15/17) with Strachan & Brown bodywork were purchased during September for use on the NDT routes.

It was agreed to renew the REO and Bristol agencies and also take up a new agency with BAT (Harris

& Hassall), but with no guarantee that they would sell any chassis.

To finish off the year, Williamson's were given approval on the 25th September for the final two acquisitions. J Saxton & Son of Heanor provided the licences for a Heanor-Ilkeston service, and E E Hamilton (Teddy Bear) also of Heanor sold his Nottingham-Heanor and Ripley service. Four or five REOs' came from the two operators. Three buses were included in the Hamilton deal, but possibly two were sold or scrapped.

Nottingham Corporation allowed certain trams, between 7am and 9am, to run to Sneinton Wholesale Market to pick up fruit and vegetable for distribution. Although it was not within the powers to operate, it was allowed as a temporary agreement for a trial period of three months, which helped to ease congestion on Parliament Street.

The cost of conversion to trolleybus operation was estimated as: 1) Heanor-Ilkeston £8.096, 2) Ilkeston tramway conversion (route mileage 3.78 miles) £16.262, 3) Fourteen trolley buses £22.050 making a total of £46.408. It was resolved by the Board that Balfour Beatty be instructed to proceed with the work.

Payments were made to the Post Master General following complaints of electrolysis affecting post office cable near to the tramway.

There was some concern that pirate buses had reappeared in opposition to the tramways, and although not reported it is assumed that Ilkeston Borough would have been advised.

Six additional NDT licences were granted by Nottingham Corporation for the operation of omnibuses on the Nottingham-Ripley service.

1930

W W Clark was appointed Manager of Mansfield & District Tramways and was released by the Board as from the 30th April. No doubt this was a sideways move so that Douglas Hays could become the General Manager of the associated traction and omnibus properties of the midland counties group from the 1st June. He was transferred from a similar position with the Falkirk Tramways and Scottish General Omnibus Co. The Balfour Beatty Scottish Group, which included Scottish General Omnibus (Northern), sold out their considerable interests to W Alexander & Sons Ltd, of Falkirk in June. It has been said that most of the money from this sale was injected into MGO/MDT/NDT for the expansion and improvement of operations.

By September the General Manager was to remit to the Board on the early amalgamation of local accountancy for the companies in the Notts area (would have included the Derbyshire contingents).

During the November Board meeting a merger of all the MGO subsidiary companies and Mansfield & District Tramways, was discussed. The alternative of using Williamson's purely as a goods carrying undertaking for the Derbyshire & Nottinghamshire Power Co, haulage and other business, was also considered.

Experiments were introduced with a view to adopting a universal colour scheme for the Notts area. As a trial, buses were painted red or blue and cream in various layouts, including variations on the existing green livery. Later in November a revision was considered, and it was decided to adopt a uniform standard colour scheme of azure below the waist line and white above, lined in opposite colours. Lettering was to be uniform throughout. MDT remained with the original green and cream.

A new office, additional garage space and other additions were approved for the Langley Mill headquarters.

On Tuesday the 13th May, in the House of Commons, local MP Mr Oliver drew attention to the position of private companies with regard to monopoly powers. He wished to know if those companies granted monopoly powers through the private Act of Parliament would be compelled to go to the Traffic Commissioners to obtain a licence. He cited the position of Ilkeston, Heanor and Ripley and asked

Repainted open top car No. 12 at Nottingham Road, Ripley, in the area which was to become the trolleybus turning circle. The Ebeneezer chapel is on the left and just visible to the right is the Ripley Co-operative Society store. On a dismal damp day the tram car did not look particularly appealing or attractive to intending passengers, and typifies the decline of the system.

A typical period (c1929) view of Ilkeston Market Place. The buses shown from left to right are; RA 1720 Dawson's Super Service 20 seat Laffly, R 9323, Phipps 'District' Talbot, RA 1653, Guy BB of E & J Bramley, and a Trent Tillings-Stevens TS3.

when the Bill became law would his constituency be free from monopoly. Mr Herbert Morrison, the Minister of Transport replied that this would be dealt with in a separate clause. The Road Traffic Act received Royal Assent during August. This was far reaching in all aspects of motoring and the sections affecting passenger vehicles were to make dramatic changes.

Earlier vehicles were renumbered during this period, although some with a short life did not receive a replacement fleet number.

It was resolved to acquire E & J Bramley (Prince of Wales) of Cotmanhay, in equal shares with Trent Motor Traction and enter into an agreement to operate the service, in the proportion of two MGO and one Trent, with protection being given to the Ilkeston tramways route. However, when negotiations were reported to the MGO Board, it was decided to purchase jointly with Trent, Dawson's and

Williamson's. Nine buses, spare parts, etc. were obtained in the sum of £5.000, with £2.500 each paid by Williamson's and Trent. The service between Cotmanhay, Ilkeston and Nottingham via Trowell, eliminated all competition, and was operated by two Williamson's (or Dawson's) to one Trent. Receipts were pooled and divided in two thirds to Williamson's and one third to Trent. In total four combine buses (two Dawson's and two Williamson's) were required for this operation.

Dawson's were supplied in July with two (Nos. 70/6) Tilling Stevens B10A2s with Ransome 32 seat bodies, specifically for the Cotmanhay to Nottingham service. It is likely these carried Williamson's fleet name, and then MGO, as they were loaned to both permanently, but they remained the property of Dawson's. Williamson's also obtained two (Nos.71/5) almost identical Tilling-Stevens B10A2 chassis with Ransome 32 seat bod-

ies. Six assorted Guy buses from the Prince of Wales Service also entered the Williamson's fleet, but two were quickly loaned to Carlisle & District (Balfour Beatty company), and were not returned.

The purchase of the Ripley to Heanor service operated by J Argyle of Codnor, was confirmed to the Williamson's Board on the 29th January.

During the Saturdays of August express services were run for the first time between Ilkeston, Ripley, Heanor, Eastwood and Kimberley, Skegness and Mablethorpe. These were operated by Williamson's.

MGO repurchased the four (43-6) Tilling-Stevens from Leamington & Warwick, during January for £2.742.16s.

Authorisation was given for MGO to purchase six vehicles for the statutory service, although all were not lettered with the NDT legend. They consisted of two (Nos.3/34) Tilling-Stevens B10A2s with Ransome 32 seat front entrance bodies and four (1/77/102-3) Thornycroft BC chassis, with highbridge bodies from Brush, Dodson and Strachan. The Thornycrofts were an unusual choice for the first double deckers in the MGO fleet, as Tansey & Severn already had two all Leyland TD1s. The first two were received on the 16th April, and the remaining two entered service on the 24th September.

An eight month old Commer F4 touring car with a 32 seat body (No.112) was purchased from the General Motor Carrying Co Ltd., Kirkcaldy, a member of Balfour Beatty Scottish group.

Fleet Nos. 102-3/112 were not allocated until 1932.

A Leyland TD1 with Leyland lowbridge body, and two Tilling Stevens B10A2s with Strachan? 32 seat bodies were added to the T&S fleet. No doubt these were to replace the three twenty seat buses which came to them with takeover of the W J Wright business of South Normanton. This removed the only competition on the 3 South Normanton to Nottingham service.

The hourly J G Severn (SMA) Nottingham to Alfreton service, became half hourly and the fare reduced to one shilling between Eastwood and Nottingham. However, the combine fare remained at one shilling and threepence.

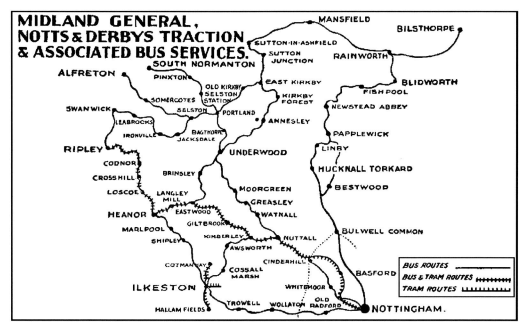

MIDLAND GENERAL, NOTTS & DERBYS TRACTION & ASSOCIATED BUS SERVICES.

Circa 1929 route map, note the spelling of Nuthall, and suprisingly Whitemoor is shown rather than Bobbers Mill, the area to which the group normally referred to. The dotted line denotes the Nottingham city boundary.

Nottingham Corporation offered an exchange of land, during early March, which the Corporation would lease at a rent of three shillings per square yard in Lower Parliament Street in exchange for the MGO site at Carter Gate leased at 2s.6d per square yard, which was accepted. Six weeks later MGO still awaited the NCT proposals. Although a draft plan for the proposed building on Parliament Street was authorised in December, the lease was surrendered on the original site a fortnight later.

Notice was given to terminate the lease on the former Midland Bus garage at Kimberley from the 29th September.

The Board discussed the need for increased garage accommodation at Mansfield, to meet the present MGO needs and a possible merger with Mansfield & District Tramways.

A Packard car was authorised, which was most probably for Mr D Hays, who was now appointed as an additional Director.

The 1 Heanor-Ilkeston statutory service was pro-

vided by Williamson's from the 1st January, on the same terms as the existing arrangement, but with a local adjustment charge per mile for operation. MGO had been running this prior to this date on their behalf, although the timetables which have been seen, except the opening day, showed only MGO not NDT. The agreed sum was an equal amount of the gross receipts taken by Williamson's.

Still the correspondence flowed and the local authorities kept up their vigil into the overcrowding on the buses. Yet it was pointed out that the Nottingham Corporation was to blame in some way, by limiting the amount of additional licences they issued. An Alfreton proprietor (SMA) was summoned for aiding in abetting his conductor to commit an offence of overcrowding, having sixty passengers on a thirty two seat bus. In defence he stated the service was inadequate, although he wanted three more licences the Corporation would not permit them. The matter was resolved by April, with the introduction of works services from the John Players

factory in Radford and the factories in Haydn Road, Basford. The introduction of double deck vehicles for the first time also helped to ease the difficulties.

Plans for the Ilkeston-Heanor trolley service were submitted and preliminary notices were served on the local authorities concerned.

From the 7th February the tram service was severely curtailed between Monday to Friday with only early morning and early evening cars being retained. On Saturdays and Sundays from early afternoon they became half hourly through to the early evening.

Balfour Beatty was instructed during March, to prepare plans and estimates for the conversion from Nottingham to a point for a turning circle, west of Kimberley railway station, including necessary arrangements with Nottingham Corporation in respect of their lines leased and worked by the company. However, these instructions were amended a month later when the board requested that the scheme be in two sections; Cinderhill to Heanor and Heanor to Ripley. Provision was to be made for turning points at Heanor Market Place, Ilkeston Market Place, Ripley, and Kimberley, plus Cinderhill in conjunction with NCT and at Loscoe on private ground to be leased or acquired.

On the tram routes the existing standards and poles were to be adapted to take the trolley overhead wiring.

The revised estimates received in September included all feeder cables, but not the vehicles. These were as follows; 1) Ilkeston to Ripley and Heanor to Langley Mill - equipment £36.600 and road reinstatement £14.100. 2) Langley Mill to Cinderhill - equipment £16.986 and reinstatements £1.4671. Once accepted notices were posted to the Ministry of Transport and the local authorities.

The main route was going to be difficult, as it had been with the trams, with railway lines passing over the route at six different points. In each instance the roadway was lowered, or it would have been necessary to obtain lowbridge double deckers. In half the cases, the cost of this work was borne by the company. In addition four sets of level crossings and two canal bridges had to be negotiated.

The Nottingham Corporation Bill of 1930 covered the conversion of existing tram routes to trolley buses with additional routes. Balfour Beatty submitted a letter with regard to this Bill, intimating insertion of Clause 8 for the protection of the NDT in line with section 14 of the Notts & Derby Traction Act 1928.

The Ilkeston tram system which should have been abandoned on the 29th December, was reprieved for a short period.

1931

The immediate affect of the Road Traffic Act was the registering of all bus services, excursions and tours, and the necessary road service licences were applied for by MGO, NDT, Tansey & Severn and Williamson's. They were successful as they only covered existing routes, and avoided any problems by not trying to extend the network. Applicants had to be working the journeys at the 9th February to be permitted to continue, subject to a decision by the Commissioners.

The Act also introduced the construction and use of public service vehicles, which required drivers and conductors to hold licences and wear numbered badges, subject to them having medical and character certificates, and additionally drivers had to pass a driving test.

Vehicles were required to have a certificate of fitness, which resulted in an improved safety standard. However, like most operators the group found a considerable number of vehicles, particularly the REOs in the Williamson fleet, did not come up to the requirements and were withdrawn within the statutory period.

Another new regulation under the new Traffic Act came into force on Monday the 1st June, which restricted the number of standing passengers to 25% of the seating capacity but not to exceed five in number.

On Saturday morning the 3rd January, at Gilthill on the main Kimberley to Eastwood road, there was an amazing series of accidents. A slight drizzle just before 8am on thawing ice made the surface of the hill impossible for vehicles to negotiate, and a thick mist restricted vision to only a few feet. Pedestrians were sliding as they tried to walk. The first vehicle down was a light lorry, followed by four buses. It was impossible to hold the road, and the driver struck the kerb on the wrong side of the road, which smashed the wheel and brought the lorry to a standstill. Of the following buses, the first was Williamson's which skidded for a quarter of mile before hitting a telegraph pole, next was again a Williamson's which hit a lamp post outside Digby Colliery offices. Then a NDT double decker (MGO Thornycroft) managed to negotiate a telegraph pole, but then shot across the road, crashed through a wooden fence, crossed a ditch and finished in a field. Finally an SMA bus had the most dangerous descent of all, sliding sideways it failed to turn at the bottom of the hill and ploughed into a brick wall in the front garden of a house. Glass flew everywhere, but no one was injured. A bus inspector made the decision not allow any further attempt to descend and vehicles were lined up for nearly two hours before they were allowed to venture on.

An additional area of 2.633 sq. yards of land was purchased at the rear of Langley Mill depot for the sum of £300 from the Butterley Co.

Floors were strengthened at Park Road, Ilkeston garage to temporarily carry trolley buses.

A tender for new offices, messroom and extensions to the garage at Langley Mill was accepted and work was completed during the summer.

All weekly, monthly and season tickets, introduced at the peak of the tram competition, were suspended in June and replaced by workmens return or normal return tickets. They had been originally introduced during the period of competition with the trams.

The Trent Superintendent for the Nottingham area, reported that the Daimler buses on the Nottingham-Cotmanhay joint service had been replaced by SOS Q and ODD models which was instrumental in improving the running of the service. No doubt the Tilling-Stevens of Dawson's and Williamson's also helped.

A further member of the holding company, Carlisle & District Transport Co, the tramway operator and its associated bus company Richard Percival Ltd, were sold to Ribble on the 21st November.

H B Hassall of Mansfield was taken over on the 5th March, together with the licence for a Mansfield to Bilsthorpe service and five buses. At the same time Thompson Brothers of Stanton Hill sold to MGO ten assorted buses of various manufacturers, the Mansfield-Clay Cross via Stretton or Pilsley and Mansfield-Stanton on the Hill services. It was decided to lease both operations to Mansfield & District Tramways, with MGO retaining option to resume possession. The agreement on both was finally signed and sealed on the 21st April. The Chairman was in consultation with both Managers and the following offers were made to MDT during December;
1) Sell the services and the fifteen buses for £13.000,
2) Lease them to MDT for five years from March 1931 at £1.600 per annum. Seemingly the second alternative was agreed, but only for a two year period.

MDT paid for the year ending £242 plus £70 insurance for the two Dennis and two Chevrolet

The only known photograph of a Cowieson bodied TSM B10A2, is this shot of No. 42 alongside No.102 a Thornycroft BC with Dodson body.

MGO 102 a Thornycroft BC collided with a former SMA Willowbrook bodied AEC Regal, having skidded on the greasy road surface following a heavy down pour of rain, on the 4th September 1931. The report of the incident appeared in Eastwood & Kimberley Advertiser the same day, stating that the Regal was from the SMA fleet, indicating they were still running in their original livery six months later.

buses loaned from 1929. During the period of the closing of Mansfield tram system many buses were loaned by MGO.

J G Severn & Co, (SMA) of Alfreton offered their three services and sixteen buses at a price of £30.000 and a freehold site of 725 square yards in Alfreton, during February. This was deferred pending a report from the General Manager on the result of of eliminating remaining competition on the Alfreton-Eastwood-Nottingham route. A quick decision was made by MGO to purchase and an agreement signed. The purchase price of £28.000 included the land (it is assumed it was sold on), plus an additional £1450 for a new AEC Regal with 32 seat Willowbrook body, which became No.81. This vehicle had been with Severn just three days when the business was taken over on the 31st March. Williamson's operated the services until 14th May, whilst the Underwood garage was being temporarily

rearranged to accommodate the SMA fleet.

Tansey & Severn then took over the operation of services; 14 Nottingham-Alfreton; 15 Ripley-Alfreton; 16 Alfreton-Sutton in Ashfield, although the SMA buses were owned by MGO.

With the closure of the MGO South Normanton garage in February, the South Normanton-Nottingham service became a sole T&S operation.

MGO acquired J T Boam 'The Ray' bus service on the 26th March , which finally removed all competition on the 1 Heanor to Ilkeston route. It also provided them with seven buses and one coach. However, the Boam service was not operated until one week later than the original planned take over date. Boam's Heanor-Blackpool express service was applied for, but commencing from Ilkeston and serving Ripley, although it would appear due to objections this was withdrawn.

It was understood by the Board that Brewin &

Hudson might be prepared to sell the Heanor to Hucknall service. This was the last of the operators of any consequence who had been allowed to continue on the NDT route, under the Act of 1928. However, nothing further was reported, until 1935.

The saga of the proposed Nottingham Depot continued throughout the year. Provisional plans were drawn up on the Parliament Street site offered by Nottingham Corporation, which had to be settled before they would proceed with the lease. In October the Town Clerk was asked for more information, due to the slow progress on the matter.

Twenty new vehicles were purchased to replace older stock. All were received during April and consisted of fifteen TSM B10A2 chassis; five (Nos. 27-9/32-3) with Ransome bodies, five (30-1/35/38/40) with Strachan & Brown bodies, and 41-5 with Cowieson bodywork. The remaining five were Leyland bodied LT2 chassis, a fresh departure for MGO.

Vehicles were now numbered, with the digits cast on a metal plate, which was fixed on the bulkhead, but if the vehicle had a Auto-vac, the plate was placed on the bonnet. Transfers were fixed to the rear of the buses.

Advertising was negotiated for the interior of all buses and between decks of double deck buses.

It was reported that the former SMA 15 Ripley to Alfreton via Swanwick service was not a paying proposition, and although a road service licence was applied for, the application was withdrawn, seemingly it last ran in December. This was perhaps a rash decision as this was to give Trent the full rights between Swanwick and Alfreton, and later MGO had to give protection to Trent, when they again operated along this route.

An Albion bus was hired for demonstration purposes and it is believed that it was WD 3338, which was eventually operated by Stratford Blue.

The Ilkeston statutory bus service was provided by MGO at 9d per mile, and the Heanor to Ilkeston service provided by Williamson's was calculated at 6.56d per mile.

Road service licences for route Nos. 3 and 10 were issued to T&S by the Traffic Commissioners during June. Although applications for road service licences were also made by Williamson's for the NDT statutory services and certain routes on behalf of MGO, the licences were issued to MGO.

From the 15th July the operations of Williamson's, Tansey & Severn and Dawson's came under the common management of MGO. The vehicles and garages remained with the original companies and were rented to MGO. It is assumed that the Davis & Hope vehicles were transferred at the same time.

Following the transfer of the management of the bus operations to MGO, changes were made to the staff; W Williamson continued at Langley Mill in the General Managers department, J Williamson was engaged from the 1st September in charge of the garage business at Williamson's in Heanor and L Williamson retired on the 31st August.

The three members of the Williamson family also relinquished their directorship, although G H Neale continued as Chairman.

Negotiations for Grail & Joiner (Stratford-on-Avon Motor Services) of Stratford on Avon were completed on the 21st April. The sum of £10.500 was paid for eleven buses, eleven road service licences and the Bridge Town service station, Stratford. The former proprietors Stanley H Joiner and G H Grail assisted in the formation of the new company, which became the Stratford upon Avon Blue Motors Ltd., and an associated company of the MGO on the 4th May. The buses now carried the fleet name Stratford Blue.

At the first board meeting Joiner was appointed chairman, with Grail a director and G A Thorpe Secretary. A further three directors, including Sir Joseph Nall, were appointed at the following meeting. Sir Joseph replaced Joiner as chairman on the 22nd July, when the registered office was transferred from 28 Wood Street, Stratford, to 66 Queens Street, London. On the 17th December Joiner and Grail resigned from the board of the company.

During June MGO loaned to Stratford five 1927 Tilling-Stevens buses (Nos.19/21/37/46/69), all remained, except No.69 which was returned in 1933 and renumbered No.83.

Bristol Tramways & Carriage Co, paid £2.000 for the Cheltenham-Malvern service, and a share of the Cheltenham-Evesham service on an agreed basis of 2/3rd Stratford Blue and 1/3rd Bristol running on a co-ordinated timetable.

The construction of a new garage at Bridge Town was approved.

At the time of the take-over, the application for stage carriage licences was before the West Midland Traffic Commissioners. All of these were granted, with the exception of a Leamington, to Stratford, Evesham and Cheltenham service, which Midland Red (Birmingham & Midland Motor Omnibus Co.) had also applied for. However, agreement was reached with Midland Red during December, when both companies reverted to their original operating territories.

Derbyshire County Council supported the objections of both Ilkeston and Heanor councils to the Market Places being used a turning circles for trol-

Midland General Omnibus Company Ltd.

(OPERATED BY WILLIAMSON'S GARAGE, LTD.)

SPECIAL
Whitsun Excursions.

WHIT-SUNDAY.

	Depart		For	Fare.
Ilkeston Market	2.30 p.m.		Afternoon PEAK TOUR through	
Heanor ,,	2.45 ,,		Ambergate, Cromford, Via	3/6
Ripley ,,	3.0 ,,		Gellia, Rowsley, and Matlock.	
Ilkeston Market	6.30 p.m.			
Heanor ,,	6.45 ,,		ROUTE AS ABOVE.	3/6
Ripley ,,	7.0 ,,			
Ilkeston Market	2.30 p.m.		DOVEDALE.	
Heanor ,,	2.45 ,,		Via Derby and Ashbourne,	4/6
Ripley ,,	3.0 ,,		4½ hours in the Dale.	
Ilkeston Market	2.30 p.m.		Half-Day PEAK TOUR through	
Heanor ,,	2.45 ,,		Ambergate, Matlock, Chats-	5/0
Ripley ,,	3.0 ,,		worth, and Via Gellia.	
Ripley Market	7.30 a.m.		SKEGNESS.	
Heanor ,,	7.45 ,,		MABLETHORPE.	10/0
Ilkeston ,,	8.0 ,,		Return 6.30 p.m.	

WHIT-TUESDAY.

Ripley Market	9.0 a.m.		Popular Short Day Excursions to	
Heanor ,,	9.15 ,,		MABLETHORPE & SKEGNESS.	7/6
Ilkeston ,,	9.30 ,,		Return 5.45 p.m.	

All Seats to be Booked in Advance at:

HEANOR: Williamson's Garage Ltd., Ray Street, Heanor.
LANGLEY MILL: Midland General Omnibus Co. Ltd., The Depot, Langley Mill.
ILKESTON: Mr. Richards, The Bon Bon Shop, Market Place, Ilkeston.
RIPLEY: Mr. Hutchison, The Cafe, Market Place, Ripley.
EASTWOOD: Mr. Hopkin, Newsagent, Nottingham Road, Eastwood.

The coaching side was placed in the hands of Williamson's Garage, and the above advertisement which appeared in May 1931, was one of last before the associated companies licences were transferred to MGO.

One of the ten AEC 662T trolleybuses with English Electric bodies at Langley Mill, prior to entry into service. The hinged dummy radiator and bonnet have been opened to show the English Electric 65 bhp motor and contactors. Contactors controlled the amount of current supplied to the motor from the resistances by switching in and out. Resembling the AEC radiators of the period, the Vee form was considerably deeper to carry the winged EE emblem of English Electric and below this the blue AEC triangle.

ley buses and to a reverser at Taylor Lane, Loscoe, on the grounds this would interfere with the free flow of traffic. The Minister of Transport gave his decision which was on the side of the Authorities. In Ilkeston trolleys either turned at Rutland Hotel or at the White Lion Square. At Heanor vehicles went on to Loscoe. The reverser was granted at Loscoe, on the understanding it was placed on private land.

Ilkeston trams stopped operating on the 7th February and were covered by MGO buses until the trolley vehicles were commissioned. It was agreed that Ilkeston Corporation would take up the rails at cost and retain the scrap. The Corporation employed their own direct labour, including almost sixty unemployed workmen, during the period of reinstatement, which cost £33.000.

The Derbys & Notts Electric Power Co, was granted permission to fix lighting to thirty poles in Nuthall, 25 poles in Ilkeston and 32 trolley poles in Eastwood at a fixed rental.

The Ministry of Transport inspection of the Ilkeston system was carried out on the 8th and 9th of December.

Contractors immediately transferred to the Ilkeston to Loscoe section, providing a reverser at Loscoe on land leased from the Butterley Co, in accordance with the Ministry request. A bay was cut into a field, which allowed vehicles to rest during layover, and once the extension to Ripley was completed, it prevented the obstruction of the mainline traffic.

1932

There was a renumbering of all the routes, with the Ripley-Nottingham service becoming No.1.

Applications for transfer of part of the associates licences, was not made until January and granted in the April. These were the former Williamson's express service from Ripley to Skegness and Mablethorpe, and excursions and tours from Heanor and Ilkeston. To these were added similar licences from Eastwood and Codnor. During November the NDT applied for licences in their own right, being journeys to cover trolley vehicle failure and works services, which would have been operated on hire from MGO.

It was now necessary under the Road Traffic Act to display the fact a vehicle was on hire to another concern. So a small blind was fitted inside the glass on the front bulkhead, when unwound displayed 'On hire to Notts & Derby'.

Approval was given to extend the existing Tansey & Severn garage on Alfreton Road, Underwood, which was directly opposite the main premises. It was built with a steel frame and brick infill with corrugated sheet roofing. The office in front of the old garage was converted to a bus shelter.

The Board decided the existing colour scheme of azure and cream be adhered to. Originally they stated white not cream! Azure, a mid blue or sky blue became the standard colour scheme.

TSM B39A7 chassis were ordered for 1932 with Beadle 32 seat bodies, and delivered in two separate batches. Nos.86-91 arriving in March and Nos.116-20 during July. A month later five (Nos.121-5) TSM D60A6 double deckers appeared with Weymann 50 seat bodywork. Finally No.46 a former TSM D40A6 demonstrator with a Beadle 56 seat body was transferred from M&DT. It had been with them for only a very short period. All these were purchased to replace vehicles condemned by the Traffic Commissioners.

Beadle also rebodied two Tilling-Stevens buses following a fire and an accident; they were No. 57 a B10B and No.2 a B10A.

The draft lease for the Parliament Street depot was amended and an alternative proposal for a site on Derby Road, Nottingham belonging to Mr Richardson was discussed. Balfour Beatty were asked to prepare provisional estimates for a suitable building on both sites. During June it was decided not to proceed with Derby Road, and Parliament Street was deferred for further report on the cost of building estimated at £13.500. Although a month later Balfour Beatty decided to use part of the site for other purposes. It is assumed the site on Derby Road was the car park at No.9, used as a coach terminal and booking office. Mr Richardson did sell the site and his tours and excursion licences to S Durham-Rowe, who never owned any vehicles. He then, in turn, sold on to Arthur Skill in April 1948.

Land adjoining the MDT garage on Sutton Road, Mansfield was purchased. Plans were drawn up for a twenty bus garage on the front half of the site, with the provision for extending on the remaining half later. The former Mellows garage on Russell Street, Sutton in Ashfield, was closed at the same time and alternative premises were provided at Mansfield, either at the former Davis & Hope garage on Southwell Road, or the MDT garage until the new site mentioned above was ready.

Williamson's garage on Derby Road, Heanor, was also closed, but negotiations for a sale was not completed.

Enquiries were made into the Davies Brothers of Sutton in Ashfield business, but it was not considered viable, as the daily service between Sutton in Ashfield and Blidworth served the Blidworth Colliery, which was closed at the time. The licences passed to R Butler of Kirkby in Ashfield in June the following year.

A new daily service 15 was introduced between Ripley and Aldercar serving Langley, Heanor and Waingroves.

The Ripley-Mansfield service of the Ebor Bus Co, of Mansfield and three buses were taken over on the 11th August. The journeys were embodied into the existing 8 route, which remained hourly except on Saturdays and Sundays when it became half hourly. The Ebor set up continued to operate the remainder of their business until purchased by MDT in March 1950.

The 9 Nottingham to Rainworth was extended into Mansfield, with MGO running all journeys, but the Mansfield to Rainworth section remained joint with MDT.

Agreement for the purchase of Crompton & Longford (Reliance Bus Co) of Bidford on Avon was reached with Stratford Blue on the 18th February. Eight vehicles were included (Bean, Ford, Chevrolet three Guy's and two Star's), the two Guy OND models being transferred almost immediately to Cheltenham & District (Nos.1-2). This gave them a further ten licences for services covering Stratford, Alcester, Bidford, Cheltenham, Tewkesbury, and Evesham area. Several of the routes were sold to Midland Red who took over from the 16th June. Those involved were Evesham to The Lenches, Bishampton, Pershore, Bricklehampton,

Cheltenham and Tewkesbury.

On the 14th June the management was transferred to Leamington & Warwick, when all maintenance and overhauls were carried out at their Emscote depot. Their manager Percy Olver also became a director of Stratford Blue. Upon reflection it seems rather strange that SBM was not originally placed with Leamington & Warwick or Cheltenham & District, as both were connected by SBM operations, although the sale of routes to Midland Red and Bristol was obviously territorial agreements.

The first part of the trolley system opened between Bridge Street, Cotmanhay and Hallam Fields, Ilkeston on the 7th January as service No.13. At the termini a reverser was provided at Crompton Street, Hallam Fields and at Cotmanhay. At White Lion Square an extension ran to the Park Road Garage. Power was supplied from the Park Road sub station to the Market Place by underground feeder cables. Six, (Nos.300-5), all English Electric 32 seat front entrance vehicles, were purchased at a total cost of £9.700, operating the route on a very regular headway (certain times every seven or eight minutes). Large fleet numbers being painted at both front and rear, on this batch.

Balfour Beatty had estimated the cost of erecting the Station Road, to Ilkeston Junction branch at £1.570, but it was decided to abandon this as the MGO Ilkeston-Eastwood and Kimberley services provided adequate coverage. They decided if necessary they would operate omnibuses as and when required.

The Church Street, Cotmanhay line was estimated at £1570 and would give the Heanor vehicles a second route into Ilkeston.

On the 2nd August the Ilkeston (Manor Road) to Heanor and Loscoe (Crossing) line was opened following the approval of the Ministry Inspector. Ten (Nos.306-15) AEC 662T EEC trolley chassis with English Electric single decker bodies were allocated to this route which was numbered 6. Again a frequent service was provided, varying from six to twenty minutes intervals, covered at an high average speed of 11.4 mph. A complete turning circle was provided at Manor Road/Granby Street (Rutland

Hotel), where the timings allowed transfer to service No. 13 serving Cotmanhay, Ilkeston town centre and Hallam Fields. These trolley buses were the first to have metal cast fleet numbers, which like the motor buses were fitted at the front only.

A sub station on Loscoe Road, Heanor provided power by underground cables to three points at Sheldon Road, Loscoe, Holbrook Street and Ilkeston Road in Heanor

Balfour Beatty then proceeded to estimate for the completion of the final sections; Ripley-Loscoe and Heanor-Cinderhill. This amounted to £55.000, excluding vehicles, and included payment to Nottingham Corporation in respect of the abandoned tramway.

Notts County Council agreed to the lowering of the road under a bridge at Cinderhill and the LMS bridge at Kimberley to a depth of twelve to fifteen inches. They however, refused to alter the LNER bridge at Kimberley as it would have increased the gradient, into Kimberley and, cause traffic difficulties

It was resolved by the Board, that in the event of the Nottingham Corporation failing to agree to the companys proposals, notice would be served on them to proceed with the conversion of the leased line, in accordance with section 10 of the Traction Act 1928.

With the presentation of the Nottingham Corporation Bill 1932, a petition to protect NDT rights was submitted. NCT agreed to the protective clause in the Bill and NDT withdrew their petition accordingly.

The Nottingham Transport Committee refused NDT their request to prohibit other operators from picking up passengers within 440 yards of the city boundary.

On the 23rd May the the trams ceased operation temporarily allowing the trolley vehicle equipment to be erected. However, the Ministry of Transport informed them by telegram on the 26th May that the tram service had to be reinstated immediately.

The Loscoe to Ripley section was completed and was awaiting Ministry of Transport approval on the 20th October. However, it was not until the 7th

December board meeting that it was reported that a certificate of fitness had been issued. This was a temporary extension of service 6, which only ran until the completion of the Cinderhill to Heanor line. A turning circle was provided in Nottingham Road, Ripley,

The tram service within the City boundary (Cinderhill - Parliament Street) was withdrawn on the 3rd September. A replacement was not provided, until the trolley service was introduced.

Road reinstatement appeared to be on the expensive side when Derbyshire County Council advised NDT that they were liable to pay 5s.6d (27.5p) per yard for the removal of 28.458 yards of track. It was, however, recommended acceptance of the County Council's quotation of £408.15s, for the value of materials left in situ in lieu of removing the track.

It was agreed to hire for six months a Guy trolleybus at 2d per mile, with the company paying insurances tyres and any replacements, whilst Guy paid the licence fee. The 1930 model all Guy single deck vehicle was an ex demonstrator which received the fleet No.316. It was in fact purchased on completion of the hire for £825 and survived until 1949, albeit that it did not run very regularly in its latter years.

MDT were charged £20 for the hire of the two tram cars for 9 months up to the 30th September.

1933

It was recommended that approved advertisements be accepted on the back panel or emergency door. These were to be circular in form, being a similar size to the company monogram and colours. Window adverts were to be permanent and transparent, but not to exceed 7 inches in depth and the width of the window.

The first staff dinner was held at company's expense which was similar to those held for many years, by Derbyshire & Notts Power Co.

With the Williamson's parcel division working at a loss, it was decided to carry them by MGO bus.

Commer coach (No.112) was exchanged with Stratford Blue No.20, a Tilling-Stevens bus, formerly MGO No.69, but on return was renumbered 83.

As late as April 1933 consideration was being given to the fitting of an oil engine in one of the Tilling-Stevens.

Following management reports in February, it was decided to take up the lease on Nottingham Corporation's Parliament Street site, subject to the obligation to build being extended to three years. A month later they proceeded on the condition the lease was transferable to the Midland Counties Electric Supply Co.

Further excursion and tours licences from Blidworth and East Kirkby were obtained.

Certain journeys on the 5 from Ilkeston were extended from Eastwood Market Place, to Bailey Grove, New Eastwood.

From Thursday 20th April the 17 Ilkeston-Nottingham timetable included Sunday afternoon and evening journeys previously provided by F U Charlton between Ilkeston and Kimberley.

It was as late as July before application was made to the Traffic Commissioners for the 2 Cotmanhay-Nottingham (joint with Trent), and Heanor-Matlock services previously licensed to Williamson's. There was also a Cotmanhay-Nottingham works service which diverted via Strelley to the Haydn Road factories, which was again joint with Trent.

Negotiations with Chesterfield Corporation for the joint acquisition and operation of independent services in the Alfreton, Clay Cross, Chesterfield and Tibshelf area was approved, subject to final estimates. Chesterfield were very keen to establish a joint Chesterfield to Alfreton service, which the General Manager was to negotiate. Previously this area had been served by Trent from 1910 until 1914 and also by W T Underwood from a garage at Tibshelf. However, following the change of the company name on the 1st July 1927 to East Midland Motor Services Ltd, they withdrew from the area. The Tibshelf base was closed, and services between Alfreton-Chesterfield and Clay Cross-Mansfield were withdrawn.

If territorial agreements had been made, it would appear that neither Trent nor East Midland had made any claim to the area. This provided MGO with the

One of the 1933 AEC 661T-EEC trolley buses at the turning circle introduced at the Ripley terminus.

opportunity to complete their expansion programme which had been achieved in five years. Although it is doubtful if they had ever anticipated gaining a foothold in this area.

It is not known if Chesterfield Corporation had influenced the agreements, but MGO had proceeded to negotiate independently with several operators in the area concerned. The following had signed and sealed their sales by the 4th or 17th July. Although the changeovers were registered in July, they continued to operate separately until the 1st October, (the service Nos. shown were also added at this same time);

E Wharton (Morton Bus Co), Morton supplied a Dennis EV (No.130), and a Morris Viceroy (No.132) plus a stage carriage service 26 between Alfreton, Morton and Clay Cross. Although MGO registered excursion and tours from Morton, they did not include the express Morton to Blackpool service.

F Porter & Son, Stonebroom, sold to them five Leylands (69/84-5/112/127) and six Guys which were withdrawn. The routes consisted of 21 Mansfield-Chesterfield, 23 Alfreton-Chesterfield via Tibshelf, 24 Alfreton-Chesterfield via Shirland, 25 Sutton in Ashfield-Chesterfield, Alfreton-Morton colliery service and Higham-Lea Mills factory.

Leah Brothers, Huthwaite provided two licences only; 20 Sutton in Ashfield-Tibshelf via Huthwaite and Huthwaite (CWS factory)-Tibshelf.

E Viggars, Alfreton, who had three buses (two W&G L20s and No.128 Leyland PLSC1), decided to sell and included his licences for 22 Alfreton-Clay Cross via Shirland service and a Clay Cross-Belper works service.

R Fearn, Alfreton and Severn Bros of Swanwick joint operations between Alfreton and Heanor via Riddings, were given the service number 27. Of the vehicles they provided; two (Nos.131/3) Morris Viceroys were ex Severn and two Crossleys came from Fearn.

A Pilsley-Clay Cross service was obtained from Mrs Whitworth of Lower Pilsley during May and this was transferred to MDT for them to operate, albeit for only a period of about five months. It was then possible to take back the former Hassall and Thompson Bros services between Mansfield and Clay Cross and six buses from MDT during July, but again not operated until the 1st October. The journeys via Pilsley, which included the former Whitworth route, were given service No.12. Journeys via Stretton were cut back to Sheppards Lane, Tibshelf Wharf, and many of the shorts rationalised between Mansfield, Sutton in Ashfield and Stanton Hill, as they were already well covered by the newly acquired operators licences.

To cater for all the extra vehicles shared garage accommodation, for ten to eleven vehicles, was leased from Mr.Kenning at the Alfreton Motor Transport depot in Angel Yard, Alfreton. This came into effect on the 1st October, but there some problems for a few days, whilst drivers and conductors got familiar with new surroundings and schedules. Angel Yard had a very narrow entrance off the High Street, and visiting drivers delivering replacement buses regularly broke the glass window louvres, due to the restricted access. The more apprehensive asked the local drivers to take the vehicles into the yard.

The three months delay in taking the acquired businesses into the main fleet, may have been necessary to allow the completion of the Sutton Road, Mansfield garage, and the leasing of suitable premises in Alfreton.

The Board wished to purchase fifteen new vehicles, but Balfour Beatty did not approve of this, as they must have felt they were already well committed with the spending on acquisitions, and trolleybus conversions.

The auxiliary fleet contained vans, tower wagons, snow plough, staff cars and a motor cycle, which had been added to the fleet from the time MGO had been established. There was also a unit of small lorries, worked mainly on behalf of the Derbyshire & Nottinghamshire and the Leicestershire & Warwickshire power companies, transporting electrical equipment and workmen. The earliest lorries dated from 1925, although there were more additions when several of the Dawson's Thornycroft bus fleet, were converted to lorries during this period, and a new Dennis Lancet lorry was also purchased.

Although Stratford Blue was now under the control of Leamington & Warwick, MGO authorised the expenditure of £3.700 for a new garage on the Bowling Green site at the junction of Warwick Road and Guild Street, replacing the proposed Bridge Town site approved earlier.

The Derby Road, Heanor garage was leased to Ilkeston Hosiery Furnishing Co Ltd, in January. Trent Motor Traction, had been interested, asking for a seven years lease, but MGO required a longer lease.

NCT loaned a Karrier Clough double deck trolleybus for trial purposes during January. These trials were obviously successful as the Board recommended that Balfour Beatty purchase fifteen double deckers at an estimated cost of £1650 each.

The order was placed for the double deckers, Nos.317-31 with AEC 661T chassis, EEC equipment and 55 seat MCCW bodies. Like the AEC single deckers they were received with the rather unusual, for a trolleybus, half cab and dummy radiator.

Road reinstatements in Nottinghamshire, were agreed at the same terms as those of Derbyshire reported in 1932.

The tram track between Langley Mill depot and Ripley was abandoned at the end of January and it was proposed to abandon the remainder on the 31st March. In fact the Cinderhill to Eastwood Market Place section closed on the 13th February, and from Eastwood Market Place to Langley Mill depot on the 9th March. However, it was decreed a statutory service should be provided until the trolley buses were introduced, and a very basic service, mainly for workers, ran between Heanor and Cinderhill.

From the end of January the Langley Mill depot was connected at Heanor to the existing trolley system, allowing vehicles to be based at the headquarters. Interestingly the garage wiring was not connected to the overhead in the road. Trolleybuses had to leave the depot, providing the roadway was clear, either by battery or gathering up speed inside the building and coasting into the road with the booms held down with bamboo poles controlled by attendants or the conductors.

A turning point for the colliery works trolley buses was approved at Pit Lane, Shipley during April, and the agreed rent was £10 per annum. Although the work was not put in hand, until 1934.

The Church Street, Cotmanhay overhead was completed in accordance with Balfour Beatty's original estimate of the 28th September 1931 and the Board were informed on the 27th September that the Ministry of Transport Inspectors report had been submitted. It is understood that this became operational on Monday the 1st October. The reverser was converted to allow a turn from Cotmanhay Road into Church Street. A layby was provided by extending a leg of the reverser into Bridge Street, for the short journey vehicles. With the Loscoe service now passing through Cotmanhay this was linked to the Hallam Fields service, and in consequence the whole route became No.6. The use of the No.13 disappeared, although it would have been sensible to have used it for the far less frequent direct journeys, although on Saturday it ran hourly.

The final section opened on Goose Fair Thursday the 5th October, between Langley Mill and Nottingham (Queen Street). The changeover was not a success by any means according to the local press, who felt the fog may have been partly responsible for the early morning problems. They said "inconvenience is but a poor word for the conditions that ruled, and what some of those who have to rely on the buses to get to work said, is not printable". As a footnote they added; "the tram(?) post, would leave from Eastwood at 9.19pm"!

Thus trolley buses now ran the 15.4 miles between Nottingham and Ripley as service No.1. Despite being of a hilly nature, combined with high operating speeds, sixty six request stops and six compulsory stops on the 11.29 miles of inter-urban route between Ripley and Cinderhill, it was still possible to keep an average speed of 14.41 mph. It was claimed by the company that it was the fastest trolleybus schedule in Great Britain. Within the city boundary the speed was slackened, but they still maintained 10.7 mph between Cinderhill and the terminus. Trolleybuses frequently covered 250 miles daily, and with a restricted turn round time imposed

at Nottingham, a round journey of 30.8 miles was completed, almost without interruption. With only three minutes allowed for the loading of passengers on Queen Street, trolleybuses laid over either on King Street itself, or at the intersection of the two streets.

A substation on Walker Street, Eastwood provided a very short underground service to Nottingham Road, Eastwood and another at James Street, Kimberley supplied an underground service to points at Nottingham Road (near Maws Lane), and to Greens Corner, both in Kimberley.

The motor bus service renumbered 1.P (quoted in the timetables as petrol bus) from the original 1, supplemented the trolleybus service, but only on Mondays to Saturdays at peak times. Peak times being mornings, Monday to Friday evenings, and Saturday lunchtimes. This gave a combined service interval, with duplication, of just over two minutes. The normal headway was fifteen minutes during the week reduced to ten minutes on Saturdays for the trolley vehicles.

All receipts taken within the City were passed to the Corporation, less 10.5d per mile working expenses. Originally this agreement was for an experimental period, and the company reserved the right to go to arbitration on the subject of carrying local traffic within the city. From the 10th October NCT did provide occasional journeys on the 1.25 mile section between Valley Road, Basford and the boundary, which commenced from the city centre, with their route No. 41. At one time joint working between Queen Street and Kimberley was considered, but was not pursued. The trolleybus service between Valley Road and Queen Street was adequately covered by NCT services 36/37/48, and in fact, during 1927, was the first route to be opened.

The Provisional Order 1933 was passed without amendment during July and was awaiting Royal Assent. The order gave powers to construct circular terminals and reversers at Ripley, Heanor, Kimberley and other places incidental to the system, which were constructed the following year, except at Heanor. This meant that with service 6 continuing to turn at Loscoe, there was considerable duplication

with service 1 between Heanor and Loscoe.

Unsuccessful representations were made to the Traffic Commissioners on the 28th June, opposing competitors licences on the line of the trolley route, but restrictions were not imposed on them.

Although the Ilkeston section had been completed for over eighteen months, representations had to be made to the contractors to remove the redundant overhead equipment on Station Road, which had not been converted for trolley bus operation.

Regulations and Byelaws made by the Minister of Transport, were printed in a Statutory Rules and Orders book, displayed on each trolley vehicle in use. These had been issued on the 9th May 1932, 18th October 1932, end February 1932, and the 22nd June 1933, being updated for each new section. Of particular interest, was the listing the speeds that a trolley vehicle could operate, varying from 30mph on the following; a) In Nottingham Road, Nuthall, between Greens Corner, Kimberley and Broxtowe Inn, Cinderhill. b) In Nottingham Road, Ripley, between Codnor Gate Farm and Butterley Colliery Railway Bridge. Then reducing at various section from 25mph, 20mph, 15mph or 10mph with a 5mph limit on the following; all turning circles and triangles, passing through junctions and crossings, entering Bath Street from Market Place, Ilkeston, passing through Church Street, Heanor junction from all directions and over the level crossings in Loscoe Road and Mansfield Road, Heanor. If this was not an inconvenience to other road users, then the bringing of the trolleybus to a complete standstill, must have been really frustrating. These were specified at; Bath Street, Ilkeston and Church Street/Prince Street, Cotmanhay both on the descending journeys, and in Nottingham Road, Nuthall, near Pole No.258 (church layby) on the east bound journey.

Although Mansfield & District Tramways continued to hold road service licences after the closure of the tramway system, some were registered to Mansfield & District Omnibus Co Ltd, (MDO) from June 1933. However, in 1937 these two companies were merged into the Mansfield District Traction Company, which itself was formed in 1929 from the Mansfield & District Light Railway Company.

Chapter Five:
Hays Days

1934

The General Manager reported that he had not been satisfied with a Beardmore oil engine on trial, and it had been returned to the manufacturer. This may have been fitted to a Tilling-Stevens mentioned the previous year. However, he did add that he was hiring a an AEC single decker at 2d per mile.

It was reported on the 27th March that J H Booth of Westhouses had sold his business (effective from the 4th July), giving MGO nine vehicles. There were licences for; the Alfreton-Chesterfield via Tibshelf service which became 28, a Westhouses-Glapwell Colliery service, an Alfreton -Blackpool express service and excursion licences from Westhouses and Alfreton. The Alfreton excursions were sold on to Trent, under agreement. Only three buses were taken into the fleet, No.134 a Leyland LT2, No.135 an Alexander bodied Leyland TS1 and No.136 a Morris Dictator. The remainder that MGO operated for a short period were; three GMC T42s, two T30s and an Albion.

The acquisition of the Booth, service saw the rationalisation of routes, with the withdrawal of service 23 (ex Porter) between Alfreton and Chesterfield, as both covered the same route as far as Holmewood, but the 28 when on to cover Temple Normanton. To cover the section between Holmeswood and North Wingfield, the 21 Mansfield-Chesterfield was diverted by deleting Pilsley, which was already covered by service 12.

On the same date the Ripley-Pinxton service oper-ated by W E Topham of Leabrooks was acquired, together with an Albion and two Guy OND Cowieson bodied 20 seat buses. The Albion (RB 5318) was loaned to Leamington & Warwick from the 20th March 1935 for an unknown period, although it was returned and sold on by MGO in July 1937.

George Shaw & Sons of Ironville, the other oper-ator of the Ripley-Pinxton service sold out on the 26th April. The deal included two Dennis G buses dating from 1928.

Both the former Shaw and Topham buses remained un-numbered, during the period with MGO, and it was the 19th July before MGO com-menced operation on service 13 Ripley-Pinxton.

Jointly with Chesterfield Corporation MGO pur-chased the business of J Cresswell of Clay Cross. This gave them the excursion and tours from Clay Cross, and a summer Saturdays and Sundays express service between Clay Cross, Heath, Glapwell to Skegness and Butlins Holiday Camp.

F U Charlton of Ilkeston sold to MGO his Cotmanhay to Shipley Colliery service for £50. It was last operated by Charlton on 31st December, as the journeys were already covered by NDT trolleys.

An MGO application was submitted, but subse-quently withdrawn, for a Ripley to Nottingham direct express service, although it was limited to one journey each way on Monday to Saturday.

Garage premises at Sutton in Ashfield, South Normanton and Southwell Road, Mansfield were sold in June.

Due to illness J.F.Petry was appointed Secretary, in place of W.C.Bryden.

The Nottingham Corporation (Trolley Vehicles) Provisional Order 1934, provided for a direct route from Nottingham City Centre to Stockhill Lane, Cinderhill from Bentinck Road via Alfreton Road and Bobbers Mill. This never came into existence, possibly as it was felt by NCT that this was more for the benefit of NDT, although there was not the intense development on the main road as most of the other routes.

In June, Nottingham Corporation wrote to NDT complaining of de-wirements when operating with-

BME 520 an AEC Regal 4 demonstrator in the Langley Mill paint shop, for a little touch up work in company with No. 124 a Weymann bodied TSM D60A6. BME 520 was fitted with a 5.35 litre 4 cylinder oil engine.

The interior of Ilkeston Park Road garage, c 1934, clearly shows the timber flooring which has been laid in the far bay to cover the pits and the tram tracks in the near bay. Of the rear views it is possible to identify two of the three Ransome bodied Tilling-Stevens B10A2s, from the left as Nos. 76 and 71.

in the City and suggested that they supplied them with a pair of Corporation pattern trolley heads, to overcome the problem. In reply, it was stated that they had considered this for some time, but the difficulty arose in the fact NCT used a 4 inch wheel and they were compelled to use a 5 inch wheel by reason of the speed they operated between Ripley and Cinderhill. They added that the situation was difficult and they were loathed to make drastic changes for fear of upsetting the balance of operation. They did have a good record on their own section and if they changed it might improve on the city lines, but have an adverse affect on their own lines. Again on the 3rd October, the Corporation informed the company of a de-wirement of trolley No.329 at the top of King Street. The pole short circuited the overhead, causing a delay of fifteen minutes before power could be restored. It was suggested that they withdrew the vehicle in question, as they were under the impression that fault existed on one or other of the trolley poles. Since there was no known reply, the suggestion may have remedied the problem. The Corporation changed from trolley wheels to carbon sliders during the War.

During severe weather, the trolley heads were liable to freeze up, but this was overcome by adding a little glycerine to the lubricating oil. To prevent delays these were attended to during layover, when trolley wheels or heads were replaced. Some years later cutters were fitted in frosty weather, and one enthusiast well remembers the early morning vehicles, showering the ice from the wires, which glistened in the rays of the morning sun.

Trolleybuses were docked at 80.000 miles, having their motors removed and dismantled. New or reconditioned armature shaft bearings were fitted, and the contactor equipment overhauled. The front axle, steering gear, transmission lines and the rear axle differential were reconditioned. All insulation was tested and renewed as required.

Colliery traffic, was catered for by the early vehicles with the first trolley leaving Langley Mill at 4.45am.

Further turning points were introduced, with reversers provided at Pit Lane, Shipley (£282.13s6d), Hill Top, Eastwood (£149.15s4d) and a revised turning circle at Ripley (£580.16s7d). Although the original Ripley circle on a wide section of Nottingham Road adjacent to the old tram terminus was retained, the later construction allowed

vehicles to turn from Nottingham Road, into New Street then Park Street and load in Beighton Street. The MOT statutory rules and orders, issued a little later in June 1935, deemed there should be a 10mph speed limit on this new section. Three more were referred to the Chairman, and it is assumed that Station Road (£265) and Green Lane (£360) Kimberley and Nottingham Road/Watnall Road, Nuthall (£290), were completed within a few months. At Nuthall a full turning circle with a layby was built on the North side in front of the Parish Church. The Ministry of Transport submitted their report on these in May 1935, and they were in use shortly afterwards. The primary purpose of these installations was to enable a shuttle service to be worked in case of obstruction or damage to the overhead equipment.

In Nuthall and Kimberley, the D&N Electric Power Co, were granted permission to suspend street lights centrally from the trolley standards.

Quotations for a further fifteen trolley vehicles were agreed, but nothing was ordered.

1935

The deaths of A H Beatty and the former Company Secretary W C Bryden were reported to February meeting of the Board.

Fun and games commenced when MGO signed a purchase agreement on the 17th January, with Frederick Nelson Billingham for the Billingham Bros, of Ilkeston business. Immediately objections were raised by Barton, who had taken over other operators who ran in the same area. The main contention was the 15 Long Eaton-Ilkeston service, on which Barton had competed with the Ilkeston independents since 1927. Special conditions were imposed by the Traffic Commissioners relating to this and the proportion that Barton, E Poxon and United Bus Service (five businesses, including Billingham. Poxon was taken over in 1934 by Grainger one of the other members) could operate. By the time MGO had negotiated with Billingham, Barton had already acquired S Pounder and F U Charlton, and established a base at Ilkeston. During May it was reported that Barton would be acquiring the business and agreement reached in June was; 1)

MGO to sell to Barton all the Billingham vehicles. 2) To sell the services, but retain the excursion and tours from Ilkeston and an Ilkeston-Derby football match day service. An agreement as to operation in the Ilkeston was also approved. It would appear that the territory allocated to Barton was defined roughly to the south west of Ilkeston, with MGO taking all the excursion and tours business. Barton thus surrended to MGO the former Pounder and Charlton excursions licences as a matter of course.

The saga continued when in February, Barton agreed to the purchase of F W Chambers, Ilkeston operations. Although there is nothing now to substantiate the assumption, it would appear this was used as a bargaining point by Barton, as again licences covered both companies territories. Since Barton did not apply for the licences until August it virtually confirms that Chambers was a part of the equation. Two licences passed to MGO, who applied for them in January 1936.

A month later the Pinxton Bus Co, of Sutton in Ashfield was obtained for £9.650 and the agreement was signed and sealed on the 18th February. The Huthwaite to Rufford Colliery licence was sold to MDT for £100. Their daily service between Alfreton-Pinxton-Mansfield became route 11. Also the tours and excursion licences from Pinxton and Sutton in Ashfield were included. Although ten buses were purchased only five entered the fleet. Of the five, three were Crossleys (Nos.94-5 Eagle models, No.96 an Arrow), one Maudslay No.129 and No.137 a Dennis Lancet.

Although reported to the Board on the 14th May the signing of the agreement was delayed for the Brewin & Hudson business of Heanor. The fleet was made up of three Ford AA models and an A model, which were consigned to the rear of Langley Mill, until sold later in the year to E H Allday. The bulk of the purchase price of £3.000 must have been for the Heanor-Hucknall via Langley Mill service which became route 20. This was the last of the opposition which had been competing with the trolleybuses.

Service 29 Sutton in Ashfield-Tibshelf via Whiteborough had been obtained from Albert Scott of Huthwaite, together with a 1929 GMC T30 20 seat bus on the 30th October. This vehicle was quickly withdrawn, but remained in storage until sold in April 1937.

An agreement for the purchase of the Supreme Motor Coach Co, was signed on the 3rd December. The proprietor George Swain was retained on a service agreement. Included were two stage carriage routes, two express services, tours and excursions from Mansfield and Teversal, eight vehicles and a garage at the junction of Oxford Street and Woodhouse Road, Mansfield.

It was decided to provide accommodation for a sports and social Club at the Mansfield garage, and a site was purchased at the rear of the premises, for that purpose.

Negotiations opened, in May, with Midland Red for the sale of Stratford Blue as a going concern for £15.000. On the 12th December the sale of the MGO shares was completed.

Following the decision of the Ilkeston justices to find a conductor guilty of permitting a trolley bus to be over loaded, an appeal was made before a Kings Bench Divisional Court. It was stated the 32 seat trolleybus was one of the service run in the Ilkeston district, and forty passengers were found to be on it at the time it was stopped. NDT contended that a trolleybus was excluded, because there was no statute which brought it within the category of stage carriage as the Road Traffic Act 1930 exempted tramcars and trolleybuses. It was argued that under the NDT Act of 1928, these vehicles were not classed as omnibuses or motor cars. The Court dismissed the appeal with costs, saying it was obvious that the vehicle exhibited all the marks of a stage carriage vehicle, which came within the Act of 1842. It was not taken out of category for the purposes of road transport, although excluded from the definition of a road service vehicle.

The turning point at Heanor was still an issue and discussions were held with the UDC, to see if this could be resolved. Consideration was given to a Heanor UDC proposal of the 5th December, to effect a settlement of the objections on various terms. These included the payment of £800 for highway works, and the consideration for a turning point at a corner site in Heanor or near the Midland Hotel, Langley Mill. In reply NDT stated their preferred option was to pay £800 for road works.

Agreement was reached with Barton to give protection to the trolleybuses in Ilkeston.

The Alfreton Road and Bobbers Mill, Nottingham route was still concerning the Board, and it decided during May to seek running powers in addition to the Nottingham Road, Basford, route. The Traction Bill 1935, in the form of a draft for powers to run on certain additional routes and extend the Company powers of running vehicles. Nottingham Corporation advised NDT that they were unable to accede to the Bobbers Mill route. However, representations from local authorities and an enquiry from the MOT regarding the alleged crowding out of through passengers at the King Street, Nottingham terminus, proposals were laid before NCT again, to persuade them to build the new overhead through Bobbers Mill.

1936

An agreement was made between MGO, MDT, MDOC and NDT for promoting and protecting services.

The bus replacement programme was submitted to the Board as follows;- 1936 - 8, 1937 - 34, 1938 - 14, 1939 - 23, 1940 - 23, 1941 - 28, 1942 - 17, 1943 - 1. Two were added to the 1936 order making a total of ten (Nos.156-65) with very attractive Weymann coachwork on AEC Regal chassis. Obviously the 1934 demonstrator must have impressed the management, to see this change in vehicle purchasing.

Overhauls and major repairs were carried out at Langley Mill. Running repairs, including greasing and semi-docking being undertaken by the night or day mechanics at Alfreton, Ilkeston, Mansfield and Underwood. Each depot had one spare vehicle each to cover any problem or major defect. Between 25 to 30 buses were housed at each of these garages. Between 9am and 4pm, during offpeak, a considerable amount of the fleet was available for repairs, consequently reducing the amount of night staff required.

Following the acquisition of G Swain they considered the following proposals;- 1) Dawson's

The interior of No. 164 one of the ten AEC Regals with Weymann coachwork. The provision of moquette seats finished with leather headrests, sliding roof, and luggage racks was quite an advancement in luxury and styling of the earlier buses. It was possible to provide five seats across the rear, by moving the emergency exit to the offside rear.

Stanton Hill, X3 Mansfield, Sutton in Ashfield-Blackpool and eight vehicles; four Leyland coaches (Nos.139/41 TS1s, 147 a TS2 and 143 a TS6) supplemented by four buses; Leyland PLSC3 No.153, LT1 No.149. KP No.151 and an Albion PMB28 No.145. Two of these vehicles were loaned to MDOC pending delivery of their new coaches. The intended sale of the former Swain garage was delayed due to shortage of space. It was, however, sold by auction by the 1st July.

Swain's Skegness service was embodied into the former Cresswell service X4 from Clay Cross, which now picked up at North Wingfield, Hardstoft, Huthwaite, Sutton in Ashfield and Mansfield.

Ripley and Swanwick were added to the 24 (D4) Alfreton-Pilsley-Chesterfield, with protection given to Trent, between Swanwick and Alfreton, which must have annoyed them as they had relinquished this section, in 1931.

Although agreement had been reached in October 1935 for the purchase of Alfreton Motor Transport Co Ltd, the takeover did not take place until the 1st April 1936. Shares were transferred from George

Enterprise be transferred to MDT and renamed Supreme Tours Ltd, a new company formed on transfer of shares, 2) Excursions and tours from Mansfield, and contract work to MDT, 3) The Blackpool express service to MGO, 4) Excursions and tours from Teversal to MGO. 5) Supreme Tours to act as tours and private hire department of MDT. Eventually, it was agreed that the following be introduced. Pick up points on seven tours licences from Blidworth, Rainworth, Mansfield, Sutton in Ashfield, Stanton Hill and Teversal transferred from MGO to MDT, and George Swain be employed by MDT as tours agent. Following the take over from the 23rd April, MGO were operating the 23 (D3) Mansfield-Teversal, 30 (E1) Sutton in Ashfield-

No.315 AEC-EEC with English Electric body at White Lion Square, Ilkeston, prior to the installation of a traffic island. The signpost in the centre of the picture, which must have been rather vulnerable, indicates London 131 miles. Just above the trolleybus an engineer carries out some adjustments to the overhead system.

Kenning, Anthony Stewart, and Frank Kenning, these being taken up by MGO and their nominees, including Sir Joseph Nall, W McGill, Aubrey Edward, and D Hays who were made directors. Ten of the eleven vehicles entered the MGO fleet; Nos.142/8/50/2/4 Leyland PLSC3 with Leyland 35 seat bodies, No.146 Leyland LT1 also with Leyland body, Nos. 138/40 Gilford 1660T and 1680T, No.144 Karrier JKL and No.155 Karrier Chaser. A Commer bus was not used. The licences were; 31 (E2) Alfreton-Matlock via Crich, 32 (E3) Alfreton-Matlock via Tansley, 33 (E4) Alfreton-Brackenfield, also 33 (E5) Alfreton-Wheatcroft, three routes to Lea Mills from Alfreton, Wessington and Whatstandwell. There were also tours and excursions from Alfreton, sold on to Trent by agreement. The new company retained the freehold garage and two dwelling houses at Angel Yard, Alfreton and vehicles which they leased to MGO.

F W Chambers licence for the Ilkeston-Matlock Wednesdays only express, was successfully applied for in January, with a revision to serve Ripley in lieu of Derby, from Horsley Woodhouse. Also at the same time a lunchtime works journey between Ilkeston Junction (Lewis's factory) and Station Road was applied for although, Barton continued to work this until the 4th July. The tours and excursions licence from Ilkeston was surrendered by Barton.

Negotiations were completed on the 24th April for the purchase of Straw & Fletcher (Pride of Ilson Coaches) of Ilkeston. This consisted of the tours and excursions from Ilkeston picking up at Heanor, which were transferred into the existing licence, but the Heanor, Ilkeston, Derby and Blackpool summer Saturdays X8 express was amended, by deleting Derby and commencing from Ilkeston to Heanor. Trent, who already ran a similar service from Derby, acquired the pick up point. Three Guy coaches taken into stock became Nos.166-8.

A cross town extension to the 7 (B6) at Ilkeston, from Manor Road, via Lord Haddon Road and the Market Place, to Wade Avenue, Larklands, opened up an area to traffic to the west of Bath Street

Conditions were imposed upon MGO, Trent and Naylor to give protection to MDT on the Mansfield

to Nottingham and Alfreton services.

During August a new system of route numbering was introduced with NDT having the prefix 'A' and MGO 'B' onwards. With 9 numbers with each letter of the alphabet, it gave a potential of 234 alternatives, using only two lines. These prefixes did not indicate any variations of route, as the suffixes implied on other systems. The highest number reached was the newly acquired E5 Alfreton-Wheatcroft, previously sharing 33 with Alfreton-Brackenfield which became E4. Express services received an X prefix, but the works services remained unnumbered. The 1933 AEC trolleybuses had number apertures, but they had remained blank until they introduced this, and probably the same applied to the MGO AEC Regal coaches received during May and June. Numbered 156-65 they introduced navy blue into the single deck fleet.

The inter availability of tickets with Trent was confirmed on the 14th May and was in force until the end of the year and thereafter at one months notice.

It was decided to relinquish the lease at Parliament Street, Nottingham site and it was termi-

nated from the 24th July.

Further land was purchased fronting Sutton Road, Mansfield, and also a plot to the rear.

The staff at Underwood depot requested better accommodation for their sports and social club which was approved.

Heanor UDC accepted the earlier NDT offer to pay £800 towards cost of the reconstruction of a road necessary for the extension of the trolley routes. This was then embodied in the N&DT Bill 1936, which received Royal Assent on the 21st May. Immediately a new overhead system gyrating from Ilkeston Road into Mundy Street and Wilmot Street Heanor was approved, and put in hand. Upon completion of the necessary roadworks service 6 was cut back to Heanor Market Place.

A gyrating traffic system at White Lion Square, Ilkeston, involved alterations to the overhead system in connection with traffic islands, at a cost of £420.

It was quoted in the AEC Gazette that the trolley buses were working a twenty hour day, covering annually a distance of up to 48.000 miles. Up to the year ended 31st December, the AEC-English Electric units travelled 1.442.000 miles and carried

An atmospheric view from a cobbled Huntingdon Street, Nottingham of the bus station, showing the variety of operators. On view are buses of Trent, East Midland, Barton and in the centre MGO No.4 an AEC Regent with Weymann front entrance body. The ice cream vendors transport was one of the original Walls 'Stop me and buy one' tricycles.

8,771,000 passengers.

Consideration was given to the conversion of Nos. 306-15 the AEC single deck trolleybuses to diesel engine and to replace them with double deck trolley vehicles. Nothing further is reported, so it is believed cost may been a major factor with the decision not to proceed. Balfour Beatty sanctioned seven AEC 661T chassis, with English Electric 80hp regenerative equipment and Weymann 56 seat all metal rear entrance highbridge double deck bodies, at a cost of £14070. However, initially the order was placed for two only.

1937

Estimates were accepted for extensions at Ilkeston garage.

Dawson's land and garage at Cotmanhay Road was sold during October to the Derbyshire & Notts Electric Power Co, for £720. Leaving vehicles as the only assets

The character of the fleet was changed with the new vehicles purchased during the year and was to set the purchasing policy up to World War 2. Oil engines were fitted for the first time, and became the standard, with the delivery of twenty five (Nos.4-6/9-10/12/14/16/18/20-1/36-7/48-50/52/54/61/5/67-8/72) AEC Regent double deckers with metal framed Weymann front entrance highbridge bodies. Double deckers with front entrance bodywork provided extra comfort for the passengers, except when the manual sliding door was left open, when it was draughty and dangerous. This layout became very popular in the Midlands with Midland Red introducing them in 1933, followed by Campion of Nottingham in 1934, Trent in 1936 and Barton in 1939.

Ten (Nos. 73/8/82-3/92/4-8) 35 seat Weymann dual purpose bodies were fitted on to Leyland TS7 chassis with 8.6 litre oil engines. These were designed for both stage carriage and longer distance services, being a compromise between a coach and a bus. The same all metal body was used, as for the previous years coach, however, the difference was mainly in the seating, and interior decoration. The sliding roof, was specified on this batch, and also appeared on some of the later saloons. On all single

deck models now had destination displays fixed above the rear window, roof mounted advert boards and rear luggage lockers, but not the roof mounted luggage racks. There were two styles of exterior moulding on this batch, each was to be adopted from the next year to distinguish between coach and dual purpose vehicles. Several were received in a off white livery with navy blue relief to the wings and side flashing, and red wheel hubs, introduced to celebrate the Coronation of King George VI.

MGO had returned to Leyland for the larger engine 8.6 litre oil engine required for the hillier parts of Derbyshire. Routes generally were 600ft. above sea level, and between Alfreton and Matlock they rise to 800ft. In winter, snow, ice and fog were the cause of delays, and so buses were equipped with non-skid chains, shovels, grit boxes and scotches.

It was rather unusual to have a high standard of vehicle whose primary purpose was stage carriage work and a very limited amount of seasonal coach work. This may have been influenced by the type of vehicle that Barton was putting into service, which Trent in particular, had difficulty competing with. The outcome was the people in the area, received a quality product from the operators, compared to most.

The lorry fleet increased to sixteen units, with the purchase of eight (G1-2/5/9-12/15?) 2 ton Morris Commercials.

East Midland Motor Services offered the Tupton-Lea Mills works services which they had recently obtained on the purchase of W Stoppard & Son of Clay Cross. Transferred during May, one operated via Shirland and the other via Higham, but they quickly amended them to terminate at Danesmoor and Williamthorpe Hotel, Holmewood respectively.

Barton acquired the stage carriage licences of E Gregory of Ilkeston. and in accordance with the agreement sold on to MGO the excursions from Ilkeston and two match day services to Derby County FC ground.

An article that appeared in the 'AEC Gazette' at the time, produced some rather interesting statistics and items, which were; total route mileage of stage

carriage services 369, which was supplemented by 190 miles of works journeys and 629 miles of express and seasonal services. The longest route was the 21.71 miles of the B8/9 Mansfield to Nottingham and then the B6 Mansfield to Ilkeston (19.71 miles). They ran 6.387.00 miles and carried 18.688.00 passengers, including 5104 on coastal express services

Mexborough & Swinton Traction Co., offered £3600 for six (Nos.300-5) English Electric trolleybuses, which was accepted. An order was then placed for a further five AEC 661T double deck trolley buses. With the two ordered the seven received became Nos. 300-5/32. They were all equipped with regenerative and rheostatic braking. Basically a standard product, except they were fitted with elec-

MIDLAND GENERAL OMNIBUS COMPANY, LIMITED.

NOTICE!

On and from Sunday, May 1st, 1938, the Brinsley—Langley and Waingroves—Spondon Services now operated by the Heanor and District Omnibus Co., Ltd., will be operated by the Midland General Omnibus Co., Ltd. The time and faretables will be unchanged, BUT the last picking up point on journeys to Spondon and the first setting down point on journeys from Spondon will be Pit Lane, Smalley.

Messrs. Barton Transport Ltd. will operate Services between the 'Nag's Head,' Smalley, and Spondon to cater for traffic on that section of the route.

Offices: Langley Mill.
'Phone: Langley Mill 201 & 292.

D. HAYS,
General Manager and Director.

Normally a basic notice of takeover was placed in the operators vehicles, but as shown above the Heanor & District acquisition was a little more complex

trical tubular heaters for the passengers comfort. It was believed at the time they were the only all metal construction double deck trolleybuses to have heating equipment installed.

A wayleave with LNER for troughing and trolley-wires attached to Bridge 61 over Cotmanhay Road, was agreed at £1 per annum.

1938

Extensions at Langley Mill provided additional garage accommodation for a further twelve double deck vehicles.

New deliveries were again all bodied by Weymann. They consisted of fifteen 35 seat dual purpose buses, ten (Nos. 53/55-6/99-101/10/3/26-7) on AEC Regal chassis with 7.7 oil engines and a further five (128-9/31/7/44/) Leyland TS8 models. Seven (151/5/69-73) 32 seat coaches were to a similar design on TS8 chassis and painted once again in the Coronation livery. Ten (174-83) AEC Regent front entrance highbridge double deckers were of cleaner lines than the previous years batch.

Additional pick up points were added to the X8 Blackpool express at Shipley, Marlpool, Loscoe and Codnor.

Purchase of shop premises and land at Alfreton, allowed an extension to the garage and the long needed widening of the narrow passageway to the garage.

The front entrance to one of the Underwood garage buildings was raised to allow the accommodation of a further five double deckers.

Jointly with Barton and Trent, MGO purchased Heanor & District Omnibus Co Ltd, of Ilkeston. All eighteen vehicles were stored by MGO pending disposal, when the sum of £400 was received for them.

The licences were split between the three. The Barton/MGO portion served Celanese works at Spondon and was a little more complex as divisions had to be made, to give Barton the Stanley Common and Smalley area. MGO remodelled the existing into three licences from Ripley, Brinsley and Langley, which the Traffic Commissioners approved. Two years earlier Trent had obtained a Heanor to Ilkeston service, which they abandoned.

A licence held by C Kirk (Blidworth Blue) of Blidworth was acquired and MGO commenced operation of a works journey between Blidworth, Daybrook and Jolley's Garage on Union Road, Nottingham.

Short journeys between East Kirkby and Mansfield on the B6 Ilkeston-Mansfield service, were taken from the main timetable, and extended in East Kirby to Diamond Avenue, on the Derby Road Estate, as route E6

The former Fearn & Severn, Alfreton-Heanor (D7) was joined with the former Inglis & Beardsley, Heanor-Hucknall (C9) to become C9 Alfreton-Hucknall, with a diversion via Aldercar. The D7 became Alfreton-New Eastwood, following the same route to Eastwood as the C9 except for

Aldercar. A new service E7 Heanor to Codnor via Langley Mill and Aldercar, ran on Fridays, Saturdays and Sundays pm only, as did the D7.

A newly introduced E8 Hucknall-Oxton via Papplewick and Calverton, again operated at pm times on Saturdays and Sundays.

The Board agreed to purchase from Llanelly District two 35 seat AEC Regals for the sum of £1573 each. With an additional payment for the fitting of heaters and they also offered to fit standard MGO seating in the price. These were virtually brand new and had identical Weymann dual purpose bodies to their own 1938 batch. Fleet numbers Nos. 184-5 were allocated to them.

Ilkeston Borough agreed to pay 21shillings (£1.05p) for the use of the overhead equipment for suspended street lighting.

1939

Cheltenham & District Traction Co, was sold to the Red & White group of companies from the 1st July, leaving only Llanelly and the three east midlands companies within the Balfour Beatty group.

Introduced in the summer the X2 operated New Brinsley, Underwood, Selston, Pinxton, South Normanton, Alfreton- Blackpool and the X3

Former Llanelly District (ABX 79) AEC Regent with Weymann dual purpose body which received fleet No. 185, was completely at home in Midland General territory. In this instance it is seen at Awsworth Road approaching the junction of Eastwood Road, Kimberley, working the B5 to Eastwood. In the background a freight train crosses the brick arched viaduct (known locally as forty bridges) over the Giltbrook valley, on the branch line from Awsworth Junction to Pinxton.

Bilsthorpe, Blidworth, Rainworth, Mansfield-Blackpool

Exchange of licences with MDT, gave MGO tour and excursions from Teversal (originally MGO) and Southwell, and it was suggested that services east of Mansfield be transferred to MDT.

An application was made during August to run between Ilkeston and Strelley during weekend evenings, but with the outbreak of war it never saw light of day.

War was declared with Germany on 3rd September and reservists were called up immediately, but it also affected employees who were being conscripted into the forces. Both companies responded by paying two months wages to the monthly paid staff and six clear weeks pay to the weekly paid. At the the discretion of the Directors, allowances were made for extra payment in special cases. It is assumed that this was a one off payment, as it was generally felt that it would be a short period of war and staff would return to work very quickly!

Although the Board requested thirty five Leyland TS8 models with the usual Weymann 35 seat bodies, the order was actually amended to ten (Nos.135-6/8-40/9-50/2-4), and five (142/5-6/66-7) 32 seat coaches. The remaining twenty (Nos.13/5/7/9/39/47/51/62/6/9/74/9/80/5/104/112/5/130/2-3) were fitted on to AEC Regal chassis.

A general complaint from the major operators was that the impressment officer for the War Department always selected the best vehicles, and again there was no exception at MGO when five (157-60/2) of the 1936 AEC coaches were acquired. Of these No. 158 was returned quite quickly, but Nos. 157/62 are believed to have been lost at Dunkirk, when they were driven into the sea to escape possible use by the enemy.

From Sunday the 24th September restricted timetables were introduced on all routes, with the recently E7 and E8 being completely withdrawn. As it transpired the restriction to conserve fuel and labour may have been too stringent, and so from the 21st October some of the restrictions were lifted. Journeys previously covered by a works service to Silverhill Colliery were embodied into the D3 Mansfield-Teversal.

NCT applied to extend the time by two years on the Bobbers Mill route (Alfreton Road), under the Nottingham Corporation Trolley Vehicle Act 1934. The Board was advised that the MOT was to make an order extending the period of time by six months, until 12th January 1940, for NCT to construct this line. In December a further application by NCT to extend the expiration date until the cessation of hostilities was approved.

Mr A A Edwards was appointed a director from October.

1940

Weather conditions during early part of year were very bad, with the whole country being covered with a great frost. The drivers suffered a lot of discomfort, and on Sunday the 4th February, the adverse weather saw the withdrawal of all services after 7pm. It must be remembered that at the outbreak of war, the Government had imposed blackout restrictions due to possible air raids, which forbade anyone to show a light which was visible from the air during the hours of darkness. Motor vehicles were restricted at first to the use of sidelights and a hooded single headlamp. Street lights were switched off, or only showed a very dim light on street corners. To distinguish vehicles white bands were painted around the edges of the mudguards. These restrictions, plus the weather must have been quite stressful to a driver with a heavy load of passengers, who were travelling in buses with blacked out windows.

As more and more male workers were enlisted into the armed forces, so women staff were recruited, as they did in the First World War. Mostly in those days they were employed as conductresses, but there was a strict ruling they must wear skirts. There was always some feeling at Mansfield garage as the MDT allowed the girls to wear slacks. Interestingly 'Modern Transport' carried an article on the situation at MGO showing how the male had dominated the workplace, and was rather surprised at womens adaptability. This read on the following lines; "The labour element in the workshops had been upgraded and has seen the younger workers being given more responsible work, and women

Photographed at Gregory Boulevard, newly delivered No.333 an AEC 661T-EEC trolleybus with Weymann bodywork, is painted in the wartime livery of grey. An NCT 1934 trolley bus passes in the opposite direction. White markings, to assist night driving with dimmed lights, have been applied to lamp posts and trees.

introduced where possible. One woman who had trained as a welder, became fully employed in building up worn parts by electric process, releasing a skilled welder for work of a more demanding technique".

MDT recommended co-ordination on certain stage services in the Mansfield area, as suggested in 1939. It was agreed and MDT took over completely the short journeys on B8, B9 Mansfield, Rainworth and Blidworth and the C1 to Bilsthorpe previously jointly operated. MGO retained the through journeys to Nottingham. Allocation of revenue on the pooled routes with MDT was MGO 40%, MDT 60% on the Mansfield-Blidworth section of the B8/9 service and MGO 20%, MDT 80% on the C1 Mansfield-Bilsthorpe.

A licence for a works service between Selston and Kirkby Bentinck Colliery, was transferred from T M Mitchell of Selston during June. Around this time Barton obtained the licences of T Winfield & Son (Star) of Awsworth, from which MGO purchased a works service between Lewis's factory Ilkeston Junction and Ilkeston Brook Street, and tours and excursion licence from Awsworth, which they did not take up until May 1948.

The MGO Mansfield depot was requisitioned for military purposes as from the 14th October, and garaging of vehicles was transferred immediately to the adjoining MDT depot.

NCT trolleybus services stopped running during air raid alerts, due to the possible sparking when passing through breakers or crossings, but strangely the the same restriction was not imposed on NDT who continued operating throughout. Initially the problem was overcome by painting white circles in the roadway, below the crossing, to indicate the problem and drivers coasted over them. Then the points were covered with an asbestos shield, but eventually the problem was solved by the fitting of carbon sliders. NDT experimented with sliders, but found the ice on the wires at the higher points of the route wore out the carbons after a single journey.

Approval from the MOT dated the 14th June was received for ten double deck trolleybuses and an order was placed accordingly.

1941

Priority for permit holders was introduced on the 10th November. With the restricted amount of vehicles and emergency timetables, non-essential travel was discouraged and so these were introduced to allow workers to travel to and from work. Timetables on stage carriage services, showed journeys which were reserved completely or partly for the accommodation of workers.

J F Petry the Companys' Secretary since 1934, was replaced following his death by Polydore Henry De Keyser. A little later in the year on the 26th September George Balfour JP, MP, passed away. Tributes were paid to him at the MCESCo meeting and it was through his auspices that an association was formed of several derelict companies in 1912. Balfour Beatty was now a great undertaking and one of the leading public utility companies.

MGO agreed to purchase from Dawson's four Thornycroft lorries and Tilling Stevens Nos. 70/6 (later requisitioned by the RAF) from the 1st January

An agreement was reached with Basford RDC to use part of the single deck garage at Underwood, as a fire station.

Northern Command of the armed forces, requisitioned the following during April; Tilling- Stevens Nos.29/38 and Leyland LT2 No.23 and the Royal Air Force obtained Tilling Stevens No.3/70/6.

With the purchase of Blue Service (Grainger Bros.) Ltd of Ilkeston, Barton had eliminated competition from their Ilkeston-Long Eaton service. This also gave MGO the monopoly on excursion and tours from Ilkeston, although these and an express service to Skegness were not registered until 1945.

The first four of the 1940 order for trolleybuses were received as Nos. 333-6 AEC 661T-EEC with Weymann H56R bodywork, having an improved styling to the 1937 batch, and they were painted all over in an austere dark grey livery.

A through running agreement was signed with Nottingham Corporation on the 17th June regarding adjustments to the original arrangements concluded in 1933

1942

MCESCo approved the purchase an 'unfrozen' Leyland TD7 with Leyland 56 seat highbridge body which entered service as No.186 on the 6th July.

The wartime allocation of utility vehicles was rather haphazard and very often operators received buses which did not fit into their fleet. MGO were no exception, although Leyland and AEC chassis were not available due to their other commitments in the war effort. Guy Arab I chassis with Gardner 5LW engines were supplied in an all over grey livery and the first No. 187 arrived in July with the standard Brush utility highbridge bodywork. However, during October No.188 was delivered with a body originally intended for Manchester Corporation with typical drop end window styling. The metal frames had been constructed at Metro-Cammell with others for Manchester when war broke out, and the project was shelved. The Ministry of War Transport (MOWT) later released these bodies which were transferred to Weymann for completion, but they were nowhere near the pre-war specification.

MCESCo agreed to a proposal, subject to Regional Transport Commission (the wartime body which replaced the Traffic Commissioners) approval, that MGO be authorised to pick up within the MDT protected area between Mansfield and Huthwaite, on the D1 service to Chesterfield. MDT provided 1d and 2d tickets and two thirds of the proceeds was paid to them. This continued throughout the period of the war. Protection was re-introduced after the war.

The balance of the 1940 order for trolleybuses were received as Nos.337-42, again with the same chassis and style of bodywork.

On the 1st April 1935, the boundary of the city of Nottingham had been expanded to include the villages of Bilborough, Strelley and Wollaton, which included the area of land between Middleton Boulevard and Coventry Lane. With this now within its boundaries the Nottingham Corporation decided to obtain powers to run trolleybuses from Middleton Boulevard along Wollaton Road and

Russell Drive to the junction of Russell Drive and Trowell Road, Wollaton, which of course was already served by MGO buses.

A MOWT public inquiry was held on the 24th and the 29th September. On the 4th December, the Ministry of War Transport (MOWT) reported that the Minister was satisfied there was a need to improve passenger transport facilities between Nottingham and Wollaton, which should be provided by trolleybus. The Minister stipulated that MGO and Trent should have a part financial interest.

1943

NCT made an application to extend a further 0.96 miles to Balloon Houses, Wollaton. The MOWT drafted proposals for- 'The continuance of the companies present through services, by the companies only, between Cotmanhay, Ilkeston and Nottingham, and for the provision of shuttle services between Nottingham and Balloon Houses, Wollaton by the companies and by Nottingham Corporation'. These stressed the Minister's view with regard to the need for economy in the use of imported fuel, the services should be provided by trolleybuses.

Based on the MOWT proposals NDT promoted their own Bill. This entailed the MGO purchasing Trent's share of the B2 Nottingham-Cotmanhay service, including short workings to Wollaton, for £8.000, and NDT extending the trolley system from Ilkeston via Trowell and Wollaton to connect at Middleton Boulevard, Nottingham with the NCT system. NCT was to provide one half of all necessary shuttle services between Nottingham City Centre and any point west of Middleton Boulevard, but not west of Balloon Houses.

It is rather interesting that the MOWT considered all the costs of providing the trolley system to be a preferable option so that imported fuel could be used for the war effort. Although in his proposals he did allow the possibility of providing motor buses by both MGO and NCT. Further proposals allowed the NCT to retain all revenue between the City Centre and Middleton Boulevard. Corporation tickets would have been provided on both the through and the shuttle services, for the section between Eton Grove, (stop before Middleton Boulevard) and the City Centre, with an apportionment of the revenue. There was to have been provision to cover the costs of electricity, use of the lines and facilities within the Corporation area by NDT.

NCT refused to participate in the MGO proposals of the MOWT to construct the system, particularly the use of the Corporation overheads by the company vehicles.

The NDT Draft was put before the Board on the 2nd October and was formally lodged, not knowing the intentions of the Corporation.

On the 3rd October a new bus station was opened on Mount Street, Nottingham, and most of the services serving the west side of Nottingham, north of the River Trent were transferred. MGO took platform 4 which had a small corner piece for additional parking. Barton and Trent took platforms 5 and 6 respectively, with Midland Red at the head of Trent vehicles. The new site not only reduced congestion at Huntingdon Street, but also saved in consequence a lot of motor fuel, which was at a premium. Built in the time of war, the shelters were utilitarian but served their purpose very well for over twenty five years. Just below the site was an old factory unit, which was converted to canteen facilities. Jointly leased with Barton and Trent, MGO provided £20 for utensils, which was repaid from the canteen profits.

In the meantime the Trent portion of the B2 was taken over from the 3rd October, but with a shortage of vehicles Trent continued to provide vehicles until the 31st December, by which time further Guy utilities had arrived.

The Ministry of Supply requested the release of W

On the 25th October 1945 NDT and MGO provided a luncheon and cheques for the long service employees of the companies. Those present left to right were:- Front row, G Horsley (8/1/14), R W Burley (15/7/13), T Walker (5/7/13), D Hays (General Manager), G H Lapworth (2/8/13), A G Hayes (4/8/13), B B F Hancock (1/8/14), W Basford (30/8/14). Back row, A Greensmith (1/10/16), C Patrick (25/10/14), J E Blackwell (1/10/15), J H O'Connor (27/9/16), W Williamson (Chief Engineer), K Laing (Traffic Manager), G Bullock (1/8/16), H Oldroyd (3/4/20), W Ford (18/3/20), A White (5/7/20). The dates in brackets indicate commencement of service.

Williamson to take charge of an important tank design branch. The Board replied that Williamson was essential to the operation of the company, but was temporarily released from the 4th January 1943.

All the 1943 deliveries of Guy Arabs were fitted with Weymann bodies and again the first two (Mark I chassis), were rather different. No.189 was identical to the earlier 188 and No.190 had a body intended for Liverpool Corporation which had again been in store, this time at Weymann's, following the outbreak of war. The remaining six (Nos.191-6) were standard utility design on Mark II chassis again with 5 cylinder Gardner engines.

One (No.158) of the 1936 AEC coaches was returned from the MOWT along with Tilling-Stevens No.29 and No.23 a Leyland LT1.

Six Sunbeam trolley vehicles from the 1944-5 programme for the production of 100 vehicles were allocated to NDT for the new route.

With effect from the 1st July, D&NEPCo, revised the rates, in connection with conversion to AC from DC. They had to pay a fixed charge of £100 per month to cover the conversion at five substations. This resulted in an estimated saving of £800 per annum.

1944

Sixteen gas producer units were purchased in the sum of £1701.1s.6d. As early as 1942 they had received licences for the acquisition of these, but only hired one for trial purposes. It was noted in the 1942 minutes that the opinion of the representatives of the omnibus companies was that these were unsuitable, but the MOWT had intimated that bus operators would be required to make use of 10.000 units. However, at the time of purchasing these, a MOWT directiive had reduced the fleet to be converted from 10% to 5%, and six months later abandoned the scheme. The producer gas units were introduced to save fuel on petrol engined buses. These two wheel trailers units had a water heater to which was added anthracite to produce a gas which drove petrol engines.

The Guy Arabs were now supplied with six cylinder Gardner 6LW engines, no doubt for the hillier Derbyshire terrain. The first five (Nos. 197-9,1-2)

had standard highbridge Weymann bodies, whilst the remainder Nos. 3/7-8/11/22-6/9-30 had the Northern Counties derivative.

Difficulty was being experienced in providing increased services due to the shortage of labour, which was being conscripted into the war effort. However, it had been possible to put on additional evening journeys on the Cotmanhay-Nottingham service, by utilising crews who were catering for US Forces based at Wollaton Park, during the daytime. There was also a saving in engine fuel with the opening of Mount Street bus station and cutting back the short workings from Nottingham to Birchwood Avenue, Wollaton in lieu of Balloon Houses.

Guy B No.166 and Leyland Cub No.151 were both converted to tower wagons for the NDT overhead system, tree lopping and D&NEPCo work.

NCT deferred the application for the extension to Wollaton until after the War and consequently decided to withdraw the Bill. NDT also withdrew their Bill following opposition from NCT. The six trolleybuses allocated the previous year, were not now required, following the withdrawal of powers to extend the system. Sanction was received from the MOWT to transfer them to Llanelly District. They were delivered to Llanelly in 1946 as Karriers (badged Sunbeams) with Park Royal utility bodywork and became Nos.43-8 in their fleet.

From the 1st June the AC supply of 11.000 volts, was increased from 1.000KW to 1.500KW. The charge for conversion to DC being £12.000 per annum.

1945

The final two (Nos.31/4) highbridge Guy 6LW Arabs with Northern Counties bodies arrived in January along with nine lowbridge versions for the

Five lowbridge versions of the Weymann metal framed body (Nos. 416-2) were received on the AEC Regent chassis during 1947. The lowering in height resulted in the loss of three seats on the upper deck. No 416 is seen proceeding along the northern end of the cobbled Huntingdon Street during August 1948. The only services using this part of the road were the B8 and B9 to Hucknall, Rainworth and Mansfield.

B8/9 and the Alfreton area. Of these five (200-4) were bodied by Weymann and four (Nos.205-8) had Roe bodies. For the first time a vehicle type was put into separate block of numbers. In the Alfreton area, these reduced height double deckers were required for operating under a lowbridge between the Corner Pin at Morton and Pilsley. Even then they were restricted to the centre of the road, due to the arching of the railway bridge.

Six Morris Commercial 3.5 ton lorries added to the lorry fleet replaced stock which was around twenty years old. Fleet numbers did not appear on these later vehicles, and the fleet now consisted of Morris Commercials and one Dennis Lancet.

The National Fire Service lease was terminated at Underwood from 31st January.

The company was still interested in having a base for a bus and coach station in Nottingham, and a plan was prepared for a site abutting Canal Street and Broad Marsh, which was remitted to the chairman for consideration. Interestingly if this had proceeded it would have been adjacent to the third Nottingham bus station which opened in 1952. Also the company had this desire to have a base in the city, which is somewhat difficult to understand, as all of the services minimised dead mileage with the existing bases. Even today the former MGO routes are maintained from outside Nottingham.

A Fridays and Saturdays E9 Matlock-Riber via Tansley village was introduced jointly with North Western who numbered the service 179.

The former Blue Service (Grainger Bros) tours and excursion licences, and the Ilkeston-Skegness express service obtained in 1941 from Barton were registered. They were embodied into existing licences, but the pick up points in Sandiacre and Stapleford were not included.

As late as December the MOWT issued licences for the purchase of eight AEC double deckers, plus four AEC and two Leyland single deckers.

Stanton Ironwork Co Ltd, advised NDT of the road repairs required at the reverser in Crompton Street, Ilkeston. They agreed to this at cost not exceeding £100. A little later Stanton requested an annual rent of £15 and £2 right of way rental for the

same place, no doubt to cover further road maintenance work.

The Nottingham Corporation Town Clerk indicated that a Provisional Order could be obtained for the Wollaton trolleybus extension, but stated that the case for the powers was not a strong one.

D&NEPCo. fixed 250 lamps to the overhead system in the Heanor Urban District,

1946

The Transport Bill was introduced in the House of Commons on the 27th November, and had a second reading on the 18th December.

A roundabout was constructed at Cotmanhay Road, Cotmanhay, to give access into Skeavingtons Farm for a new council housing development, which saw the reconstruction of the overhead wires to provide a full circle, and a layby in Cotmanhay Road.

By April the final five Guy Arab II 6LW buses had arrived in dribs and drabs. They had lowbridge bodywork by Roe (Nos. 209-10) or Strachan (Nos. 211-3). A further two transferred from MDT with Weymann lowbridge bodies had the smaller 5LW engines, and became Nos. 214-5.

Additionally the eight (Nos. 60/3-4/70-1/5-7) highbridge double deckers were delivered with Weymann rear entrance bodies on the new AEC Regent II chassis. Weymann was unable to supply the single decker requirements due to pressure of work, so four AEC Regals received Duple dual purpose timber framed 35 seat bodies numbered 41-4.

A further two Morris 3.5 ton lorries were added to the fleet.

Pooling arrangements on the B8/9/C1 Mansfield-Blidworth and Bilsthorpe were terminated at the 1st January. MDT had operated the journeys solely since 1943.

A meeting was held on the 17th December to wind up the subsidiary companies. This included the following which was purchased by MGO. Williamson's; freehold land and buildings at Derby Road, Heanor. Tansey & Severn; freehold land, buildings and garage equipment at Underwood and Freizeland, Selston. Alfreton Motor Transport; freehold land, buildings and equipment at Angel Square, Alfreton. Dawson's had already ceased trading.

The D9 Sutton in Ashfield-Tibshelf was with-

Duple provided rather attractive D type wooden framed saloon bodies for six chassis, four AEC and two Leyland over the 1946/7 winter, which has can be seen from the photograph, was rather cold and snowy. This rear view of Leyland PS1/1, fleet No. 45, JRB 13, shows the Duple influence on the Balfour Beatty specification.

drawn as journeys were covered by the D1 or works services.

On the 20th September it was reported to the Board that the Nottingham Corporation had under consideration the promotion of a Bill, in the ensuing session of Parliament, to extend the existing trolley system to the Parish of Trowell. MCESCo gave authority to the Managers to take such steps as necessary to protect their interests. NDT had 'locus standi' for objecting to the proposal, unless the company promoted a Bill for similar powers. It was remitted to the Managers to take steps for the promotion of a Bill in the present session of Parliament on the lines of the 1943-4 session, subsequently withdrawn. Nottingham Corporation deposited a Bill with Parliament for the construction of a trolley vehicle route. This was to commence at the junction of Wollaton Road and Middleton Boulevard, via Russell Drive and Trowell Road to a point 8.58 chains west of the City boundary (Balloon Houses). The Companys Bill was also deposited and both Bills commenced in the House of Commons.

In the Parish of Kimberley thirty lamps were fixed to the overhead and a further fifty four at Nuthall.

Balfour Beatty approved for delivery during 1948 of fifteen double deck trolleybuses at an estimated cost of £53.250.

They were informed the renewal of the signalling equipment at Langley Mill level crossing was to cost £296, but they did not believe this was justified. Nothing further was reported, so it is assumed that it was not replaced.

1947

The Electricity Bill had a second reading on the 4th February, which provided for vesting in the British Electricity Authority, properties, rights, liabilities and obligations of MCESCo, including shares in MGO/NDT. Royal Assent was given on the 13th August. The Transport Bill had received Royal Assent on the 6th August.

After seventeen years in office, Mr D Hays decided to retire on the 31st October, having passed his seventy first birthday. However, this was deferred until 31st December, no doubt to allow a smooth change over of the business.

AEC Regal No. 160 which had been impressed by the War Department in 1939, was re-purchased, but was sold on almost immediately.

Vehicle replacements for 1949 and 1950 was agreed as; twenty Leyland single deckers and thirty AEC Weymann double deckers, but this was later amended to thirty five single deckers.

Two new models were introduced to the fleet in the form of two Leyland PSl/1 again with Duple dual purpose bodies (Nos.45-6) and six (Nos.103/5/14/34/41/8) of the ubiquitous Bedford OB with the almost obligatory Duple coachwork. Fifteen AEC Regent IIs were fitted with Weymann rear entrance bodywork. Nos. 121-5/157/9-60/2/8 being of highbridge layout and Nos. 416-20 were lowbridge. Lowbridge Guy utility buses were also renumbered from 2xx to 4xx. It was now possible for all the remaining Tilling-Stevens to be withdrawn.

Preliminary meetings took place during March to discuss the possibility of extending the Mansfield garage on to adjoining premises, but this was postponed for further consideration.

The E7 Heanor-Codnor was re-introduced with an extension from Codnor to Ripley.

A new D9 was started between Nottingham and Balloon Houses, operating via Russell Drive Wollaton. This was an amendment to the original application which included Coventry Lane and Strelley as the terminal. It was quickly extended to Trowell. A counter NCT application was refused.

With the NCT trying to get powers to operate trolleybuses to Balloon Houses, it was felt necessary to cover this route, to protect their own interests. Russell Drive. although it does not sound it, is a single lane carriageway which bye-passes Wollaton village. Demand for post war housing saw this area being developed by the Nottingham City Council with several housing schemes including the large Strelley site which was still to be completed.

At the same time an application was made to operate between Nottingham, Wollaton Village to Wollaton Vale (Bramcote Lane junction). Immediately the NCT objected and made a similar application, which terminated further along at Derby

Road. The interest by both parties was again due to a development that was re-housing families from Nottingham, which the local authority felt were still their passengers, although they were not in their territory. Both applications were refused, as they were considered premature.

An application for a Pinxton, Eastwood-Great Yarmouth express service was refused.

A petition against the Nottingham Corporation was lodged by NDT and MGO on 29th January. The Examiner of Petitions decided NDT had failed to comply with standing orders of both Houses, so they asked for Standing Orders to be dispensed with. On the 15th March it was reported to the Board, that a resolution was passed approving The Bill proposed, and was being introduced in the current session of Parliament. However, the Select Committee decided not to grant powers to Nottingham Corporation for the extension of the trolley system between Middleton Boulevard and Balloon Houses. In consequence NDT withdrew their Petition against the Bill, but they agreed to proceed with the Bill in respect of administrative and financial powers only. This was considered by the Unopposed Bills Committee on the 14th May, and received Royal Assent on the 18th July.

Chapter Six: Nationalisation

1948

Following the retirement of D Hays as General Manager of MGO and W W.Clark as Engineer and Manager of MDT, it was decided to consolidate the positions. W Williamson was appointed Chief Engineer and Manager of the Group, and K Laing Traffic Manager of the Group. P H De Keyser and G A Thorpe resigned as Secretary and assistant Secretary, to be replaced by H J Beatty and J A F Kelly respectively

MCESCo was dissolved on the 1st April, with the introduction of the Electricity Act, being replaced by the British Electricity Authority (BEA), which included the share capital of NDT and MGO. Following the Ministers consultation with BEA, he gave the Authority direction as to the use or disposal of any assets which were not connected with generation, transmission or distribution.

All matters previously with MCESCo were now referred to C R King Senior Executive Officer representing the BEA. Management agreement with MCESCo and the subsidiary traction undertakings, under an agreement of 17th June 1941 (management of MCESCo by Balfour Beatty), would continue between BEA and Balfour Beatty from the 1st April, allowing them to meet all existing commitments.

The MGO/NDT shares were then transferred from British Electricity Authority to Bishopgate Nominees Ltd, on the 27th September.

It was possible to find metal framed bodies for this years batch of twenty five (Nos. 200-24)

Leyland PS1/1 chassis, fitted with SEAS dual purpose bodies. Twelve were 32 seat coaches and thirteen 35 seat saloons. These were received prior to nationalisation.

Payment was made to Balfour Beatty for the supply of fifteen (Nos.27-8/86-91/108-9/116-20) Weymann highbridge bodied AEC Regent III with, for the first time, pre-selector gear boxes. The utility buses delivered in 1942-5 were upgraded with seat replacements and conversion of destination indicators to standard layout.

A wartime model Ford was purchased and converted to a breakdown recovery lorry.

Following an investigation into garaging facilities it was decided to proceed with Mansfield (45 buses), Tibshelf (30 buses) and Nottingham area (30 buses). It is assumed the last two would have replaced Alfreton and Underwood depots.

The C7 Alfreton-Sutton in Ashfield was extended by adding the E1 journeys to Skegby and Stanton on the Hill. Also the E8 was reintroduced between Hucknall and Oxton, with Barton having protection on the Calverton to Oxton section.

A new service F1 between Mansfield and St. Andrews Estate, East Kirkby followed the same route as the E6, but turned off Lowmoor Road to serve the Alexandra Street area.

MGO were successful when reapplying to operate between Nottingham and Strelley but only as far as Bilborough Road/Strelley Lane junction. This became E1 and it had been hoped to use Cockington Road, but was not at the time suitable for vehicles. However, it was granted upon completion of the development. Within a year it was diverted through Wollaton village in lieu of Russell Drive.

Nottingham Corporation objected to a second application to run between Nottingham and Wollaton Vale, as the City Engineer considered Bramcote Lane unfit for PSV operation. The licensing Authority refused the application, solely on these grounds.

The High Spania district of Kimberley was connected with Nottingham, taking the main road route on Mondays to Fridays as the F2.

An express service X5 between Alfreton and

Leyland PS1/1 No.206 awaiting collection from the coachbuilders- Saunders Engineering and Shipyard Co, (SEAS), Beaumaris, Anglesey. The metal framed bodies were built to the pre-war Weymann styling.

Matlock was introduced on August Bank Holiday Sunday. The only intermediate stop being at Wessington.

Although the Winfield licence for excursions and tours from Awsworth had been registered at the time of the purchase in 1940, an application was not made until April 1948, when it was granted.

The NDT through running agreement in respect of working and administration, was settled with NCT during September.

1949

Shares were transferred to Bishopgate Nominees Ltd, the holding company to the British Transport Commission on the 18th January, with the balance of 500 shares in each company going to five newly appointed directors.

The management agreement with Balfour Beatty was cancelled as from the 1st April.

Following a meeting held at 22 Marylebone Road, London, it was resolved that the principal office be transferred from 66 Queen Street, London EC4, to Station Road, Langley Mill, as from the 11th April, with common directors for both companies. Sir Joseph Nall resigned and G Cardwell was appointed as Chairman.

The plot of land purchased in 1943 directly opposite the Langley Mill Offices, became the site for the company office, which was a wooden hut. This housed a very small staff, including Jack Kelly who was moved from London. This outpost remained in isolation until 1969 when the new office block was built, and the Secretary and his staff (including Mr Kelly) were transferred.

At the Board Meeting held at Euston Station on the 28th July, two directors resigned and one of the replacements was W Vane Morland. After an absence of twenty five years he was to renew his acquaintanceship with the old companies.

Working arrangements between MGO and NDT were revised, with MGO continuing to operate existing services over the statutory routes of NDT as from 1st January 1949 as follows; MGO to operate on behalf of NDT at the charge of 1 shilling (5p) per mile, except the proposed limited stop A4, which would be calculated from the annual accounts. MGO to pay NDT £50 for the rights to operate on its own behalf over parts of their services.

Loans which MGO had made to MDT were repaid and taken over by BTC.

A direct service C1 Mansfield to Skegby, Stanton Hill and Teversal was introduced using Skegby Lane for the first time.

The certain journeys on the C8 from Ilkeston were extended at Kimberley to Watnall or Swingate.

With the introduction of the F1 the previous year, it was decided to re-route the E6 via Station Street and the Greenwood Drive area of Kirkby in Ashfield and extend the F1 to cover Diamond Avenue.

The popularity of the X5 Alfreton-Matlock saw the frequency increase from hourly on Sundays and twenty minutes on Bank Holiday Mondays to every ten minutes, if required.

After almost ten years with the War Department AEC Regal No.159 was repurchased and immediately sold on to Camm of Nottingham.

Balfour Beatty was notified that the outstanding order for thirty five Leyland single deckers and twenty AEC Regent Mark III double deckers had been cancelled for 1950 delivery. In fact there were no deliveries during 1949. Instead the complete batch of Leyland PS1s with Weymann dual purpose bodies were taken into the fleet of Crosville, a fellow BTC company. The Weymann bodies were very similar to a batch of twenty four supplied to MDT, still to the groups standard design evolved in 1937, although the Crosville vehicles did not carry roof mounted advert boards. The twenty AEC Regents with Weymann lowbridge bodies were purchased by London Transport, becoming RLH 1-20. MGO recovered the capital from both operators.

Of the six Bedford ML 2/3 ton lorries received, four had Perkins diesel engines, and the remainder later received Ford diesel engines.

Plans were drawn up for a new garage to hold eighty vehicles at Sutton Road, Mansfield, which included alterations to the facade of the existing. This decision resulted in the Tibshelf and Nottingham garage investigation being abandoned. It would have been interesting if a garage had been built in Nottingham, as the BTC had no representation in the city except the United Counties services to London and the South Coast! United Counties garaged vehicles overnight at the Trent Nottingham depot.

Agreement was reached with Balfour Beatty to loan buses for the conveyance of their employees to and from work, for not less than 26 weeks. Balfour Beatty were at this time involved in power station installations across the East Midlands.

Fifteen (Nos.343-57) BUT 96611T-EEC trolleybuses with Weymann 56 seat bodywork were supplied by Balfour Beatty for £76.481.10s 4d almost a 50% increase on the 1946 estimate. They replaced all the remaining single deckers (Nos.306-16) and the half cab double deckers (Nos.317-331), making

BUT 9611T with Weymann body No. 345 picks up a good load of passengers at Codnor Market Place, one typically dull Autumn morning.

a total of twenty six in all. Latterly very little had been seen of these vehicles and all were sold to Rhodes a Nottingham dealer. Although it would appear there had been a change of chassis manufacturer, this was not really so as British United Traction Ltd, of Hanover Square, London, was a company set up jointly by AEC and Leyland, in June 1946, to design and build trolleybuses. The 96611T model was a four wheel model based on the AEC Regent chassis.

The NDT A4 Nottingham-Ripley daily limited stop service commenced on Monday the 14th March. The first stopping point was Hill Top, and then only once in each town or village, so that an overall timing of forty two minutes was achieved. Comparisons showed there were savings in time, as this followed the same route as the B1 bus service which took 53 minutes or 69 minutes on the A1 trolleybus. MGO provided the vehicles on hire as the normal practice.

1950

Ten (Nos.421-30) Weymann lowbridge bodied AEC Regent III entered service, being the balance of the 1949-50 order, and identical to twenty diverted to London Transport.

Although a decision was approved to convert premises in Church Square, Heanor to an enquiry and booking office, it was leased to another tenant, the following year.

The MGO Managers recommended to the Railway Executive that Ilkeston Town (Midland) station, which had closed in 1947, be retained as site for a new garage.

Stanton Hill was deleted from the C7, as all vehicles now terminated at the Healdswood Estate, Skegby.

The remote area of Moorwood Moor gained Monday to Friday journeys on the E5, albeit that they were serving the Lea Mills factories.

1951

W Williamson was appointed General Manager, and E Jowett Chief Engineer from the 1st September. J A Allen was appointed Secretary from the 1st April. Mr Williamson who had come into the business, following the takeover of Williamson's

Garage in 1928, now found himself at the pinnacle of his career.

An attempt was made to obtain permission to work between Cotmanhay, Ilkeston and the new Kirk Hallam Estate, however, following objections from Barton, it was granted as far as Little Hallam Lane, some 440 yards from the Estate. The licence was surrended within an a month of its approval.

The Festival of Britain which was opened on 4th May, was the Socialist Government's idea to give the people a pat on the back, or a pick me up following the dark days of the war and the early postwar blues. It included a skylon, a dome of discovery, the Festival Hall and pleasure gardens, located in London on the South Bank of the Thames. Perhaps as a concession to the remainder of Britain it was decided to have a festival village. To everyones surprise Trowell was chosen. A strange choice, or was it seen as a typical ideological working village? Even the name Trowell, portrayed this, and as it overlooked the large Stanton Ironworks, it was exactly what they were looking for. A public house which was built at the time, still carries the name in its title; The Festival Inn. Although there were no attractions, MGO offered tours and excursions to various destinations, during the period of the festival for visitors to the village. Excursions also departed from various points for the celebrations in London.

The F3 service came into being, offering direct facilities between Rainworth, Blidworth, Redhill and Nottingham on Saturdays only.

It had become increasingly obvious that the trolley system required either expanding or closing. The factors against were; Renewals of the overheads due to the age; Affects of mining subsidence on certain sections; An unpopular detour around Nottingham; The charge made by Nottingham Corporation for every passenger carried in their territory, resulting in a complex fare system, which at one time, required the conductor to have 47 different types of tickets; The lack of flexibility to cater for new development; The supply which provided a good base load for the Spondon power station in Balfour Beatty days was based on an an acceptable 'in house' charge, but this changed when the East Midlands Electricity Board

realised they had a substantial captive customer who had no alternative than to meet any considerable charges that might be demanded. Although trolley buses gave good service and were popular with the short distance passengers, it was felt these were outweighed by the disadvantages, and so, it was decided motor buses should be introduced.

The Nottinghamshire and Derbyshire Traction Bill 1952 was prepared as follows; 'To authorise the NDT to discontinue their trolley vehicle services; to redefine the objects of the company; to amend or repel certain entractments relating to the company; to confer further powers on the company; and for other purposes.' This was prepared to bring it into the then current session of Parliament.

1952

Llanelly District Traction which had been managed by South Wales Electricity Board since nationalisation, was sold to the South Wales Transport Co Ltd, the local BET subsidiary.

Rehabilitation of twenty five bodies was sanctioned in February, and Nudd Brothers & Lockyer of Kegworth were awarded the contract to rebuild the whole of the 1937 batch of AEC Regent double deckers.

The completion of the new garage at Sutton Road, Mansfield, was reported at the 18th June Board meeting. MDT were charged for part occupation of the new premises.

Trolleybus No. 353 (NNU 234) stands at the Beighton Street, Ripley terminus. In front is No.345 waiting to take up duties, on the 6th April 1953, less than three weeks before closure of the system.

Great Yarmouth was reached on summer Saturdays with the X6 Mansfield, Rainworth, Blidworth, Bilsthorpe and Southwell service being introduced.

A second E7 route introduced was the Heanor-Marlpool Farm Estate-Heanor circular. A further local Heanor service was the E8 to Langley with the occasional extension to Langley Mill and Aldercar. The old E8 Hucknall to Oxton, became the F8.

The X9 (later renumbered X15) Ilkeston-Chesterfield (Walton Sanatorium) ran on three days of the week, for visitors only.

Whilst the Bill was before the select committee, it was argued that the system lacked flexibility and the company's only statutory obligation was to operate between Ripley and Cinderhill and by adjusting its operation Nottingham Corporation could cover the local traffic. Nottingham Corporation claimed compensation for the possible closure, which would have to be met by higher fares. The trolley bus loadings across the city boundary averaged eighteen whilst the bus averaged thirty one. It became obvious to the NDT that NCT had been short changing them for years under the 'Through Running Agreement'. It was, however, decided there would not be a compensation clause. Royal Assent for the Traction Bill was received on the 1st August .

Expenditure was agreed for twenty five double deck buses as trolley replacements.

Licences were issued for the replacement bus services between Loscoe-Cotmanhay-Hallam Fields and Loscoe-Ilkeston (White Lion Square), as temporary cover, as required, until completely fresh applications were made in 1953.

1953

Following the cessation of trolleybus services it was resolved MGO would take control of receipts, maintain assets, make payments on their behalf, and transfer to NDT at the end of each financial year average receipts, less expenses. MGO/NDT joint services were introduced on the 26th April, which was rather surprising, as it had been expected this would see the end of NDT, once the conditions of the 1952 Act had been fulfilled.

BTC acquired the share capital from British

Trolleybus No.336 (HNU 829) at Cotmanhay Road, Cotmanhay on the 6th April, painted in the livery of Bradford Corporation. Having negotiated the turning circle, it was waiting to operate the short working to Hallam Fields

Electricity Authority of MGO/MDT and NDT as at the 1st April 1948 for £1.4 million, provisionally allocated between the three companies.

Bristol Commercial Vehicles Ltd., and Eastern Coachworks were both part of the Tilling group who voluntarily sold out their bus interests to the British Transport Commission in 1948. The former Balfour Beatty group was now a part of the Tilling group, within the BTC. It was decreed that all the state owned bus companies would be supplied with Bristol chassis and ECW bodies, which would not be available to any operator outside the BTC.

It was reported that the British Road Services (the nationalised division of the road haulage companies)

Five of the withdrawn trolleybuses, parked in the former Williamson's garage, in Derby Road, Heanor, prior to delivery to Bradford Corporation. From the left to right the vehicles are Nos301/0/3 (DRB 617/6/9), 338 (HNU 970), and 305 (DRB 621)

Guy Arab No.199, on the A2 town service between Cotmanhay and Hallam Fields. The passengers would be in no doubt that this was the replacement for the trolley service, withdrawn months earlier. It is not difficult to make comparisons of a smooth trolleybus, and the solid mounted, vibrating 6 cylinder Gardner engine, particularly when climbing the steep Bath Street, in Ilkeston. Note the trolley poles had been retained for the street lighting.

garage on London Road, Nottingham might be available for disposal, and the General Manager was instructed to advise them of their interest.

Having a comparatively modern fleet it would appear BTC concentrated on other operators fleets, and when the first vehicles in almost three years came they were ex Hants & Dorset stock dating from 1939-40. The three double deckers (Nos.431 3) were Bristol K5G with ECW low bridge bodies .

Over the next three years the 1937 batch of AEC Regents had their seating increased from 52 to 54 seats. Several of the half cab saloons, including pre-war vehicles, were remodelled, with the removal of the side flashing which were replaced by straight lining out, which gave a more up to date appearance, being very similar to the post war Weymann bodies

supplied to MDT. At this time the cream Coronation livery was reintroduced, and also during repaints the navy blue was omitted, and several saloons received a white roof.

Setright Speed ticket machines were introduced at all garages from the 14th March replacing the elderly Bell Punch units.

The Matlock express services were renumbered in the stage carriage list, the X5 to Alfreton became F6 and the X9 to Heanor became F7.

At last they were granted permission to operate the F5 Nottingham-Wollaton Vale (Sheraton Drive), which overcame the problem of Bramcote Lane, by using the recently completed Arleston Drive from Wollaton Village. Albeit for a very short period as it was transferred to joint working with NDT, along

with several other routes.

The change over date for the trolleybus replacement services was intended to have been the the 25th March. However, when the MGO/NDT applications came before the East Midlands Traffic Court on the 6th March, the official shorthand typist did not appear and so it was therefore adjourned until the 30th March, delaying the changeover by a month.

One of these for a Hucknall-Nuthall-Nottingham service, was refused as Trent had opposed on the grounds that this would abstract from their own service. But this did not affect the overall restructured plan, which was to be the largest and most coordinated that either operator had attempted. However a month later an F4 service Watnall-Nottingham service was granted, being a shortened version of the above, which served the Basford, Huntingdon Street and Broad Marsh, Nottingham

Of the old NDT services the A1 remained but only at peak periods, with only one journey each way to Ripley, and the remainder to Langley Mill or Heanor. The A2 and A3 were cut back to Cotmanhay to operate as town services to Hallam Fields or Longfield Lane, on the Middleton Estate. A new A5 Hallam Fields-Cotmanhay-Heanor-Langley Mill ran mainly at peak periods.

Former MGO routes were also altered. The B2 was extended from Cotmanhay to Heanor, and Ripley via Codnor or as the C6 via Waingroves, now ran via Russell Drive at Wollaton. The D9/E1/F5 served Wollaton village. The C8 short journeys to Kimberley and the F2 were linked to become the F2 Ilkeston, Awsworth, High Spania, Nuthall, and terminating at Nottingham (Broad Marsh). The A1/F2 and the F4 ran via Stockhill Lane and Nottingham Road, as the trolley service, but from Mansfield Road, they turned into Huntingdon Street, where the A1 terminated. The other two ran on to Canal Street and Broad Marsh Bus Station. All remaining services terminated at Mount Street, Nottingham. The A4/B6 remained unchanged, and the B1 now had far more extra journeys, and they were all now jointly operated.

NDT placed orders for fifteen (Nos.300-14) Bristol KSW6G chassis with ECW highbridge 60 seat bodies. The balance was made up of twelve (Nos.315-26) AEC Regent III with Weymann high-bridge bodies from MDT which dated from 1948-9. It had been suggested that the ten remaining Bristols not required from the original order, be transferred to MGO or MDT, but this never transpired. These were the only KSW6G's to be operated by the three companies, and the first buses to be purchased by NDT.

There was no special celebration to mark the end of the system, although a commemorative 1½d ticket was issued during the final week.

The overhead system closed on the evening of the 25th April. As the trolleybus were withdrawn, they were driven to White Lion Square, Heanor, detached from the rails, coasted down Derby Road Hill, into the former Williamson's garage. They were then stored in the yard until all thirty two (Nos. 300-5/32-57) were collected by Bradford Corporation who paid £62.500 for them. Although it is understood one trolleybus from each batch had gone to Bradford earlier. Some of the trolleybuses which had been repainted, into the Bradford livery actually continued to run for NDT. These were all finished with blue roofs, which Bradford adopted for the rest of its fleet.

ACV Sales Ltd, had taken over the tenancy of the former Williamson's Derby Road, Heanor premises, the previous year. However, an agreement was reached with Heanor UDC to sell to them the premises but this was not concluded until 1960.

It was reported on the 21st October that the dismantling of the overhead had almost been completed.

1954

Plant, machinery, furniture and fittings were purchased by MGO from NDT, but they still retained the former tram depots at Langley Mill and Ilkeston.

The distinctive cast metal fleet number plates fixed to the front end, were not fitted on new deliveries, being replaced with gold transfers as those fixed at the rear.

The first new deliveries to MGO since 1950 and from the new stable were six LS6G 39 seat coaches (Nos.226-31) and two LD6G 58 seat rear entrance door double deckers (Nos.434-5). These double deckers were commonly known as Lodekkas, which had been developed with the highbridge layout, but with an overall height 13ft. 2ins. of a low bridge bus. This was achieved by using a drop frame chassis, which gave a lower saloon gangway that was level with the rear platform.

Over a period of four years, many of the wartime Guy double deckers were rebuilt by MGO, Willowbrook and Bond in the original style, but with rubber mounted windows. Part of the fleet of Leyland PS1/1s with SEAS bodies were fitted with new ECW seats, which increased the capacity from 32 to 35. The 1936 AEC Regents were also rebuilt in the MGO workshops. The coaches were the last to be applied with the navy blue relief. All future coaches were in a cream livery with mid blue relief.

A Ford 500E 2 ton truck was delivered along with an ex MOF Supply Ford 7E 5 ton tipper. Both had oil engines fitted.

The C9 terminus at Wood Lane, Hucknall, was extended into the Beauvale Estate.

For a trial period of one month a licence was issued for a Saturdays only Alfreton-Somercotes-South Normanton service, it was obviously not a success as there was no request for an extension of time.

The F1 Mansfield-East Kirkby was amended to cover Hermitage Lane and Hamilton Road to Sutton Junction, giving a more direct route than via Sutton in Ashfield. The terminus became 'The Nags Head', on Station Street, East Kirkby.

A Chesterfield-Derby service joint with East Midland and Trent commenced operations on the 29th August. This was achieved by linking of the three concerns routes, MGO provided the D2 Alfreton-Clay Cross section. This had only been made possible with the East Midlands recent purchase of the Clay Cross-Chesterfield service of A Heeley Ltd, of New Tupton. Chesterfield Corporation objected on the grounds that it would abstract from their own Chesterfield-Clay Cross service, and argued there was no demand for a through service to Derby. The route number 44 was

Lodekka No. 480 at Derby Bus Station, working on the joint service with Trent and East Midland to Chesterfield.

NDT 316 the AEC Regent Mk III rebodied by ECW operating the F5. It is seen leaving the Sheraton Drive terminus, when the area was in the early stages of development.

shared by all three, and for the first time MGO displayed route numbers without a prefix.

A second Great Yarmouth express Saturday service was introduced as the X9 from Sutton in Ashfield, Kirkby and points south of their territory to Kimberley. The X6 was amended to commence at Shirebrook and covered Church Warsop, Market Warsop and Mansfield Woodhouse, before Mansfield.

The F8 now commenced at Heanor on Saturday and Sunday, and additional Monday to Friday journeys ran between Calverton and Westville.

In consequence of the introduction of Setright ticket machines, it was not possible to issue MDT tickets on the protected Mansfield-Huthwaite route, and so it was agreed that it be based on a proportion of the amount paid.

On appeal the Traffic Commissioners decided to shorten a Barton service to Moorbridge Lane, Stapleford, and Nottingham. Originally this had been granted to operate between Kirk Hallam Estate and Nottingham. However, Barton reapplied in October to reinstate the complete service, to which MGO/NDT proposed an alternative. In the event both were granted and the F9 operated via Longfield Lane, Gallows Inn and Russell, Drive, Wollaton.

The amount of expenses due to NCT for through running of the trolleybuses had not been resolved

and the Town Clerk proposed the appointment of an arbitrator.

1955

Sir Joseph Nall and Mr Vane Morland ceased to be directors from the 29th June, after long associations with the companies.

The bus shelters owned by MGO were offered to the local authorities, and four were transferred to Eastwood UDC.

MGO Lodekkas (Nos.436-48) were again LD6G models, but the single deckers (Nos.232-241) although LS6G's were 43 seat dual purpose models.

Seven ECW double deck replacement bodies were sanctioned and allocated to six (Nos.405-10) Guy Arab II models, originally fitted with Roe low bridge bodies. They were renumbered 102-7. The seventh was fitted to NDT AEC Regent III No.316, which had been severely damaged following an accident and had the distinction of being the only Regent Mark III to receive an ECW body. Seven AEC Regent coaches dating from 1938 were increased to 35 seats over a period of two years.

An unsuccessful Saturday and Sunday service ran jointly with East Midland between Alfreton and Ashover over a three month trial period.

Nottingham Corporation settled on the sum of £500 for through running expenses for the period 1st April 1948 to the end of running powers.

1956

Upon instructions from the Traffic Commissioners fuel for stage carriage services had to be reduced by 5% from the 17th December, to save fuel, following the Suez Expeditions. This was overcome by foreshortening services and reducing Sunday frequencies.

It was reported to the 21st June meeting that E Naylor & Sons Ltd, of South Normanton had offered their business and the General Manager was asked to negotiate. The main attraction being a Mansfield-Alfreton via Fulwood service. It was reported two months later that this had been sold to Trent, who already covered the route with their service 100.

The demand for more destinations to seaside resorts saw the introduction of more summer Saturday express services; The X10 operated to Clacton from Sutton in Ashfield, Mansfield and Southwell. Jointly with East Midland an X5 (EMMS 90) Chesterfield-Great Yarmouth express Saturday service was launched, serving Glapwell and Pleasley. Again with East Midland the X11 (EMMS 89) ran to Llandudno, Colwyn Bay and Rhyl from Market Warsop, Mansfield, and Alfreton. At the same time the X13 Alfreton, Ripley, Heanor, Ilkeston-Great Yarmouth was started with Trent as partners.

The A5 was extended from Langley Mill to New Eastwood.

Dual purpose 43 seat L6SG models were numbered 242-53 and Lodekkas 449-58 in the MGO fleet. The balance of the 32 seat SEAS bodied Leyland PS1/1s were increased to 35 seat capacity.

1957

It was possible to resume services, to the level of those provided before the oil fuel crisis, by running on creosote fuel produced from coal, which was not rationed. Experiments had been carried out previously, Barton Transport being an early innovator, with coal produced oil, but they had found it difficult to mix the fuel with diesel oil. However, the oil shortage made these difficulties of secondary importance. The oil was a by product of production gas taken from coal, which came from the new Wingerworth coal carbonisation plant, where cre-

The arrival of the Lodekkas gave MGO the opportunity to place them on the X service to Skegness. They had been granted permission to operate double deckers on this route in 1950, but the lack of suitable vehicles had led to the delay. Bristol LD6G No. 436 is seen at Heanor Market Place with a good load of passengers. The lack of luggage suggests this may have been the Sunday journey which catered for the day trippers.

osote type fuels were produced as part of the extraction of tar and pitch. This was also a by product of ordinary small gas works, which were prevalent at the time. A secondhand Fordson oil tanker dating from 1951 was purchased, to transfer fuel between depots or store fuel as required.

Unofficial strikes affected the group during the early part of the year, when it was reported that services had been severely disrupted. After the first on the 29th January, the Traffic Manager, K Laing said agreement had been reached on all items except one, which had not been given priority. Again in February only sixteen crews, including a number of union officials, reported for work. The majority, however, remained on strike over their demands for revised work schedules, which they claimed were too exacting. Mr Laing stated that a section of the employees had made new demands for paid meal breaks, which the company had refused. Mr R

Harvey chairman of the local branch of the T&GWU said that he had negotiated with the management and reported back. He added that if the employees had abided by the promises he had made, and not inconvenienced the public, they would have been alright and the matter could have been settled by negotiation.

This was followed by an official national strike, which the T&GWU called over wages, from Saturday the 20th July until the 28th July. Lost receipts amounted to approximately £34.000, which was a net loss of £18.000, and a reduction in passengers in the weeks following.

Ten Bristol Lodekkas LD6G models with ECW bodies for NDT were sanctioned as a part of an order for fifteen from the MGO programme.

Consideration had been given to raising the roof on the single decker garage at Alfreton, but it was decided to provide additional accommodation for

thirty nine double deckers.

The Mansfield garage was sold to MDT for £53.779 and MGO then paid them rent for part use.

A former Ministry AEC Matador was obtained for conversion to a breakdown truck.

Of the 1957 programme five LD6G Lodekkas were delivered as Nos.459-63. Just one LDL6G Lodekka (No.464) a 70 seat 30 feet long model with rear open platform was received during 1957, which entered the NDT fleet.

Three 1936 AEC Regents with Weymann highbridge bodies arrived from MDT and became Nos.4-6. Although rather elderly they had been fitted with 7.7 oil engines during the war, and completely rebuilt in 1953 by Nudd Bros & Lockyer of Kegworth.

With the addition of a few journeys the F3 Nottingham-Rainworth became a daily operation.

The Heanor-Marlpool Farm Estate circular was renumbered A7 from E7 and the E8 Heanor-Aldercar became A8. The second E7 service continued to work between Heanor, Aldercar and Ripley. Also a new service A6 was introduced in conjunction with the A5/A7 and A8, which ran Heanor-Eastwood (Church View Estate).

1958

Sir Joseph Nall, perhaps one of the most influential people in the Balfour Beatty group, passed away on the 2nd May.

A single lane road and footpath which passed under the Cossall Marsh aqueduct had been controlled by traffic lights, and with restricted height allowed only single deck buses to pass through. However, on the 22nd October, after rebuilding the new structure was opened, with a double decker driving through one way and a single decker in the opposite direction.

As a part of the improvements to the Alfreton garage, Nos. 34/36/38 King Street, Alfreton had been purchased and demolition of these and No.40, bought in 1957, was put in hand. The height of the single deck garage at Underwood was increased to give access to double deck vehicles.

A new style dual purpose body was fitted to the recently introduced MW6G models given fleet numbers 254-63. Three Lodekkas (Nos.474-6) were to the usual layout. The remaining nine NDT Lodekkas (Nos.465-73) of the 1957 sanction, again had open rear platforms, but were only 27ft. long and seated 62 passengers.

Twelve (Nos. 174-185) 1949 AEC Regal IIIs with Weymann dual purpose bodies, came from the MDT fleet. These had seen very little service with MDT and were the only Weymann bodied saloons supplied after the War to the group.

Five Ford 502E 3 ton and one 500E 2 ton trucks were received to replace the early postwar Morris Commercials.

For the first time works and schools services were numbered and received the prefix W.

The Ilkeston railway station site was purchased after some eight years of negotiations for £11.000, They also obtained 1.728 square yards of land at North Street, Ilkeston and additional land at Langley Mill on the garage site.

1959

Although seventeen MW6G dual purpose saloons (Nos.264-80) were delivered during the summer, two (Nos.279-80) did not enter service until June 1960. Lodekkas numbered 477-89 were received during the year.

Land at Dark Lane, Cinderhill which had been used for the tramway was conveyanced to Nottingham Corporation.

1960

The former Williamson premises on Derby Road, Heanor were sold to Heanor UDC on the 15th March.

The opening of the M1 London-Birmingham Motorway (as it was then known) was considered an attraction and operators were offering tours of this new road. MGO were no exception running the whole length from Crick to Watford where the coaches turned and returned back to Crick. These excursions were short lived, and as we all know now there is no novelty travelling on Motorways!

Five Lodekkas (Nos.490-4) arrived in 1960, similar to the previous deliveries, except these were new FS6G models. They had 60 seats whereas on the earlier deliveries 58 seats had been specified, being

unusual as they were only supplied to MGO/MDT/NDT and Bristol Tramways. MGO had continued to receive the 27ft. long versions even though a 30ft. long version had been available since 1957, although NDT did have the solitary model numbered 464. the previous year.

A single Ford 502E 2 ton lorry entered the fleet.

The A4 limited stop service had an additional setting down point, when it was extended direct to Alfreton from Ripley.

The Park Road garage at Ilkeston was sold to the East Midlands Electricity Board, in preparation for the move to Bath Street.

1961

The Midland National Omnibus Co Ltd, and the Northern National Omnibus Co Ltd, were dormant companies originally set up by the National Omnibus Co Ltd, to protect the names. They were retained upon acquisition by the Tilling Group and then British Transport Commission. They were transferred to MGO beneficial ownership, during December. Each had seven shares, one being held by Transport Nominees Ltd, and six of each by MGO.

A further six and the last rear entrance Lodekkas to enter the fleet, were numbered 495-500. They were superseded by (Nos.501-5) the FSF6G model fitted with front entrance bodywork. The F denoting that it had a lower frame than the earlier L model, which had been found necessary to avoid having a second step with the introduction of the front entrance design.

AEC Regal No.172 was converted to a snow plough. Two Ford 502E 2 ton and one Ford 504E 4 ton lorries were purchased.

Limited stop journeys on the F6 between Matlock and Alfreton, were extended to Heanor and Ripley, and the F7 was limited to Bank Holidays only.

A Sutton in Ashfield town service was introduced between Stanton Hill, Carsic Lane Estate, Portland Square and Sutton Junction; this was given route numbers G1/G2/G3. In consequence the route of the E6 was amended to take in Skegby Lane, Dalesforth and New Cross between Mansfield and Sutton in Ashfield.

The Bath Street, Ilkeston garage was completed

on the 28th February, and vehicles were transferred from Park Road on the 12th March. Although owned by NDT, MGO was the prominent name. The allocation was forty buses, yet there was covered accommodation for fifty and for a further twelve on the hard standing. There was a large area of land at the front, which was dedicated to a new by-pass, but in the event was not built until thirty odd years later. There were separate entrance and exit drives, and landscaped areas with grass, shrubs, roses and trees.

1962

Following the death of the Secretary J A Allen, he was replaced by G C Smith.

Again only Lodekkas were delivered, five (Nos.506-10) being FSF6G type as the previous year, and the last to the shorter 27ft length. Five (Nos.511-5) FLF6B models introduced had a seating capacity of 70. On these F models the L denoted 30ft. long and 6B signified a 6 cylinder Bristol engine, rather than 6G the standard Gardner engine fitted to all previous MGO Lodekkas.

Two Thames Trader 2 ton lorries were the years additions.

Proposed alterations to the Alfreton garage were experiencing some difficulties, as the local authority refused planning permission for the frontage as this conflicted with the town plan and extensions to the rear infringed the Park. It was , therefore, decided to offer this recently acquired plot to Alfreton UDC.

The X12 Ilkeston-Scarborough was operated for the first time serving Eastwood, Underwood, Kirkby, Sutton, Mansfield, Bridlington and Filey.

Permission was given to MGO/NDT to operate a second service to Wollaton Vale, this was the E8 from Nottingham to Wollaton Village, Bramcote Lane and Kevin Road. At the same time they diverted the E5 off Bramcote Lane to Glenwood Avenue, and Arleston Drive to terminate at Wollaton Rise.

1963

Under the provisions of the Transport 1962, The Transport Holding Company (THC) took effect from the 1st January, taking over the BTC. This included the Tilling and Scottish bus groups, British Road Services, shipping and travel agencies. Other than this there was no evident change.

Of the nine FLF Lodekkas delivered, Nos. 516-20 had Gardner engines and Nos. 626-9 were fitted with Bristol BVW engines. The delivery also included the first coaches since 1954, which were six (Nos.281-6) 39 seat MW6G types.

The final purchase of lorries arrived in the form of Thames Traders, one 3 ton and two 2 ton versions.

1964

G McKay was appointed Chairman on the 1st June.

It was reported to the Board that, except for those over ten years old, all Lodekkas were now fitted with power operated doors and fluorescent lighting had been installed in the Lodekkas, LS and MW single deck models.

The X5 was extended to commence from Dronfield on the Chesterfield-Great Yarmouth service.

An attempt was made by United Counties and Trent to operate between Alfreton and London, to which Yelloway put in a counter application for a Derby-London service. Yelloway who had an old established seasonal Blackpool and Blackburn to London services, which also served Derby, were preserving their rights. However, the railways as usual objected and a second application was made with all three joining forces together with MGO, but this was again refused.

Casualties from the Beeching Plan, included the closure of the former Great Northern line between Nottingham and Derby. Jointly with Trent and a British Railways Board guarantee, a Monday to Friday peak hour service was introduced on the 7th September between Derby (Friargate Station), West Hallam, Ilkeston, Kimberley, Basford, New Basford (Meridian works) and Nottingham (Broad Marsh). There was one morning departure from Derby and two early evening departures from Nottingham. The Nottingham terminus was the bus station which was in close proximity to the Midland Railway Station. The train service had terminated at Victoria Station, which was also closed. However, the new service served the adjacent Huntingdon Street to cover this.

A further three coaches, were Nos. 30-2 newly introduced RELH6G models, being the first rear

engined vehicles in the fleet. These were also 36ft. long, the maximum permitted length introduced in July 1961. FLF Lodekkas numbered 630-4 came during the year, of these the first three had Bristol engines.

1965

J Niblock was appointed General Manager and director on the 1st May. This followed the retirement of W Williamson who had been with the company thirty seven years, following the Williamson's Garage takeover.

Forty eight Setright long range ticket registers were obtained.

MGO deliveries for 1965 were (Nos.291-7) 43 seat dual purpose MW6G's and the usual mixed engine FLF Lodekkas (Nos.642-5). NDT received seven FLFs (Nos.635-41) and two MGO 1964 FLFs (Nos.633-4). In exchange nine (Nos.318-26) ex NDT AEC Regent III double deckers were taken into MGO stock, but disposed of over the next two years. Originating with MDT, they had passed to NDT on the trolleybus replacement programme.

It was possible to introduce a MX4 Alfreton-Derby-London service jointly with Trent, United Counties and Yelloway, by applying for a Alfreton-Derby-Loughborough licence. From Loughborough it then ran on the times of the United Counties Nottingham-London service. Marketed as the 'Derbyshire Express', it offered a daily service by the M1 Motorway from Northampton, or by changing at Northampton it was possible to take the old route via Luton and St.Albans. An early morning journey from Northampton to Derby and an evening return were withdrawn quite quickly. However, the Fridays and Sundays journeys were extended on to London, retaining the timings. The four companies operated in rotation for fixed periods. Yelloway drivers had overnight lodgings at Alfreton and the coaches were garaged at the MGO Alfreton depot.

Both the X8/12 to Blackpool/Scarborough respectively, now commenced from West Hallam and also served the large Kirk Hallam Estate before Ilkeston.

The F6 Heanor-Matlock also became a Bank Holidays only operation. The numbering of the variants G2 and G3 on the Stanton Hill-Sutton Junction

service were dropped, making G3 the highest stage service number reached

MGO/MDT introduced a four day extended tour to the Lake District and the Yorkshire, being the first operated by the companies, as were inclusive coach holidays for elderly people.

The level crossing was closed at Langley Mill and the existing rail traffic was diverted to the railway line under Heanor Road. The railway line adjoined the Langley Mill garage and negotiations were opened for purchase of the land.

1966

The X11 Llandudno express was amended to start from New Ollerton by extending from Market Warsop, and Edwinstowe.

The X12 West Hallam-Scarborough became a joint service with Trent, with an additional route added from Ilkeston, Heanor, Ripley and Alfreton, before joining up again at Mansfield.

On the Great Yarmouth service additional pick up points were added on the X5 when it was extended to Dronfield from Chesterfield

The railway replacement service was reduced in the early evening to operate between Basford and Ilkeston, and the later journey to serve points between Nottingham and West Hallam only.

Ten FLF6G Lodekkas were introduced as numbers 660-9. Four MW6G's with B45F bodies, were the first true single deck buses for thirty five years, being taken into stock as Nos.101-4.

Three (Nos.89/119-20) 1948 AEC Regents passed to MDT

The combined name of MGO/MDT was introduced to the single decker fleet names, and also a new livery of cream, with a black waist rail and/or window surrounds.

A provisional estimate of £65.000 was quoted for a new head office at Langley Mill and instructions were given to proceed with the plans.

An enquiry office in the garden of the Ilkeston garage premises, facing on to Bath Street, was opened on the 1st December.

1967

R G Howe General Manager of Lincolnshire Road Car was also appointed General Manager of

MGO/MDT/NDT from the 1st February, replacing J Niblock who became Chairman in place of G McKay. It was rumoured that Lincolnshire was to be added to the MGO/MDT fleet names on the single deck buses, but it never transpired.

J A Stevenson became Deputy General Manager on the same day. M J Holmes was appointed Secretary from the 1st December, following the resignation of G C Smith who took up a similar appointment at Eastern Counties.

The very considerable interests of the BET bus empire were sold to the THC on the 22nd November and this was to have a particular affect on the former Balfour Beatty group of companies.

At last it was possible to travel between Cotmanhay Farm and Kirk Hallam, with the introduction of a half hourly daily joint service with Barton (52) when the A2 was extended from Ilkeston Market Place. Taking the normal Barton route this travelled via Cavendish Road, and Little Hallam Hill, Ilkeston.

A second rail replacement service ran between Westhouses & Blackwell Station and Ilkeston Market Place with stopping points limited to; Alfreton (Bus Station), Pye Bridge (Station Approach), Jacksdale (Picture Palace) and Langley Mill (Milnhay Road). This followed the closure of the Erewash Valley railway stations on the 2nd January.

MGO MW6G No. 101 at Wharncliffe Road, Ilkeston in Mansfield District livery, working the C8 to Watnall, late in April 1968, just prior to transfer to MDT. The rear destination display reads One man operated vehicle"

Additional pick up points were added on the X6 Great Yarmouth service, when it was extended to Bolsover, Clowne and Eckington, and it also became jointly operated with East Midland (91).

Relaxation of the vehicles purchasing policy allowed MGO to obtain three (Nos.219-21) Bedford VAM14 Duple bodied 41 seat coaches. There were also two (Nos.133-4) rather unusual dual purpose 43 seat RESH6G buses and the standard FLF6G Lodekkas, which received fleet numbers 670-82.

The hiring of lorries to the East Midland Electricity Board ceased on the 9th June and the Ford and Thames Trader lorries were disposed of.

At an extra-ordinary meeting on the 11th April The Midland National Omnibus Co Ltd, name was changed to Amalgamated Passenger Transport Ltd. By 21st September the seven shares (six MGO and one Transport Nominees) had been transferred to Transport Holding Co.

A proposal to provide new washing and refuelling bay, engineering workshop and garage maintenance facilities, depot office, and canteen block at Langley Mill was estimated at a cost of £140.000. A dwelling house at 34 Station Road. Langley Mill was purchased for £2.000. This was to be demolished as a part of the overall scheme.

1968

BET UK-based bus operations became subsidaries of the THC, as from the 1st March. Statutory Authority had to be obtained to increase the borrowing powers of the THC, which meant a delay before Royal Assent was received.

The Transport Act, 1968 received Royal Assent on the 25th October 1968. The provisions of the Bill were to provide: 1) Passenger Transport Authorities, 2) The National Bus Company, 3) The Scottish Transport Group, 4) New Bus Grants 5) Subsidisation of rural bus services.

Following an approach by Trent (now a part of THC), with a view to garaging their buses at Alfreton, the Architect was asked to draw up plans. This included the replacement of the single deck garage and modernisation of maintenance facilities, fuelling, and new administrative and enquiry offices, canteen, etc.

More (Nos.307-13) FLF6G Lodekkas appeared during the year, along with three (Nos.222-4) Bedford VAM70 Duple 41 seat coaches. Six Lodekka FLF6G's from the MGO 1968 programme, became Nos. 301-6, in the NDT fleet.

Added to the MGO fleet was more MDT redundant stock; Nos.211-5 MW6G 39 seat dual purpose buses; Nos.533-4 FS6G's with rear entrance doors; Nos.535-44 FSF6G Lodekkas. In return, four Lodekkas Nos.267/95-7 and MW6Gs Nos. 101-4 were transferred to MDT during April, but No.267 was returned in the December.

Ten of the 1956 LS6G's and one 1955 model were converted to buses from dual purpose vehicles.

FS6G Lodekkas Nos. 490-520 were renumbered 590-620.

Three pre-war MDT AEC Regal dual purpose buses (MDT Nos. 29/33/47) were obtained and converted to snow ploughs.

The X3 Blackpool was extended from Blidworth to Southwell, for the season only. Both the X5 and X6 were extended from Great Yarmouth to Lowestoft.

Friday journeys on E9 Matlock-Riber were withdrawn during February.

The F7 Heanor-Alfreton-Matlock limited stop was withdrawn at the end of the season. Since 1966 journeys on both the F6 and F7 had been limited to Bank Holidays only. The ex Chambers, Ilkeston-Matlock summer Wednesdays service was withdrawn at the end of August.

The licence for the Westhouses-Ilkeston railway replacement service was surrendered in December. Similar services had been introduced following the implementation of the Beeching Plan, which proposed the closure of almost 5.000 route miles and 2.363 stations on the British railways system. Although there were many closures it was never, as extreme as originally planned. More often than not, the railways provided a guaranteed subsidy, but very little publicity was provided. It has been impossible to find details of the above service displayed in either the British Railways or MGO timetables of the period. The imposition of pick up points which had to be close to the stations restricted development, and was most probably a deliberate policy, as these services were introduced to appease the travelling public. Several colliery works journeys had been introduced during the period of railway closures, but usually on contract to the National Coal Board.

There were, however, more permanent benefits from these rail closures. as it allowed many operators to introduce express services to more coastal resorts. As it will be noticed earlier, MGO had already taken advantage of this additional opportunity

The opening of the East Midlands Airport at Castle Donington on the 1st April 1964, introduced another form of travel close to MGO territory and the opportunity was taken to provide summer weekend services jointly with Trent. For the one year only the X24 ran from Mansfield, Sutton, Kirkby, Heanor, Ilkeston, including intermediate points to the airport. The timetable listed connections with various flights, although it was only possible to pick up Basle passengers on the return flight.

The six MGO shares in Northern National passed to THC Bus Nominees Ltd, on the 28th May.

1969

The National Bus Company came into being on the 1st January taking over bus interests in England and Wales of the Transport Holding Company, with the exception of areas covered by the new Passenger Transport Authorities.

R G Howe continued in the position of General Manager to the Lincolnshire & Midland General Group

Premises in Church Square, Heanor were sold to Heanor UDC to provide car parking and access.

Two different styles of single deck bus came in the form of Nos.111-6 LH6L's with 45 seat front entrance bodies and Nos.135-9 dual entrance 44 seat RELL6G types. The first rear engined double deckers were VRTSL6G with 70 seat front entrance bodies, numbered 315-20

Bristol RELH6G's numbered 30-2 were renumbered 130-2 and reseated as C47F.

Six FS6G Lodekkas (Nos. 595-600) passed to MDT, and two Lodekka LD6G's from MDT became driver training vehicles Nos. T1-2

Rainworth became the terminus of the X3 and Underwood on the X2 Blackpool services. West Hallam was deleted from the X8 Blackpool, so all journeys started from Kirk Hallam Estate.

Closer ties with Trent, saw revisions and rationalisation on the Mansfield-Alfreton corridor. The MGO C2 becoming the 42 and the Trent 100 became the 43. Additional journeys were provided on the X43 limited stop service running directly between South Normanton and Sutton in Ashfield, but this withdrawn before the end of the year.

In consequence of the above, the MDT service 3 Mansfield- Alfreton (formerly Ebor) was cut back from Alfreton to Blackwell or South Normanton and renumbered 4. This became a joint service with MGO, and also the D1 Mansfield-Chesterfield became joint with MDT, although this was not shown in the timetable books.

Additional journeys were granted on the C9 which gave Hucknall a town service between Bernard Avenue, Papplewick Lane Estate and West Street.

Breadsall was introduced on the morning journey from Derby (Friargate Station) to Nottingham rail replacement service. Breadsall station had closed in April 1953, some eleven years before the line was closed.

From the 2nd October the F5 became circular from Arleston Drive, Wollaton Vale, Bramcote Lane, then Woodbank Drive, to Wollaton Vale, Arleston Drive and back to Nottingham. With the introduction of one man operated single deckers on one of the two journeys per hour on the E8, it had turned in Rivergreen Crescent and Denewood Avenue, whereas the double deckers continued to reverse into Kevin Road. This was in accordance with the standard requirement that single crew vehicles could not reverse. There were, however, protests from local housewives, who formed a blockade, for seven hours to prevent buses passing. In consequence the E8 was drastically reduced to Monday to Saturday early morning peak journeys only from Kevin Road, joining the F5 at Woodbank Drive.

No. 291 at the new covered Broad Marsh Bus Station, working the A1 to Langley Mill, on the 8th November 1971, shortly before transfer of services to Mount Street. As can be seen loading was allowed on both sides of the recently opened platforms, but changed very quickly as a matter of safety.

On the 5th May the old offices were transferred from Station Road, Langley Mill to an adjacent new head office on Mansfield Road, Heanor They were officially opened on the 8th May. Rent was apportioned to MGO and MDT for use of workshops and the Heanor office. MGO was apportioned rent for Ilkeston, Langley Mill and the Heanor office. From June board meetings were held at the new offices in lieu of London.

1970

Brian R King formerly with Trent was appointed Assistant Traffic Manager, replacing J S Madgett, from the 1st July .

The E9 Matlock-Riber was withdrawn in its entirety during November.

Sutton in Ashfield town centre was reinstated on the F1 route as the section along Hamilton Road was withdrawn in its favour.

Tours and excursions from Mansfield were reorganised and the licences of MDT, MGO and East Midland were jointly operated.

Although the Nottingham-London express services were advertised as United Counties, the licences were amended to include MGO and Trent as joint operators. Thus they were able to provide coaches, without the usual on hire stickers and logically they were better placed for the work than the Northampton based United Counties.

A further two (Nos.230-1) of the lightweight Bedford VAM70 coaches arrived with Duple 41 seat bodies. Again there was the usual mixture of Bristol/ECW combinations; Nos.146-7 RELL6G's with dual entrance bus bodies, Nos.117-21 LH6L's with 45 seat bus bodywork, and Nos.321-2 VRTSL6G double deckers.

The A8 became a Heanor-Langley-Heanor circular on Mondays to Saturdays, extended on Sundays to Langley Mill, Eastwood and New Eastwood.

Seven 1967 Lodekkas (Nos. 676-82) were transferred from MGO to NDT.

1971

It was intended to split the Lincolnshire & Midland General Group as from the 31st December. The management of Midland General becoming a part of Trent Motor Traction, with the NDT operational element transferring to MGO. MDT was placed under the wing of East Midland MS. R G Howe resigned as Director and General Manager of the group from the 31st December.

The original programme requested Bedford VAM coaches with Duple bodies, but they received Nos.232-3 Bedford YRQ (mid engined chassis) with Plaxton coachwork. It also stated that nine Leyland Nationals would replace nine RELL's. In the event they were supplied with six (Nos.148-53) RELL6G's dual entrance buses and three (Nos.122-4) LH6L's with 45 seat bus bodies.

Very modern single deckers were obtained from MDT as follows; Nos.287-8 MW6G with 39 seat coachwork, Nos.143-5 RELL6G's with dual entrance 44 seat bodies, Nos.234-5 Bedford YRQ with Plaxton coach bodies, Nos.216-8 Bedford VAM14/Duple coaches and Nos.225-9 Bedford VAM70 again with Duple bodies. In exchange two MW6G's (Nos.258/63), and FS6G No.594 went to MDT and Bedford VAM70/Duple coaches Nos.225-9 were returned within four months.

Following the closure of Huntingdon Street bus station, the A1/B8/F3 were extended to Broad Marsh early in the year and shared the new bus station facilities, opened in October, with the F2/F4. However, after a period they were all diverted on Mansfield Road, Nottingham, to Milton Street, Upper Parliament Street, and the new Mount Street bus station.

What remained of the F3 Nottingham-Rainworth was extended to Mansfield. It consisted of a journey each way Mondays to Saturdays. The A4 limited stop service between Alfreton and Nottingham was withdrawn.

The former Ormonde Colliery line was purchased. It ran between the office block and workshops, covering an area of 4.000 sq.yds.

Phase 2 of the redevelopment of Langley Mill (New depot maintenance facilities, washing and refuelling bays) was authorised to be constructed. However phase 3 (new workshops, depot offices, and canteen) was rescinded.

All the NDT fleet was transferred to MGO on the 31st December as follows; Nos. 633-4/7-9/76-82/301-6 FLF6G's and Nos. 635-6/40-1 FLF6B's.

1972

Although L Waller General Manager of Trent was also appointed General Manager from the 1st January 1972, the operational side of MGO continued as a separate entity until the 1st April.

On the 28th March a combined meeting of MGO and Trent was held at the Trent headquarters on Uttoxeter New Road, Derby. The final General

The new Mount Street Bus Station, Nottingham opened during October 1971, and during the period of construction MGO/NDT buses had stops allocated on Maid Marian Way. Seen on the 18th December 1971 with a line up of MGO/NDT filling the allocated bays. Shown are the rears of Bristol/ECW 114 (BNU 676G) LH6L, 2149 BNN 102C) MW6G ex MDT, 664 (JNU 984D) FLF6G, 682 (SRB 80F) FLF6G, 305(TRB 572F) FLF6G, and 665 (JNU 984D) FLF6G.

Meeting of NDT was held on the same date and at 10 am it was in voluntary liquidation.

Work was in hand for the new garage at Alfreton, which had involved the purchase of a dwelling at 32 King Street and a printing works at 42 King Street.

The final delivery was four (Nos.154-8) RELL6G models with dual entrance bodies.

The E1 was amended to terminate at Balloon Wood Flats in lieu of Strelley Lane.

The 1972 programme included three Leyland Nationals, which were received after transfer of operations to Trent.

The joint MGO/MDT licences granted in 1968 for the D1 Mansfield-Chesterfield and the 4 Mansfield-Blackwell, were reapplied for separately during 1969, but with joint running. These references were retained and a further twenty nine applications were made during October 1971, and granted early in 1972. A further five applications made in January may have been withdrawn. It would seem that the intention was to make the two into one larger unit, which was the NBC policy at this time. Although it

was stated, that this was a policy decision to make the interchange of vehicles simpler. Looking at this in retrospect the decision to switch MGO into Trent, and MDT into East Midland, seems to have been rather hastily arranged.

1976-7

The Midland General Omnibus Company Ltd, became a dormant company, following the transfer of vehicles to Trent in October 1976.

1978

G F Harvey the Secretary to Trent, was advised that the Nottinghamshire & Derbyshire Traction Co, name had been available from the 22nd June 1978 three months after the final notice. United Automobile Services, applied for the change of name Bell's Services Ltd, to Nottinghamshire & Derbyshire Traction Co. Ltd (the original statutory company was dissolved on the 31st December with the new company becoming Limited) which took effect from the 29th November.

1980

On the 8th December the title Nottinghamshire &

Derbyshire Traction Co Ltd, was changed to Amalgamated Passenger Transport Ltd (dissolved on 22nd November 1990). This title had derived from The Midland National Omnibus Co Ltd, in which MGO had a vested interest from 1961 until 1967. At the same time the Amalgamated Passenger Transport Ltd, became the Nottinghamshire & Derbyshire Traction Co Ltd.

1986

Privatisation of the members of the NBC, saw the formation of many companies, to purchase parts of the group. A management buyout of Trent under the name of Wellglade Ltd, was incorporated on the 21st January. Other subsidiary companies were formed including Bilmore Ltd, on the 25th April and Adelian Ltd on the 4th November.

1987

The Nottinghamshire & Derbyshire Traction Co Ltd, became Countryside Tours Ltd, on the 9th February, and Adelian Ltd, was renamed Notts & Derby. Five days earlier The Midland General Omnibus Co Ltd, exchanged names with Bilmore Ltd, and Bilmore was dissolved on 4th August 1992. This apparently convoluted procedure was undertaken on the advice of solicitors so that Wellglade could acquire the Midland General and Notts & Derby names without incurring any liabilities, which the original NBC companies might have had as they were not under Trent's management and the MBO team were offered no warranties.

Postscript

Both companies still survive under the Wellglade umbrella, and in April 1998 NDT became operational again, trading as 'Blue Apple', The vehicles ex Trent Leyland Nationals and Olympians painted in pale green and blue, are a low cost operation initially providing transport for students at the University of Derby, an area never previously covered by NDT. During the Autumn of 1998 more work was obtained when Derbyshire Council contracts were awarded. Schools, contract and local bus work has been transferred from Barton Buses Ltd (Barton Transport operations and vehicles being acquired in July 1989). So NDT lives on, and we may yet see the dormant MGO name on buses again!

Derby Road, Nottingham, May 1973 and a pair of FLF6Gs. No. 719 (MGO old No. 662) in NBC poppy red and white livery, tries to keep abreast with No. 745 (NDT No. 306) in the old livery of mid blue and cream. From September 1972, buses were painted in blue and white, being changed to red from November 1972.

NDT Trams

United Electric Car Company of Preston built all twenty four trams each having Peckham P22 trucks and two BTH GE67-3T motors rated at 40hp. Two GE K10D controllers per car had 5 series and 4 parallel notches, but lacked rheostatic brake notches and had emergency brakes only.

(Right) During the early part of the twentieth century groups of inquisitive onlookers gathered more interested in the arrival of a photographer with his camera and tripod than the tram? At Hill Top, Eastwood, there was the usual gathering for the arrival of open top car No. 1 on a trial run, but it is only the young boys who fixed their attention to the new tracked phenomenon. Both were to become a regular part of the every day scene, although the camera was somewhat later. All the first twelve [Nos.1-12] were received with open tops, but cars 1 to 3 received top covers in 1922.

United Electric Car Company Ltd, of Preston [previously The Electric Railway & Tramway Carriage Works Ltd, until 25th September 1905], was a part of Dick, Kerr & Co Ltd, which amalgamated with other companies to become the English Electric Co Ltd, on 14th December 1918.

(Left) Again on a trial run and a mixed reaction from the crowd, when No.14 posed for the cameraman opposite Losoce Road Post Office, Heanor. Although displaying Nottingham, it would at this time, only have been able to reach Cinderhill. But was this the closed top tram that became trapped under Midland Railway bridge at Kimberley, as the engineers had calculated the height with an open top car? Very quickly the road was re-excavated to lower the road once again!

(Right) The Ilkeston system was detached from the main system, and generally never had the glamour or notoriety of the main system, which was and still is often referred to as 'The Ripley Rattlers'. This may have been the reason for the rather limited amount of photographs taken of the Ilkeston cars, following the purchase by NDT. However, a shot which was taken of No.12 is shown on the right. One of the second batch of four [Nos.10 -13]with Milnes body and Westinghouse equipment, they differed only slightly from the originals around the top of the staircase. This was cut off abruptly, whereas on the Electric Railway & Tramway Carriage Works units it continued further round giving a shorter squared off appearance. The Ilkeston Corporation Tramway name had been removed, but it is possible to see where the borough coat of arms had been applied.This view is of particular interest as No.12 is shown working on the short branch line between Station Road and Ilkeston Junction Station, with Bath Street the main thoroughfare in the background. By 1921, with the sale of five cars, the fleet was reduced to eight all of which were sent to Langley Mill, for repairs.One was converted to a single deck and it is believed all the remainder had their staircases reversed, to match the Ripley cars.

Trolleybuses

The first six trolleybuses were purchased for the Cotmanhay to Hallam Fields section of the new system, they were numbered 300-5 [RB 5568-73]. The chassis and the 32 seat bodywork were produced by English Electric with DK 121C 60hp motors. The DK reference being a throw back to the days when Dick Kerr manufactured motors for trams, before becoming part of English Electric on 14th December 1918. All the DK motors fitted, up to 1934, were series-wound with augmented field control. Originally window surrounds were painted in dark blue, as seen on the photograph (Below) taken at the Preston works of English Electric Co Ltd. (Top right) No.301 turns into Thurman Street, from Nottingham Road, Ilkeston on its journey to Hallam Fields. The changes in the livery can be seen, including the fleetname, now in the buckle style, which became standard until the 1950s. Large non standard gold fleet number transfers were fixed to both the front and the back, rather than the usual cast metal plate on the front introduced circa 1930.

A pair of unidentified English Electric trolleybuses, photographed in Bath Street, Ilkeston, shortly after the system opened.

The second order for trolleybuses again had English Electric 32 seat bodies, with half cab layout, giving the impression of a standard single deck bus, and more modern styling. AEC supplied the 662T chassis with English Electric equipment including DK 130A 65hp motors They were given fleet numbers 306-15 [RB6613-22].

(Right) No.306 on Gregory Boulevard, Sherwood, Nottingham during November 1933. Note there are two signs on the lamp post reading; Bus request stop and Railless stop here. Also note the standard fixing of the bamboo trolley pole to the cant rail on single deck trolleybuses.

No, 315 on Heanor Road, Ilkeston terminus at the opening of the section between Ilkeston and Loscoe listed as route 13, Later becoming part the route 6 then A3. Comparison between this picture and that opposite, shows the changes to the rear end, particularly the fitting of a destination display, but the large fleet number has been retained.

Fifteen AEC 661T-EEC double decker trolleybuses [317-331 RB 8951-65] delivered in 1933, again had half cab fronts, but bodywork built by Metropolitan-Cammel Carriage Wagon and Finance Ltd, [MCCW] of Birmingham. The previous year MCCW formed an association with Weymann Motor Bodies [1925] Ltd, of Addlestone, to sell their products through Metropolitan Cammell-Weymann Motor Bodies Ltd [MCW]. This resulted in Weymann producing steel framed bodies, using MCW methods. They had DK 130F 80 hp motors, but one had regenerative control with a compound-wound motor. (Left) An offside view of No.328 passing a horse and cart, outside the 'Swan' public house, situated on Church Street, Old Basford. This was part of the wires, leased from Nottingham, allowing them access to the city centre. (Below left) RB 3955 No.321 at the King Street, Nottingham, layover point during an evening in November 1934. It will be seen on both the above mentioned photographs that the route number indicator remained blank, as they were not introduced on the vehicles until August 1936, when prefixes were added. (Below) When No.322 was photographed passing under the LMS railway line at Eastwood Road, Kimberley in August 1940 the area of cream had been reduced, and wartime measures of shaded headlamps and white markers on the mudguards had been introduced.

Operating on the direct A3 service, No 302 is approaching Rutland Hotel, along Heanor Road, Ilkeston from Heanor. Again an AEC 661T with EEC EE 406A1 80 hp compound-wound motor and regenerative control, and full fronted Weymann body. This batch [Nos.300-5/32] were replacements for the original single deckers which were sold to Mexborough & Swinton Traction Company.

The layover point at Nottingham was at the Vee of the junctions between King Street and Queen Street, where No.303 shares the spot with a 1946 NCT Karrier W4 with Park Royal body. Photographed in August 1950, the Riley 1.5 litre car is making a turn into King Street, which was banned some years later, when it became a one way street.

The terminus of the A2 was at Hallam Fields, where the trolleybuses turned into Crompton Road and then reversed back on to Hallam Fields Road. This stop served the vast Stanton Ironworks complex. No.335 one of the 1941 deliveries, an AEC-EEC [EE 406J 80 hp compound-wound motors and regenerative control] with Weymann bodywork, was seen on the 15th March 1953.

No.336 at Bath Street, Ilkeston, collects a good load of passengers for Cotmanhay. This was part of a delivery of ten received in wartime grey livery during 1941 and 1942, all built by Weymann to the pre-war design. There were changes from the 1937 styling seen above; noticeably the deeper vented grille, the more upright but rounded front and the thicker pillar support on the bulkhead. Again 661T models, these were to be the last trolleybuses built at Southall, as production was transferred to Kingston upon Thames in June 1946, when AEC and Leyland formed British United Traction Ltd, which took over the manufacture of trolleybuses. These vehicles virtually replaced the remaining single deck trolleybuses, but four did remain until the early post war period, although latterly little used.

The final fifteen trolleybuses, replaced all the half cab double deckers. Numbered 343-57 they had BUT 9611T chassis and English Electric [EE410/3B 120 hp motors and EE & SD control system] equipment. The motors were compound wound, but the light shunt winding was incapable of regeneration. They had bodies similar to the wartime additions, but with a smaller louvered front grille, and a higher windscreen, giving a tidier appearance around the cab area, which was also more rounded. (Top right) NNU 234 No.353 makes a stop on Parliament Street, Nottingham, before turning into King Street and the terminus for the A1 route. Behind is NCT No.288 a Daimler CVD6 with Roberts body. (Above) No.347 leaving the suburbs of Nottingham drops off passengers at Nuthall Road, Cinderhill. The clock on the left, being a timing point for NCT departures. (Left) Shortly before the closure of the system No. 344 leaves Queen Street, under the direction of the constable on traffic duty. The Elite Cinema was showing a double bill of two long forgotten films; 'The Devil Makes Three' and 'The Story of Will Rogers'.

Establishing the Bus Fleet.

 The first vehicles to carry the Midland General name were R 8802-3 a pair of Vulcan VSC 17 seat buses with bodies constructed in the Langley Mill workshops. Although allocated fleet numbers at a later date, it is possible these were never carried. Photographed outside the Langley Mill garage is R 8803

NDT obtained an ex WD AEC Y type lorry-bus in April 1920, which in all probability came from London General who had run these in 1919, when there was a shortage of buses. They were converted by fitting wooden seats on the platform of the lorry, with an entrance through the tailboard by means of steps and framework for the canvas cover. Re-registered R 4226, it may have provided transport on the Heanor to Ilkeston route before MGO was up and running. Seen in the photograph (Above left) the driver looks remarkably like Mr Laing who became the Traffic Manager, which may be the reason for not wearing a uniform. During 1922 the chassis was purchased by MGO who fitted it with a body which had been obtained from Mansfield & District, and is seen on the top right at Langley Mill garage. It has also been said that wicker seats were fitted. Behind is a partial view of R 8802 one the Vulcans. On the right it is seen in service, possibly working the Ilkeston-Heanor service, or the tram feeder service from Underwood which connected at Nuthall. Within a year the body was fitted to No.3 NU 103 a Guy BA and the chassis returned to NDT to replace the Star tower wagon.

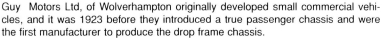

Guy Motors Ltd, of Wolverhampton originally developed small commercial vehicles, and it was 1923 before they introduced a true passenger chassis and were the first manufacturer to produce the drop frame chassis.

(Above) No.3 an early Guy BA dating from 1923, purchased new and fitted with the body from R 4226. When removed the body was completely rebuilt in the NDT workshops at Langley Mill, with three bay layout.

(Above right) Seen at the Upper Parliament Street, Nottingham terminus, is No.12 [NU 5249] working the Heanor service on behalf of NDT, in an attempt to stave off the growing competition on the route. The Guy BA with Guy 20 seat bodywork was one of seven identical buses obtained in 1925. A further Guy BB was also purchased [No.7] which again had a Guy body but with 32 seats.

(Centre) Guy BB [NU 3564] fitted with Strachan & Brown 32 seat dual door body, displays fleet No.5 on the waistrail, just beyond the front entrance. Entrance and exit are written above each of the doorways. The photograph was taken outside the waiting room and parcels office on Granby Street, Ilkeston, which was provided for a short period in 1924-5 for the transfer of passengers to the Ilkeston tramway. Afterwards connections could also be made at the new terminus on Ilkeston Market Place.

(Bottom) The same Guy BB as seen in the centre, with a much improved look about its appearance, following the fitment of pneumatic tyres and the application of a revised livery, during 1926. The original olive green was replaced by a lighter lime green, similar to the tram cars, with the cream extended from the roof to the waistrail, and black mudguards. The lining out, picked out in black, seems to have been isolated to this vehicle or type. Again parked with the nearside of the bus on to the main thoroughfare, in this instance, Parliament Street, Nottingham, which was in close proximity of the NDT tram terminus, approximately 100 yards to the east of this point. In the background are the hoardings enclosing the site for the extensions to the Nottingham Co-operative Society store.

A steady influx of secondhand Leylands came with the various acquired operators, until they purchased new in 1931. The earliest came from South Normanton Bus and then Midland Motor Bus whose NN 8868 a Leyland Z5 is shown (Above) at Wollaton Street, Nottingham. The 20 seat rear entrance body was also built by Leyland.

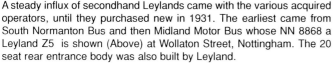

Tilling-Stevens were chosen from 1926, and became the standard for the next six years. The company was first registered as Tilling-Stevens Ltd, in 1906. Originally a petrol-electric chassis was built for Thomas Tillings Ltd, to their design by J&E Hall Ltd, of Dartford and W A Stevens of Maidstone provided the electrical equipment. This was sold to other operators as the Hallford-Stevens, but when Tillings acquired an interest the name was changed. On 21st November 1919 it was changed again to Tilling-Stevens Motors Ltd. To combat the loss of customers in the twenties, they introduced the Express chassis with a 4 cylinder engine and normal drive.

A change of policy at MGO saw the introduction of the Express into the fleet. Two [25-6] which arrived late in 1926 were the only B9B models in the fleet and they had Strachan & Brown 31 seat bodies. (Upper right) No. 26 RA 1238 with MGO abbreviated fleet name, before the change to those shown below. Both were renumbered in 1930/1 to 67 and 65 respectively. For 1927 sixteen B10B chassis were supplied with Strachan & Brown bodies. The lower bonnet and radiator made these distinguishable from the B9B, as shown in the photographs. (Centre) No. 35 at Wollaton Street, Nottingham. (Lower) A further four [Nos. 43-46] were obtained with attractive Davidson bodies, and No.45 is again at the Wollaton Street terminus. The Vee style windscreen and shaped bulkhead gave them a distinctive and modern appearance when compared with the upright Strachan & Brown design. All four had the roof mounted box windscreen blind boxes fitted at Davidsons.

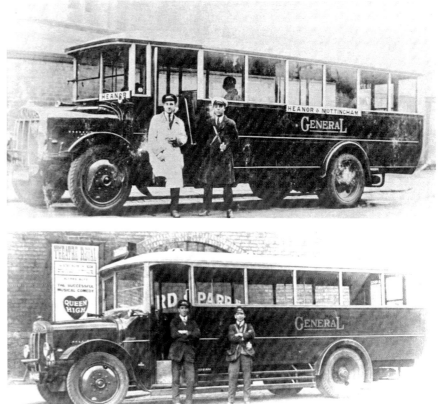

September 1929 and No. 59 a Tilling-Stevens B10A Express chassis with Strachan & Brown coachwork awaits passengers on Wollaton Street, Nottingham, before journeying to Ripley. (Below left) A bus from the same group [Nos. 56-61] was captured on camera at the Strachan and Brown Acton works. Although this was the forward control model [driver alongside the engine] there were only 32 seats adding one to the same 15ft. 6in. wheelbase normal control model. The B10A just introduced in 1927 had a lower frame, yet there was still a high ground clearance.

The Tilling-Stevens B10A was still around in 1930, when MGO received a further allocation of two [Nos. 3/34] with Ransomes Sims & Jefferies of Ipswich bodies. Williamson's and Dawson's also received similar deliveries. For the first time they were fitted with destination boxes with roller binds and reintroduced the porch style entrance, which was to be a major feature of MGO saloons. They had a revised fleet name which emphasised 'General' and the new azure and white livery to replace the olive green and cream.

Like most major operators MGO were now looking for increased capacity, however, Tilling-Stevens had not developed a gear driven double decker, although a petrol electric was available, and so they turned to Thornycroft. Based at Basingstoke Thornycroft was an unusual choice in retrospect, as they were rather late themselves in producing a double decker chassis in 1929. Apparently MGO placed the largest order for their four BC models, all supplied in 1930 in various experimental Notts and Derby liveries, and at least two had wooden slatted [ex tram seating?] upper deck seating.

Two [Nos.1/103] of the Thornycroft BC chassis were received with Dodson 52 seat bodies. It is assumed No.1 was identical on the known seating capacity, thus making No. 77 the Brush bodied model. No. 103 was photographed on Parliament Street adjacent to the Queen Street entrance, which was to be the trolleybus terminus, with a REO of Williamson's following up closely behind. The Dodson body was typically 1920s, with the upper deck finishing behind the drivers cab and yet there was still seating for 28 in the upper deck. Note a further variation on the NDT experimental livery. All four were sold in November 1944 to a Leeds dealer.

As yet unidentified as either No. 1 or 77, but facts point this to be 77 with a Brush of Loughborough 54 seat body, as the other two bodies can be identified by the seating capacity.

No. 102 the Strachans bodied Thornycroft BC at Langley Mill garage shortly after being repainted in the now standard MGO blue and cream livery.

No. 102 seen outside the Strachan works in Acton, shows a different style of livery, from the above two Thornycroft BC models. The glazed section directly above the bonnet was unusual feature, as were the painted dignity strips on the rear window opposite the staircase

During August 1930 Tillings-Stevens changed their name to T S Motors Ltd, (TSM). It was felt this change would dispel thoughts that they only produced petrol electric vehicles and the association of the Tillings name with the operator Thomas Tilling. The large name applied to the top of the radiator was replaced by a small oval plate carrying the title TSM. The Express chassis continued with a 2 suffix now added. Orders were placed for fifteen B10A2 chassis with bodies by Ransomes, Strachan, and Cowieson. They introduced rear destination indicators and the illuminated display above the destination aperture, which either showed 'General' or 'Traction'. W Brown left Strachan & Brown to join Duple in 1928 and in consequence the company became Strachan (Acton) Ltd.

No. 35 one of five with Strachan bodies, at Huntingdon Street, Nottingham during March 1932. It survived with MGO until 1945, and was working for a showman by 1947.

A further five [Nos.27-9/32-3] came with Ransomes bodies, strangely these were the only buses from this bodybuilder to have the normal folding entrance doors. Although a monochrome photograph the impression is given that these were painted in the new uniform group livery of azure below the waistline with white lining and white above, although the window surrounds were a darker blue and the mudguards black.

Vehicle development during this period was quite rapid and several of the manufacturers lost favour with outmoded designs, and then were slow to react to the situation with Leyland, AEC, Bristol and Daimler taking the bulk of the orders. Inevitably the group was now also looking around for a suitable manufacturer. Firstly they bought Leyland then AEC, and both became their main suppliers until the sale of the business.

No. 25 one of five Leyland bodied Leyland LT2s, appears to be painted in the board of directors approved uniform livery of azure and white. The fleet name was now placed within a belt, which was common practice for the period. This lasted until 1950s, when they reverted to something similar to previous style.

It was August 1931 before TSM introduced a double deck chassis designated type D, which did not prove be particularly popular, but MGO decided to take five Nos. 121-5. They were received as type D60A6 with the 60 defining the engine as 6 cylinder. They were the first of what was to be a long standing relationship with the bodybuilder Weymann of Addlestone. No. 124 is shown on both the above pictures in Nottingham, working for NDT (Left) on Parliament Street, and (Right) an the junction of Huntingdon Street and King Edward Street.

Although the double deckers received the new style squared radiator shell the TSM B39A7 Express chassis still retained the earlier style complete with protection bars. This final delivery of Tilling-Stevens products introduced a new bodybuilder; Beadle of Dartford and was possibly influenced by the purchase of No. 46 shown on the right. No. 88 represents the eleven vehicles delivered in March [Nos. 86-91] and July 1932 [Nos, 116-20] seen at Huntingdon Street bus station, Nottingham on the Ripley service.

KJ 2917 was purchased by Mansfield District on the 31st October 1931, possibly as an ex stock TSM vehicle, which had a Beadle of Dartford 56 seat body. It was transferred to MGO early in 1932 [No. 46] to replace vehicles condemned by the Ministry as not complying with the new traffic act. Described as a D40A6 model, indicates this was fitted with a type 40 engine, being of 4 cylinders possibly a 39 type increased from 69.5 bhp to 75.5 bhp which gave 2200 rpm. Seemingly it would have been underpowered for MGO routes, compared to the 60 type engine with 109 bhp developing 2500 rpm, although it may have been the 49 type of 96 bhp that was uprated

Dawson's Enterprise fleet

Dawson's Enterprise Omnibus Co Ltd, came into being on the 4th November 1927, with the amalgamation of Dawson & Co [Ilkeston] Ltd and Dawson's Super Service Ltd. A. E Dawson who had run as the Enterprise Bus Service, then as Dawson & Co, provided a fleet of Thornycrofts. (Top left) One of the three A1 models-either NU 6704, 7955 or RA 1608, with rather upright Challands Ross 20 seat bodywork, which was typical of the 1925 period. (Below) A Thornycroft A2 seen when with Dawson's Super Service at the Wollaton Street, Nottingham terminus. (Bottom left) They acquired the business of R W Dixon during March 1928, who had run as the 'Imperial Service' with this 14 seat REO 'Speedwagon', however, by the time they sold up, they were running two De Dion JE2 20 seat buses.

(Right) One of the two Tilling-Stevens B10A models [Nos.70 and 76], with bodywork by Ransomes, Sims & Jefferies Ltd, of Ipswich [Ransomes]. Although the Dawson's operation was transferred to Williamson's in July 1929, they still retained the vehicles. It is not absolutely certain that the vehicle shown is one of Dawson's, as there is a complete lack of legal lettering by which to identify it. To add to the confusion Williamson's were providing vehicles for Notts & Derby Traction, making it possible for a Dawson's bus to be in this livery.

Williamson's fleet.

The following shows a selection of vehicles, represented by what was possibly the biggest fleet of REO buses in the United Kingdom. No doubt these were supplied through Williamson's own agency, as were the later Bristol chassis.

The REO Motor Car Co, of Lansing, Michigan was established in 1904. Headed by Ransom E Olds, who had just retired from Oldsmobile, they produced their first truck in 1911. During 1915 the 'Speedwagon' model was introduced, which was also adapted as a passenger vehicle. By 1923, along with Ford and Chevrolet, they were finding a considerable demand for vehicles in the British Isles. These chassis were light and fast, although there were speed restrictions, they competed with the slow and cumbersome home grown models. Demand for the company's commercial vehicles saw the formation of REO Motors (Britain) Ltd to import and assemble chassis from the United States. However, within a couple of years demand had fallen, when the British government imposed restrictions on imported vehicles.

(Above) NU 3556 a REO 'Speedwagon with 14 seat bodywork by Hartshorn of Heanor. Dating from 1923, this was the third bus in the fleet and apparently was dark blue with black window surrounds and roof.

The new longer REO 'Pullman' was introduced to the fleet in 1925, dramatically increasing the seating capacity. The first to be received (Bottom) NU 6419 was fitted with an Eaton 20 seat body, identical to smaller models already in the fleet. A deeper skirt, replaced running boards, and a larger painted radiator showed the changes on RA 573 when photographed (Top) at Langley Mill depot. RA 2280 dating from 1927 (Above), received unusual Hartshorn bodywork, with a clestory roof which provided the ventilation. Although Williamson's Garage Ltd, was formed in 1924, vehicles continued to display the old name, and as will be seen they eventually painted out part of the the old name to leave Williamson only.

The Bristol chassis was added to Williamson's agency possibly prior to the purchase of six 4 cylinder B types with Roe 32 seat bodies. They now had the capacity of the combine and no doubt a real threat to them. All four remained with the subsidiary company until January 1937 when they were sold on to F. Lewis of Hanley a dealer for £17 10s 0d [£17.50] each. Numbered haphazardly by the combine as 20/61/18/36 RA 4516-9, the last numbered is seen here whilst on service, yet the crew had time to pose with the vehicle. Bristol Tramways & Carriage Co Ltd, started making motor bus chassis mainly for their own use in 1908. From the early twenties these were being sold more generally. It would appear there were very few sales by Williamson's to other operators in the locality, The same could be said of the BAT chassis which Williamson took on latterly, along with the REO whose sales also dipped dramatically during 1928, when they themselves only purchased four. Williamson's agency strangely had a Bristol based connection as Harris & Hassell Ltd, of Bristol were the sole concessionaires for Reo in the UK, and following the decision by REO to assemble and distribute, they decided to produce their own chassis, the BAT [British Associated Transport], using standard proprietary parts.

Once under the jurisdiction of the combine, they had to follow policy decisions. Therefore the new vehicles for 1929, were the standard Tilling-Stevens B10A models with Strachan & Brown 32 seat bodies, very similar to the MGO delivery, but with rather less fancy front canopy bracket support. Six were received, of which No. 15 RA 9652, is seen at the bodybuilders Acton works. They were painted in Notts & Derby livery, to work on their behalf, jointly with MGO, between Nottingham and Ripley on the statutory omnibus services, giving a degree of protection to the tram service.

The final two vehicles Nos. 71/5 RB 2039/40 arrived in June 1930 with No. 75 surviving until 1951 when it was purchased by a showman. Again on a Tilling-Stevens B10A chassis they were fitted with Ransome, Simms & Jefferies 32 seat bodies, similar to those for Dawson's and MGO, with the external difference being the position of the folding door handle and canopy support bracket. Although sporting the Williamson's name, the livery appears to be that applied to NDT vehicles at this time

The rapid expansion of the Williamson business was helped by the purchase of the Henshaw & Brookes business. Operating from their Ilkeston base as the 'Newell on the Cotmanhay to Nottingham service. Although only established in January 1926, they were operating three buses when they sold out 18 months later. RA 662 (Above) a Thornycroft A1 with Challands Ross rear entrance body had a rather dated running board, giving the impression of a large motor car. (Top left) J Saxton & Sons REO NU 3606 was not included upon takeover of the business in 1929. At the same time E E Hamilton 'Teddy Bear Service' was also purchased, but it is doubtful if the early REO Speedwagon shown (centre left) was included.

Tarlton & Brown of Codnor, sold out to Williamson's during September 1928, together with five REOs, of which RA 2501 a REO Major with twenty seat body is shown above. There is a distinct possibility all the secondhand REOs had been supplied by Williamson's agency. The employment of young conductors, the one above probably aged fourteen, was banned after the implementation of the 1930 Road Traffic Act, and both driver and conductor had to be licenced. The story goes that a small conductor, off duty, talking to the driver on a crowded bus, was asked by a lady passenger if he would like to sit on her knee.

E & J Bramley 'Prince of Wales Service' of Cotmanhay ran nine buses on the Cotmanhay service, which Dawson's, MGO, Trent and Williamson purchased jointly. Trent took three of the buses with Williamson having the balance and also shared the route with Trent. All six were Guys, and all possibly had Guy bodies, as NU 7973 seen above in the Royal Blue livery and fleur-de-lys motif of the Prince of Wales.

Tansey & Severn Fleet.

Like Williamson, Tansey & Severn had proved formidable opposition to the combine, again using speedy and efficient machinery. The decision to purchase Leyland was a major factor of their success, obviously a decision taken by them after running a Thornycroft and a Crossley in the early days.

No. 110 [RR 7716] a Leyland PLSC1 again with Leyland body at Huntingdon Street bus station in September 1934. Identical to RR 3206 opposite, but was a year newer being delivered in 1927. An illuminated sign displaying 'General' had been fixed above the destination box, making it a little unwieldy

Miss Elsie Severn the conductress stood apart from the drivers, one from an accompanying Tansey & Severn bus, when asked to pose in front of RR 3206. The original stance in Wollaton Street was in front of the 'Snackery' which was well frequented by the crews. Buses always stood with the passenger entrance facing into the street, not a practice recommended today. This Leyland LSC1 with Leyland bodywork received fleet No. 99.

A pair of the newly introduced Leyland Lion LT1 models entered the fleet in 1928, providing seating for 35 passengers within the Leyland bodies. (Above) VO 1827 at the Wollaton Street, Nottingham terminus, during August 1929 four months after being acquired. It was to remain in the red livery with cream roof, until at least July 1931, when it received fleet No.115. (Left) Some four years later, VO 1828 No. 64 at Huntingdon Street bus station. The only obvious changes other than livery was the removal of the roof mounted boards, and the fitting of the illuminated sign above the destination display.

With the introduction of two double deckers into the Tansey & Severn fleet in 1928, they really stole a march on the combine, as it was 1930 before MGO introduced double deckers, and as mentioned in the text they were desperately required. Also at this time it was an achievement for Leyland to have double deckers capable of working the hilly terrain of the Alfreton route.

(Left) RR 9948 a Leyland TD1 with Leyland bodywork and rear open staircase. Seen at Huntingdon Street Bus Station, Nottingham during August 1936, carrying the fleet No. 105. The sister vehicle, possibly a demonstrator, was returned to Leyland in 1929 who sold it to Sheffield, becoming WE 4371 and fleet No. 1.

(Below left) By the time VO 4386 arrived Tansey & Severn Ltd was an associated company to the MGO. Although bearing fleet No. 109, and MGO livery it was still owned by Tansey & Severn. Again photographed at Huntingdon Street, the Leyland TD1 had a enclosed staircase fitted to its Leyland body. Behind is No. 115 a Leyland bodied LT1 of Tansey & Severn.

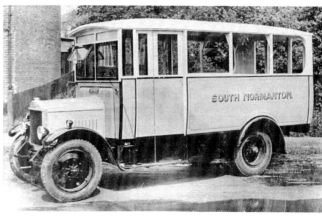

The acquisition of the W J Wright [South Normanton Bus Co.] business of South Normanton introduced two [NU 9260 /RA 3732] Dennis 30 cwt buses, one at least with Dennis 20 seat body, as seen on the photograph above. Both were sold for scrap on the 29th June 1931, just two two months after the takeover, yet both passed to other operators! The third bus, a Karrier [RA 5845] remained until May 1933. The absorption of Wright removed the final competitor from the Nottingham to South Normanton route.

Acquisitions

J G Severn [SMA] of Alfreton was renowned in the area for the quality of his main fleet of ADC or AEC buses, although there was also a mixed collection of earlier vehicles, none of which received MGO fleet numbers, although they probably only ran for a very short time with MGO. ADC or the Associated Daimler Company Limited was formed on 25th June 1926, to market both AEC and Daimler motor and commercial chassis, previously sold by AEC and Daimler. A standard radiator was used on all models produced at both factories, which were fitted with AEC or Daimler engines. The venture came to an end in July 1928.

(Above) An ADC 416 with Hall Lewis 32 seat body dating from 1929. Seen on Huntingdon Street, Nottingham during March 1933, No.53 [RA 8791] had received the MGO style destination display.

This former AEC demonstrator was under a year old, when obtained by SMA. Seen here at Alfreton in MGO livery No. 108 [JA 1291] the AEC Regent had a rather distinctive Short body. The angled upper deck windows set back from the mid deck seems a compromise between the piano front, which had recently come into fashion, and the earlier canopy type styling.

No.81 [RB 3864] a Willowbrook bodied 32 seat bus fitted to an AEC Regal chassis, had just been delivered when SMA sold out. It is seen on Kent Street, Nottingham, during October 1933, prior to taking up its stance on Huntingdon Street Bus Station for the Alfreton service. The destination display had been rebuilt to include an illuminated General sign.

The takeover of J T Boam [The Ray] of Heanor, saw the introduction of seven quality Leylands, dating from 1927 and 1930. There was, however, a 1925 Durant 14 seat bus, which was withdrawn quickly, but survived a further three years before it was sold off.

Unidentified specifically, as either MGO No. 49 or 58 RA 2061 or 4661. Dating from 1927, both were Leyland PLC1 [Lioness] and had Leyland 28 seat bodies. With a 25ft 2in chassis length and a 5.1 litre Lion engine, they were quite capable of giving competitors something of a run for their money. The styling of the vehicle gives the impression of a racier model than the norm of the period.

Number 63 survived in the MGO fleet until November 1945, over 16 years after its purchase by Boam. This replaced coach RA 7999 [No.60] which was relegated to stage carriage work. During its period of operation with Boam it was advertised as the Leyland Tiger saloon built solely for the Blackpool service. Received in May 1929, the TS2 model was fitted with a very handsome dual entrance coachwork by Willowbrook of Loughborough. The stylish lines with the quaint folding roof over the drivers cab gave the impression of a normal control vehicle. It is believed that by 1934, the cab area had been roofed over, and converted to standard front entrance for bus operation.

F Porter & Sons of Stonebroom business was an important purchase, giving MGO access to the Alfreton, Chesterfield and Mansfield triangle, and some important stage carriage links.

After leaving the bus stance, No. 85 RA 9628, passed the Trent Huntingdon Street offices, on its journey to Alfreton. The LT1 with Davidson 32 bodywork, would have suited MGO, with its porch style entrance. The illuminated display fitted above the destination display, blended quite nicely with the body styling.

E Wharton of Morton near Alfreton, trading as 'Morton Bus Company', sold out to MGO on the 4th July 1933. With the business came two buses and a Clay Cross to Alfreton via Morton service.

RB 5155 a Morris dating from 1931, with 24 seat dual purpose body was suitable for tours and excursions and the Morton to Blackpool express service. The licence for the Blackpool service was not taken up by MGO, but the vehicle was retained as No. 132 being regularly used on this type of work, and when seen in Nottingham was on private hire duties.

The second Wharton bus was a Dennis EV with 32 seat body, registered RB 1778 and dating from 1930. Photographed c1930 with the Curley brothers; Tommy [driver] and George [conductor] at Clay Cross. George who started work with Wharton, continued with MGO as a driver and then Trent, through to his retirement. The Dennis became No. 130, and survived until August 1944 with MGO.

R Fearn of Alfreton and Severn Bros. of Swanwick, although trading as separate businesses, worked together from 1928 on the Alfreton-Heanor service as the 'Association' and under the same title were joined by both Topham and Shaw on the Alfreton-Ripley service, which they sold to Trent .

The only known photograph of any of these four operators was Fearn's VO 7050 a 1932 Crossley Eagle converted by MGO to a carnival coach, being also used for advertising and display purposes for the group. This type of conversion may have seemed unusual, but there was quite a demand even in the early post war years, when carnivals were a regular feature of village and town life. Neighbours Barton having three over a period ten of years. Neither of the two Fearn Crossleys was numbered, yet both survived with MGO, until the outbreak of war.

Alfreton Motor Transport

Alfreton Motor Transport Ltd, was acquired on the 1st April 1936, and continued as a separate company with MGO owning the fully paid shares and their nominees acting as directors. Although the vehicles were transferred to MGO they were still owned by the company until the 1st March 1943.

RA 8499 a 1929 Gilford 1660T with 32 seat Wycombe bus body became No. 138, until it was sold in January 1939

RA 9030 again a 1929 model, but this time a Leyland Lion LT1 with Leyland 35 seat body. Numbered 146, it joined eight other LT1s, which had all been obtained with businesses MGO had acquired. It was fitted with a Beardmore diesel engine for a short period, and most probably had been replaced when purchased by MGO.

No. 155 was a lone Karrier Chaser 4 with Ransome 32 seat dual entrance body. Exhibited at the 1929 Commercial Motor Show in Alfreton livery, it joined their fleet a year later as No.18. It had a very short life with the group, remaining in service until January 1937.

Coaches

Ten coaches [156-65] made up the 1936 order. The Weymann coachwork on AEC Regal chassis introduced many features which were to become standard fixtures on future saloons; a front recessed jack knife door, luggage racks, and Clayton heaters. The seating was upholstered in moquette with leather sides, centre rolls and headpieces. Navy blue was added to the livery on these and all new single deckers.

The roof flash and roof mounted luggage rack was unusual to this years deliveries. These coaches helped keep up the standards, with the competition of the three main operators working out of Nottingham. Particularly between Trent and Barton, but Trent never quite achieved the overall quality of the other two, who more regularly operated their coaches on stage carriage duties.

Typically, just two months old and No.157 CRA 656 is working out of Nottingham on the B1 Heanor service. This coach was impressed by the Military in 1939, and it is believed to have been destroyed at Dunkirk.

(Below) Straw & Fletcher of Ilkeston Guy B [RA 6488] with 25 seat all-weather coach body dating from 1928 received MGO fleet number 166 and survived until 1944 when it was converted to a tower wagon. A further two Guy coaches [Nos.167-8] came with the business and were the last second hand buses taken into MGO stock other than group vehicles

1936 was the last year that vehicles from acquired businesses were taken into the fleet. There were seven coaches included, all of which survived until at least the outbreak of World War 2. Four of these were Leyland Tigers which came from G Swain of Mansfield who traded as 'Supreme Motor Coach Co. Above is No. 147 a TS2 with United of Lowestoft coachwork, photographed at Skegness, whilst still with Swain. The canvas covered cab was similar to No. 58 shown on page 85. To the left is VO 1417 an identical coach in the fleet of the Ebor Bus Co Ltd, also of Mansfield. VO 1010 survived with MGO until October1950, albeit in a dismantled state. A further four buses came with the Swain business.

Standardising the fleet.

Using the Weymann shell of the 1936 coaches, the basis of the standardised saloon was evolved. Chassis were now oil engined, mainly AEC 7.7 litre or the more powerful Leyland 8.6 litre units. The double deckers, were to the standard Weymann layout with front entrances on AEC Regent chassis.

The 1937 deliveries were supplied with Leyland TS7 chassis, with lining out for dual purpose saloons, although sunshine roofs were fitted. The engine was Ideally suited to the very hilly route E2. No. 96 is seen at Matlock LMS railway station yard terminus.

No. 97 is lined out in what was to be the coach styling, although the seating was for 35 passengers. The red white and blue livery was to honour the Coronation of King George V1. Again a full sliding roof was provided.

Twenty five Regents were received with 52 seat Weymann of Addlestone bodywork during 1937 . This view of No. 52 was taken in August 1950 at Mount Street Bus Station.

Typically the front entrance 'deckers, arrived with MGO at a similar time to an almost identical batch for Trent. Trent had received front entrance bodies the previous year on SOS chassis. Barton did not follow suit until 1939, but they did have a 1934 AEC Regent with Willowbrook body which they acquired in 1935. The MGO models had rear bumper bars, and like Barton, the route number provided in the destination display. The usual standard practice of applying transfers for the fleet No. 18, rather than the metal plate at the front continued until the 'fifties. The photograph taken in June 1950 at Granby Street, an additional terminus to the main Mount Street Bus Station, also shows the offside of No. 58 an identical vehicle.

(Left) The first AEC Regals with dual purpose bodies arrived in 1938. One of the ten No.53 at Broad Marsh, Nottingham, displays all the characteristics, including the roof mounted advertising. A further two, which were almost new, were made available by sister company, Llanelly District Traction Co. Numbered 184-5, they were identical to the MGO delivery, as can seen on No. 184 above.

Just five Leylands entered service in 1938, being the the newly introduced Tiger TS8 model. All had the standard dual purpose layout, as shown on No. 128 at the Lawn Park car park, Skegness. This terminus was full of activity over the summer weekends, particularly late July and August, when the holiday period was at its peak. Most coach companies in the East Midlands and South Yorkshire made a foray to Skegness during this period.

Seven coaches in the 1938 batch followed the specification completely, with lining out, sliding roof and only 32 seats. No. 151 in Coronation livery, was captured on film at Scarborough in June 1938. Marine Drive, Scarborough, was an established parking area for day excursions and later a regular photographic spot for the coach-builder, Plaxton of Scarborough. Note the narrow band of the flash extended along the bonnet.

The final ten front entrance double deckers arrived in 1938, and were to be the last until the Bristol Lodekkas were purchased. There was very little difference to the previous years delivery, except for the subtle straightening of the lines below the cab windscreen, and curving the front profile giving them whole new appearance.

No. 180 [FNU 175] displays this feature, when seen at the layover section of platform 4 at Mount Street, Nottingham.

It was 1939 before the saloons received the smoother cab front treatment, and again made a vast improvement to the looks, particularly with the flash continuing under the cab windscreen. No. 112 one of twenty Regals with 35 seat dual purpose bodies, awaits passengers on the F2 to Ilkeston from Broad Marsh. Note the MGO plate which has replaced the blue triangle on the top of the radiator, and the unusual placing of a full stop between the F and 2.

Just following receipt of the Regals, five Leyland Tiger TS8s arrived in February 1939, with Weymann 35 seat dual purpose bodies, and the coach style flash. No. 135 was parked in the street, at the rear of the Park Street, Ilkeston garage premises.

Although the order for eight saloons called coach style bodywork, only three were received with 32 seats, All were delivered during April and May and it was no doubt assumed by the management with the possibility of an imminent war, that there would be limited demand for coaches. Only a matter of weeks old No. 145 stands on the Lawn Motor Park, Skegness, whilst on private hire duties. Again the band of flashing continued along the bonnet, as on the previous years coach style layout.

War Time Stringencies

Chassis and body manufacture, in some cases, continued after the outbreak of war in September 1939. During 1940 production was stopped for the war effort. However, it was decided by the Ministry of Supply [MOS}that they be 'unfrozen', to ease the shortage of vehicles. Many were incomplete, having been unfinished, and others were just chassis or bodies. During this period the MOS and the Ministry of War Transport produced a standard specification for utility buses, which used the minimum of materials. Firstly these were made available for the 'unfrozen' chassis and then Guy was chosen to produce the Arab chassis. The original plan in 1941 was for Guy and Leyland to produce 500 chassis each. The Leylands would have been type TD8, but none were built as Leyland production was taken over by the military. Daimler was added in 1943. Although the bodies were supposedly built to a standard design, each manufacturer interpreted them in their own way and made them identifiable as their product.

Luckily although there was no choice MGO did receive all Guys and a fairly limited variety of bodies. Of the Guys received the Arab I was fitted with the 5 cylinder Gardner 5LW engine, as were the Arab II models introduced in 1943. From 1944 onwards they had the 6 cylinder 6LW engine fitted. The 6 cylinder engine was very restricted and only supplied in special circumstances. Iin MGO's case it was found that the 5 cylinder engines were under powered for the hilly terrain.

MGO did not take any single deckers, as the demands were for higher capacity buses to meet the shift workers and colliers demands.

(Above) Many of the 'unfrozen' highbridge Leyland TD7s available with Leyland bodies were built to Western SMT specification. One of these was allocated to MGO with fleet No. 186. It is seen at Mansfield with the Western SMT destination display, and later (Below) at Broad Marsh, Nottingham when it had been altered to the standard MGO layout. It remained in stock until 1960 when it was sold to dealer, before being broken up six months later.

(Top left) Brush of Loughborough provided the body for the Guy Arab 1 on No. 187. Brush provided only nineteen highbridge types, before changing production to lowbridge. The stepped sill below the cab window was their trademark as was, on highbridge only, the triangular fillet on the front pillar. The large aperture for the destination was not fully utilised, being blanked out above and below, rather than fitting the route number aperture.

(Above) Fifteen metal framed bodies built for Manchester Corporation Daimlers by Metro-Cammell were frozen and when released transferred to Weymann for completion. Two became part of the MGO fleet as Nos. 188-9. Metro-Cammell of Birmingham and Weymann had a joint sales force trading as Metropolitan-Cammell-Weymann Motor Bodies Ltd. The Manchester styling was easily identifiable with the dipped waist line, a little out of character in the MGO fleet. No. 188 was seen at Mount Street in March 1952.

(Left) The odd one out No. 190, a Guy Arab I was fitted with a metal framed Weymann, originally made to the order of Liverpool Corporation, but frozen by MOS dictate. When released all the remaining order passed to Liverpool on AEC or Guy 6LW chassis, but this one received a 5LW engine and passed to MGO. Parked at Stockwell Gate, Mansfield, with AEC Regal No. 69 in the background.

From October 1943, deliveries were received with the Guy Arab II chassis and from 1944 they had the more powerful Gardner 6 cylinder engine, and up to March 1945 were all highbridge models. The Weymann bodies on the Arab IIs were composite except for 193/5 which had metal frames.

(Top left) Weymann bodied No. 196 drops off passengers at Mount Street, Nottingham, before proceeding to the bus station. Again a large destination display is under used, but was changed early after the war.

From September 1944 Northern Counties of Wigan provided all the highbridge bodies which were metal framed. (Above) No. 23 a 1944 model showed all the signs of the National Federation specification, and is comparable with the 1945 relaxed design (Left). No. 34 now had a fuller destination layout, although the intermediate points were not shown. The window at the rear of the bays was now rounded at the top, although the rear dome was still sectional. There was also a rounded profile on the upper deck support on the bulkhead.

Delivered in August 1945, No. 203 part of a group of four with Weymann lowbridge bodywork, to the more relaxed design, although small headlamps were still being fitted . There were, however, more drop widows than the one per row previously specified. The destinations were now fully displayed, in accordance with pre-war practice.

Strachans introduced an improved specification with rounded dome and window to match. The glazing to the cab area was also more rounded, and with more pleasing lines, but still they had the utility looks. No. 212, one of the three received, at Alfreton working the C2 to Mansfield.

Between September 1945 and January 1946, six lowbridge Guy Arabs were delivered with Roe of Leeds bodies. All were to relaxed design, now without the front upper deck drop down ventilators. Number 210 [renumbered 410] at Stockwell Gate, Mansfield, These were the first lowbridge 'deckers in the fleet, being required for the Alfreton, Mansfield to Chesterfield corridor, and it was rather surprising that these were not required before. Roe had a reputation for building a quality product with teak framing, but due to to shortages, ash was substituted which was prone to rot, thus these were rebodied by ECW within ten years.

The same vehicle now re-numbered 412 this time on Stockwell Gate, shows the nearside of the Strachan body. This vehicle survived until 1959, albeit that it had been refurbished in the MGO Langley Mill workshops

Post War Deliveries

Although not a new double decker, No. 215 was one of a pair of 1945 Guy Arab IIs with Weymann lowbridge bodies, which were transferred from Mansfield District within a year.

Eight AEC Regent IIs with Weymann highbridge rear entrance bodies arrived during 1946 with a further fifteen in 1947. No. 64 [KNU 603] was caught in camera at Mount Street bus station during October 1956, after it had been fitted with a pre-war Regent nearside mudguard .

A full order book for double deckers at Weymann, following the wartime shortages, led to Duple supplying four D type body shells on AEC Regal chassis. Numbered 41-4 [JRB 127-30] they were very attractive dual purpose model with the styling very similar to the pre-war saloons, but the wooden frames did not really appeal to MGO. The difference between Duple and Weymann styling was the rake of the windscreen, the lining around the destination box finished in cream, the vee dip in the lining to door pillar, and the deeper outward flared skirt. No. 43 seen at Langley Mill, was sold to British Railways on the 21st May 1959.

Nearside view of No. 44 at the Mount Street bus station layover point, during the early 'fifties, showing the new experimental livery, from which the lighter shade of blue was omitted. The new style fleet name, really stood out in the cream lettering, but it was decided upon the more subdued gold. No. 44 was sold to a Nottingham dealer during April 1960, before passing to A Camm of Nottingham and then the 'Fabulous Beatmen' in October 1963.

The ubiquitous Bedford OB, could seen in virtually every town and city in Great Britain, in particular those with Duple 'Vista' body, which was the first coach body to be produced after the war. MGO took six into stock during 1947 and with their limited seating for 29 passengers, they were somewhat restricted in their use. Most, if not all stage carriage duties required higher capacity, and they were generally used on private hire or tours and excursions. The high back steel framed moquette seating did not compare with the pre-war seating of any of their saloons. No. 114, received with a cream roof was seen at Mount Street in August 1950.

The new Leyland PS1/1 with a 7.4 litre engine was introduced into the MGO fleet when two were obtained with Duple 'D' type bodies, identical to those fitted to the earlier AEC Regals. Noticeable changes externally were the wider squared off mudguards, and the wider radiator was now formed from chrome sheet metal, as seen on No. 46 at Granby Street, during layover.

The post-war Regents had a change of mudguard styling, which had been introduced by AEC in 1939. A further ten [Nos. 121-5/157/9-60/62/68] highbridge models received in 1947 were added to the 1946 batch. Of these No.122 was photographed at Mount Street bus station during May 1950.

No. 416 during layover at Mansfield, before working the D1 to Chesterfield. This was only one of five of the postwar Regent models [Nos.416-20] that had lowbridge bodies, although there were later Mark III models which did receive identical style Weymann bodies.

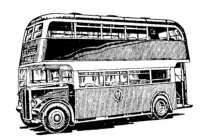

The final fifteen AECs with Weymann highbridge bodies were received in 1948, this time on the Regent III chassis. Again there was change in the style of the mud-guards, which were now angled upwards from the radiator, which was now slightly deeper. No. 41 displays these features when photographed during layover at Mount Street.

The final ten [Nos. 421-30] vehicles supplied by Balfour Beatty were AEC Regent IIIs with Weymann 53 seat lowbridge bodies. The 1950 order for twenty identical double deckers was diverted to London Transport [RLH 1-20].

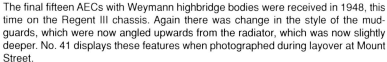

A further change in bodybuilder for 1947 saloons, saw the introduction of Saunders Engineering and Shipyard of Angelsey metal framed bodies, which were similar to earlier designs with an additional bay of windows, which rather spoilt the otherwise pleasing lines. Twenty five were fitted to Leyland PS1/1 chassis shown (Right) on No.215 at the Ship Hotel, Roman Bank, Skegness, and (Left) on Nos. 204/9 at the Lawn Motor Park again in Skegness.

Demonstrators

It always seemed rather strange that the BTC members were giving trials to demonstration buses, which they had to purchase. It would be interesting to know if anyone in the group objected to the supply of Bristol chassis and ECW bodywork.

Perhaps the most published photograph of the second prototype Lodekka. Allocated to West Yorkshire No.822, it did the rounds with the members, appearing with MGO in May 1950. It is seen operating the A4 limited stop service to Ripley, operated by MGO on hire to Notts & Derby. Already well loaded the stranded passengers await a duplicate at Mount Street .

Again working the A4 service is Brighton Hove & District, Bristol KSW6G with the new design ECW body. No. 6439 spent a month on driver familiarisation, prior to the delivery of the NDT stock. It is parked on Granby Street, Nottingham during August 1952. The terminus for the A4 was transferred from the bus station, along with Barton services 3,10 and 11 due to overcrowding.

The second pre-production Lodekka, which had been allocated to Crosville as ML 661, spent a period with MGO. It was photographed at Nottingham Road, Nuthall, on the 15th May 1953, when it was still possible to see the trolley overhead wiring. It was to be another year before MGO received the first two Lodekkas into the fleet.

Trolleybus replacements

Notts & Derby Traction had for the first time their own motor bus vehicles, ordered as replacements for the trolleybuses. Originally it was intended that twenty five Bristol KSW6Gs with ECW 60 seat highbridge bodies would be supplied. This being reduced to fifteen as twelve AEC Regent III with Weymann 56 seat bodies were transferred from MDT. Originally delivered to MDT in 1948/9 in a batch of twenty two [Nos. 135-56], with NDT taking Nos. 145-56 which became Nos. 315-26. The Board had hoped to transfer the remaining ten Bristols to MGO, but in the event this did not happen, as no doubt it was felt MGO had a comparatively modern fleet when compared to others in the BTC group.

(Above) Shortly after delivery Bristol KSW6G No. 308 is travelling from the setting down point in Mount Street to the bus station. NDT were now involved in joint workings with MGO and it is seen on the E1 service to Strelley Lane, Wollaton. The placing of the final destination at the top of the display panel became MGO/NDT standard layout.

(Above) No. 315 one of the twelve AEC Regent IIIs from Mansfield District, working jointly with MGO on the B2 service to Ilkeston, Heanor and Ripley. All the buses including the Bristols received cast metal number plates, no doubt transferred from the trolleybuses. The last time these were fitted.

(Left) Following an accident severe damage was sustained to the Weymann body of 316 and it was sent to Eastern Coachworks for rebodying. It re-entered service in 1955 and was photographed on the exit driveway of Ilkeston garage. An MGO not NDT badge is evident on the radiator.

101

Imports and Rebuilds

The lack of new vehicles, saw MGO carry out a rebuilding programme of their earlier stock. Some of the work being carried out by outside contractors. This type of work was being undertaken by many of the other operators, although it is doubtful if it would have been necessary if Balfour Beatty had retained control, with their impressive replacement programme.

To cope with shortage of vehicles, it was necessary to introduce three [Nos.431-3] former Hants & Dorset Bristol K5Gs with Eastern Coachworks highbridge bodies, dating from 1939/40. Used generally as spares and holiday relief, as seen here at Matlock, after working on the Sundays and Bank Holidays F6 from Alfreton.

The only detail change made to the postwar double deckers, was the re-fixing of the glass to the destination indicators in rubber gaskets, as shown on No. 121 in Mount Street, Nottingham. During 1951-2 Nudd Bros and Lockyer of Kegworth, undertook rebuilding work on the whole of the 1937 batch of double deckers, which externally followed the original design.

Bond of Wythenshawe a specialist in rebuilding utility bodies, was entrusted with the the overhaul of eighteen Guys during the 1954-5. This included the rounding of the rear domes, rubber mounted glazing and extra sliding windows for ventilation. (Above left) The Northern Counties bodywork on 24 had received the treatment, when seen on Bath Street, Ilkeston. The destination display arrangement was unchanged. (Above right) Lowbridge 403 similarly treated stands at Chesterfield bus station.

(Above) No. 187 with a Brush body, the first utility received, did not escape attention, being sent to Bond, who carried the refurbishment during December 1953. Photographed in the Cattle Market parking area on a football special to the Notts County FC ground. Weekend Football specials and excursions fitted into the many weekday works journey schedules.

All six of the Roe bodied lowbridge Guy Arab IIs, received new ECW highbridge 58 seat bodies in 1955. The protruding bonnet was disguised on the offside by building a stepped section directly underneath the windscreen. They were renumbered from 405-10 to 105-10 upon completion.

(Top right) A nearside view of No.105 travelling along Stockwell Gate, Mansfield, on the C5 to Sutton in Ashfield and Alfreton. (Right) No. 106 from the offside, clearly shows the bulge below the drivers window. Parked at Stockwell Gate, Mansfield terminus, before taking up duties on the C2 to Alfreton.

Rebuilding of existing stock was not confined to the double deckers, as the single deckers were treated but in varying degrees by the MGO bodybuilding department. Perhaps the most drastic was No. 156 caught on camera at Broad Marsh in July 1955, with an admiring driver looking on. The most visible changes were the removal of the roof rack, the glass louvres, rear bumper bars, roof and side flashings. Although the sliding roof was now fixed, the raised front section was retained, as it was part of the destination display. The glazing to the destination display was now rubber mounted, yet all the remaining glazing was unchanged. The straight lining out gave a modern appearance, although for some reason there was a drop in the top lining out after the emergency door. The back wheel arches were also reshaped, omitting the swept rear portion.

Of the ten AEC Regal coaches obtained in 1936, only six remained by 1950. Following the requisition by the War Department two (157/62) were believed to have been driven into the sea at Dunkirk. A further two were retained until well after the war. No. 160 being repurchased in 1947, was sold on almost immediately and eventually arrived with Ellen Wright of Southend in 1948. No. 159 was even later as it was returned in 1949 and again sold on within weeks, this time to Camm of Nottingham. A fifth coach [No. 158] returned to the fold in 1943. All were rebuilt in varying degrees, with sliding roof being sealed, and in the case of No. 165, only a change in the side flashings. No doubt when stripped down it was found the the lower panels only needed replacing. It is interesting to note that the vehicle width marker on the front mudguard had been retained.

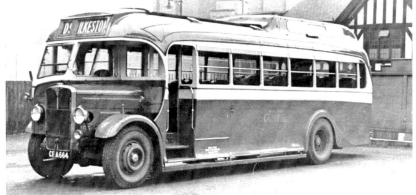

To the layman No. 100 would have given the appearance of a postwar bus, which was exactly how these were expected to be perceived by the general public. However, to the more observant the removal of the side flashings did not disguise the registration number, the roof mounted advertising boards, and the stepped section below the drivers cab. Although there were variations to the body, i.e. the removal of the adverting boards, they never tried to disguise the frontal appearance. Surprisingly, although the use of rubber mounted glazing was introduced during this period not one of the single deckers was so treated.

The change in appearance of the 1939 saloons was quite dramatic, particularly as they followed the same lines as the redesigned PS1/1s, shown below. Comparing the photographs on this page, the SEAS design followed the Weymann quite closely . The outstanding difference was the extra window, resulting in a very small and untidy end bay. No. 153, FRB 717 is seen shortly after the conversion on the standing area of Mount Street bus station, Nottingham, during September 1953.

During the early 'fifties the Leyland PS1/1s were still the main line coaches. To improve the image the SEAS bodies were re-vamped by re-lining to give the appearance of the Weymann saloons supplied to Mansfield District, and those diverted to Crosville. (Right) No. 213 passes Newark bus station with a sticker in the bulkhead screen showing No. 20, indicating it may been on a large private hire contract. A little later a larger area of white was introduced, after at least one was finished in the standard blue, and a lighter blue. (Right lower) No. 215 on Granby Street, Nottingham was photographed to show the rear, with the standard destination display. The practice of fixing metal plate fleet numbers to the front was dropped, following the introduction of Bristols to the fleet. They were replaced by transfers which were the same as those fixed on the rear of the earlier buses.

LS Models

The LS model was lighter weight than the other major manufacturers of the period being of a lightweight construction, with ECW providing a body which strengthened the chassis. An horizontal underfloor engine was mounted amidships. Although the group was now state owned Mr Williamson continued to obtain dual purpose [express] rather than bus bodies, throughout his reign as General Manager.

Six LS coaches with a capacity for 39 seated passengers, were delivered in time for the 1954 summer season, giving some relief to the PS1/ls which were now six years old, and not really front line vehicles any more. The allover white livery with blue relief was now adopted for the coach fleet. No. 230 (Above) photographed at the Lawn Motor Park, Skegness in August 1955, after working in on either the X1 from Ripley or the X4 from Clay Cross. (Top right) No. 228 seen at Blackpool on a private hire working to the Illuminations, although the general public could have travelled by MGO express services, there was only the X2 which ran until late October covering the period of the illuminations.

A total of twenty express version of the LS were used mainly on stage carriage work, providing MGO passengers with the continuing standard of comfort. All the express work was confined to summer weekends. The first batch were originally delivered with dark blue roofs, but it was omitted on re-painting. (Above) No.235, a 1955 model, at Mount Street with Barton No.638 a BTS1 with their own Viewmaster Mark1 body work, in the background. As MGO, like Barton, now ran to Kirk Hallam a place was allocated for them on platform 5. (Left) No. 246 from the 1956 batch, leaves Matlock bus station on the E2 service to Alfreton.

Enter the Lodekkas

Lowbridge vehicles, nominally 13ft. 2in high, always had an awkward layout, as a sunken gangway and a row of four seats on the upper deck prevented a free flow of passenger movement. Also in the lower deck headroom was restricted on the offside by the dropped ceiling for the upstairs gangway. Bristol designed a chassis with a drop centre rear axle, and eliminated the body underframe, which allowed the lower floor to be fixed directly to the chassis. Thus the highbridge layout was achieved, within a standard lowbridge bus.

May 1955, No. 438 leaves Huntingdon Street bus station with good load of passengers on the devious route B8 to Mansfield, via Hucknall and Blidworth. A distinct difference between MGO buses and most of the former Tilling members, was the omission of the upper deck waist line very often picked out in white as shown on the demonstration models.

The first two Lodekkas (Nos. 434-5) were delivered late in 1954, with a further thirteen (Nos. 436-48) coming in 1955. Part of the batch was received with the previous years styling as shown on No. 439 at Langley Mill garage. The front mudguards had been shortened, to allow further air circulation around the brake drums. Aluminium protection strips above the radiator became a standard feature.

A short radiator grille was fitted on to the latter part of the order as shown on No. 445, seen leaving Ilkeston Market Place in November 1955. The lamp post appearing from the roof is obviously not a part of the vehicle, although at one time enthusiasts magazines advised photographers to avoid these hazards. I cannot agree as this in no way detracts from the perfect shot of a vehicle, in its working environment.

107

Above) The only Lodekkas with rear open platforms were received in 1957, one of only six LDL6G's built was No. 464 which provided 70 seats within its 30ft. long body. The long mudguards were shortened as standard from this model onwards. The remaining nine [Nos. 465-73] were standard LD6G models. All ten received platform doors during 1964. (Top right) The cab line was revised as seen on No. 490 a 1958 model at Alfreton. (Right) No.474 seen at Mount Street, Nottingham, off loading passengers, displays the further revised cab door line which now followed the line of the main body. Hopper style ventilators were fitted to this delivery only. Note the conductors step irons have now been reduced to one larger recess, which slightly off balanced the position of the registration plate. Behind is Barton Leyland PD1 No. 513 with the very attractive front entrance lowbridge bodywork dating from 1948. One of the few companies to specify this layout immediately after World War 2 .

The Author has allowed himself to indulge in a little nostalgia with the printing of three similar pictures of the former MDT Weymann bodied dual purpose AEC saloons (Top left) No.179 must have felt quite at home on Stockwell Gate, Mansfield, working the E6 to East Kirkby. (Above) No. 174 on Wharncliffe Road, Ilkeston, undoubtedly on a Saturday, the day buses transferred from the Market Place, to allow the stall holders to sell their wares. In the background is a Barton Leyland PS1/1 with Duple body, showing the rear destination display, similar to MGO practice. (Left) No. 185 on the journey between Alfreton and Matlock on the E2, stops to pick up two passengers opposite the National Tramway Museum at Crich.

MDT excesses

Shortage of stock and the usual surplus at Mansfield District, saw the influx of twelve AEC single deckers and three double deckers. Although MGO had to sell on their postwar Weymann bodied single deck vehicles, MDT did receive twenty four that were very similar and MGO were now able to run these, giving a glimpse what might have been.

The three double deckers were rather ancient 1936 AEC Regents with Weymann 56 seat highbridge bodies, with open rear platforms. Although twenty one years old they had been fitted with AEC 7.7 litre oil engines in 1938 and the bodies completely rebuilt by Nudd Brothers and Lockyer of Kegworth during 1953. Seen working on the B3 Alfreton, from Mount Street bus station, CAL 196 had the usual MGO plate fixed in the AEC triangle and fleet No. 6 added.

MW-Medium weight class

A standard underfloor model, which was very similar in weight and layout to the AEC Reliance and Leyland Tiger Cub. MGO took up the option of the more powerful 6 cylinder Gardner engine.

The dual purpose or express version was the favoured version with the larger area of white in the livery, this was first applied to the ten taken into stock in 1958. Of these No. 255 is seen (Above) on Park Row after leaving the Mount Street bus station, on route F9 to Kirk Hallam. A further seventeen [Nos. 264-80] followed in 1959 and No. 274 was photographed (Top right) at Mablethorpe, Lincolnshire, after working in on the X1 express service from Ripley. It is seen in the same livery, with the only variation being the introduction of narrower brighter metal strips to the waist line. To accommodate the change in fleet name to include Mansfield District, the bright metal flashings were reduced in size as seen (Centre) on No. 275 at Broad Marsh, Nottingham, in January 1971, during the construction of the new shopping development and bus station. Only the F2/F4 were to use this new development, until It was decided shortly afterwards to concentrate on the new Mount Street bus station.

During 1963 six (Nos. 281-6) MW6G coaches were delivered with 39 seat bodywork introduced by ECW the previous year. However, it was now possible to increase the length to 31ft, by increasing the rear overhang, following the introduction of new legislation increasing vehicles lengths. The pronounced points of the styling was the shallow curved windscreen, with a stepped affect below and the peak above, with a vent beneath for the forced air ventilation. There was a stepped waist feature on the fixed windows and a three section window at the rear. These were the first coaches since 1954. (Above) Originally received in the style shown on the line drawing, they were altered with the fitting of roof type destination display, and an adjacent air ventilator as shown on the left. The vehicle No.282 is shown at the landscaped area on the drive of Ilkeston garage

Final Lodekka and VRT's

(Above) No. 502 at Mount Street bus station, Nottingham, was among the group of five (Nos. 501-5) FSF6G models, being the first with front entrances, which were to become the standard feature, and they were also the last 60 seat short models. The FLF with 70 seat bodies and a revised grille became the standard, as shown (Top right) on No. 633 one of a pair received in 1964. These were transferred to NDT the following January, and it is seen at Mount Street bus station shortly afterwards. (Opposite) The last new vehicles received by NDT were six FLF6G's [Nos. 301-6]. No. 305 is seen leaving Ilkeston Market Place on the joint MGO B2 service to Nottingham. MGO also received six of this batch in 1968, which were to be the last new Lodekkas in the fleet.

From the 1st July 1966 it was possible to operate double deckers with a driver also carrying out the conductors duties. With this change in law it gave Bristol the opportunity to produce a 33ft. or 36ft. long rear engined vehicle with access forward of the front axle. Introduced as the VR it had the engine placed longitudinally at the rear offside. The VRT with the engine placed transversely, was added in 30ft. and 33ft. versions, which became the standard, when they qualified for the bus grant scheme introduced in 1968. MGO took delivery of eight VRTSL6G models, the 30ft.3in 80 seat short version with the usual Gardner 6 cylinder engine. Nos. 315-20 came in 1969 followed by Nos. 321-2 in 1970, making eight in total.

No. 316 during July 1969 at the temporary Maid Marian Way terminus, shortly after delivery .

Rear engined singles - RE

The RE, introduced in 1962, with rear underfloor engine, was built to the maximum dimensions allowable for a single decker of 36ft. However, production did not commence until 1963 in two forms RELL [Low frame] for stage work and RELH [High frame] for coaches. In 1966 variations RESH and RESL became available. The S signifying a shorter version [32ft.3¼in]. All the MGO REs were fitted with the usual 6 cylinder Gardner engine.

MGO received Nos.30-32 with RELH chassis and the series 2 coachwork, seating 51 passengers, in 1964. Seen at Broad Marsh bus station, Nottingham in November 1964, No.32 had been put to work on stage carriage duties over the winter period, in typical MGO practice. The application of a larger area of blue was unique to these coaches. The following year they could be seen working on the newly introduced MX4 Alfreton-London [Victoria Coach Station] express service.

(Centre left) Nos.133-4 were two very rare RESH6G chassis, in the fact that they were the only two bodied by ECW, and also had dual purpose seating for 43 passengers, within the bus body. Delivered in 1967 No. 133 was photographed at Stockwell Gate, Mansfield, during October 1968. Further REs were received In 1969, but with 44 bus seat bodies and RELL6G chassis. They were different as they introduced for the first time dual entrances to the fleet. Shown above is No.136, during August 1969, picking up passengers outside the Trent offices on Huntingdon Street, Nottingham. Trent was now a sister company following the sale of the BET empire to THC in 1967.(Left) The only difference with the 1970 - 1 deliveries was the fitting of a re-styled front. No 152, one of the last three delivered seen in Alfreton bus station in October 1971. The forward entrance and central exit lost favour in the later years, through the difficulty of the driver [one person operation] keeping control of the centre door.

Later MW's

The affect of introduction of a combined MGO and MDT fleet name in 1966, is shown on the above two vehicles. (Left) No. 292 at the Saturday only Wharncliffe Road terminus Ilkeston, in the usual express style livery and layout. (Right) Within months this was revised to allow the display of the new fleetname, shown on No. 294. When photographed at Broad Marsh, Nottingham, it had lost the front mesh grille. The flashes on the waist rail had been removed and the blue livery replaced by more white and just a thin line of black on the waistline

The final three MW's were received in 1966, and introduced an obvious change in policy following the departure of W Williamson the General Manager. For the first time in 35 years stage carriage versions were introduced with standard bus seats, and an allover blue with white relief livery. No.102 photographed at Alfreton displays these changes.

Non Bristols - a change of policy.

Relaxation of purchasing restrictions, allowed members of the NBC to obtain vehicles from other sources. MGO deciding upon the lightweight Bedford chassis for its coaching work, giving them a short replacement period. The engine was positioned ahead of the set back front axle, to allow forward access.

Three batches of the VAM model were received with Duple Viceroy 41 seat coachwork. The first two came in 1967 and 1968 in the styling shown by No.219 (Top right) in March 1967. The final delivery in 1970, had Viceroy 37 styling, with cleaner lines, but an uglier slatted grille, as seen on No. 231 (Above) with the MDT name removed, following the split in December 1971.

Plaxton of Scarborough built the very popular Panorama Elite III coachwork on No. 235, one of a pair [Nos. 234-5] originally supplied to MDT in 1971. They joined sister vehicles Nos. 232-3 at MGO at the end of the coaching season. The Elite introduced in 1968 was the most popular coach design to be produced by any UK bodybuilder. With slight cosmetic changes it survived until 1975. The versatility of the design saw these on front line coach work, express duties, and stage carriage work. Examples were still working on every day duties into the new millennium.

Although not strictly within the confines of this history, Leyland National No. 416 seen at Alfreton garage during June 1974 was ordered by MGO. Seen in the unusual short lived blue and white livery, as the NBC liveries were either poppy red or green, with the only exceptions being MGO, East Yorkshire, Jones of Aberbeeg and Sunderland & District. It was agreed to have these Nationals at the December 1971 board meeting. and the original order was placed for six VRT's and nine Nationals on the 1972 programme. This was amended in March 1972 to VRT's [never received] and three Nationals [Nos. 415-7]. At that same December meeting it was agreed to obtain for 1973 five VRT's, five Nationals and ten RELH's [Nos.272-81]. It was revised in March 1972 to two VRT's [Nos. 762-3] and five Nationals [three only delivered Nos. 418-20].

LH - Light Horizontal

Introduced in 1967, with horizontal amidships engine, MGO took delivery of the 30ft long LH6L version with Leyland engine in three small batches.

No. 116 the sixth and final delivery for 1969, leaves the temporary Maid Marian Way, Nottingham terminus, during the reconstruction of Mount Street bus station.

An offside view of No. 120 from the five delivered in 1970, which were identical to the previous years batch, except for the lower position of the combined MGO and MDT fleet names. It is seen at the Langley Mill headquarters.

The final delivery of three in 1971, had the revised frontal styling, including the BET style windscreen. No. 124 leaves Maid Marian Way on the F2 to Kimberley and Ilkeston.

115

Auxiliary vehicles.

No 13 Guy BA [NU 6443] dating from 1925, was converted to tower wagon G13 for NDT during May 1931, before being replaced by the vehicles shown to the right and below. It was sold on to a dealer in November 1945 for £22.10shillings [£22.50]

Leyland Cub VO 7006 started life with Swain of Mansfield in 1931 as a 20 seat bus, then MGO No. 151 during 1936. In 1944 it was converted to the tower wagon for repairs to the trolley overhead, tree lopping and maintenance work on lamp posts etc, for the Derbyshire & Nottinghamshire Electric Power Co.

RA 6488 a Guy B formerly MGO No. 166 was converted at the same time, using the body from No. G13 for the same purpose as the Leyland Cub above. It was photographed on Cavendish Road, Ilkeston on the 11th May 1953, shortly before transfer to the East Midlands Electricity Board.

Photographed in the Dock shop at Langley Mill is a wheelless Morris Cowley traffic van [RA 6466] dating from 1928. It is believed the bodywork was constructed by Challands Ross & Co, of Nottingham. It was partly dismantled before being sold for scrap in November 1947.

NDT No. 466 a Bristol LD6G from the 1958 batch, the only Lodekkas in the group with open rear platform, having doors fitted in 1964. In 1970-1 when withdrawn, the other eight of the batch were transferred to either Thames Valley or United Counties, but 466 was retained as the MGO driver training vehicle. Seen here at the Huntingdon Street overflow park, it was now un-numbered, with the all over white livery with MGO and MDT fleet names, as carried by the single deckers of these fleets.

Former MDT AEC Regal No. 29 dating from 1939, became a snow plough for the group in 1954

Two of the 1955 MDT Bristol LS6G's withdrawn in 1969, were transferred to MGO in 1969 to act as driver tuition vehicles. They were numbered 207/10 and became T1 and T2 with the MGO. T1 is seen at the Langley Mill headquarters.

This AEC Matador was re-built in the workshops, with a new cab and fitted with towing facilities. This type of vehicle was regularly purchased by MGO on behalf of the Tilling group from the MOD auction sales held at nearby Ruddington.

MIDLAND GENERAL - Fleet List

Year	Fleet No.	Reg. No.	Chassis	Body and layout	New	Notes
1922	1-2	R 8802-3	Vulcan VSC	NDT B17F		
		R4226	AEC B	?B20F		chassis ex NDT returned 10.23, body ex MDT to NU103 .23
1923	3	NU 103	Guy BA	NDT B20F		body ex R 4226 rebuilt by NDT .24
	4	NU 1885	Guy BB	Guy? B26-		
1924	5-6	NU 3564-5	Guy BB	Strachan & Brown B32D		
1925	7	NU 5244	Guy BB	Guy? B32(D?)		
	8-12	NU 5245-9	Guy BA	Guy B20F		
	13-4	NU 6443-4	Guy BA	Guy B20F		13 converted to MGO lorry 15.5.31
	23	NN 499	Leyland G7	Leyland B32-	1922	ex South Normanton Bus Co, South Normanton8.7.25
	21-2	NN1533/1743	Leyland G7	Leyland? B32-	1921	ex South Normanton Bus Co, South Normanton8.7.25
	24	NN 7664	Vulcan VSC	?	1924	ex South Normanton Bus Co., South Normanton8.7.25
	17-8	NN 8868-9	Leyland Z5	Leyland B20R	1924	ex Midland Motor Bus Co, Kimberley 29.9.25
	20	NN 9236	Leyland A1?	Leyland B20-	1924	ex Midland Motor Bus Co, Kimberley 29.9.25
	19	NN 9437	Leyland Z5	Leyland B20-	1925	ex Midland Motor Bus Co. 29.9.25, to Tansey & Severn c.29 to c31
1926	15-6	NU 8131-2	Guy BB	Guy? B30-		to 32 seats by .31
	25-6	RA1238-9	T-Stevens B9B	Strachan & Brown B31F		renumbered 67/65 then 65A during 1937, to MDT 8.33 to 10.33
1927	29/27/30 /28	RA 3537-40	T-Stevens B10B	Strachan & Brown B31F		r/n 73/69/68/78 A suffix added 1937. 27(69) to Stratford Blue No. 20 11.31 until 1.33 and then No.83. 78 to MDT 8.33 until 10.33
	33-4/31	RA 3724-6	T-Stevens B10B	Strachan & Brown B31F		renumbered 9/10/4 then 4A, all to MDT 8.33 until 10.33
	32/35-6	RA 3750/89-90	T-Stevens B10B	Strachan & Brown B31F		r/n 5/12/57. 57 rebodied by Beadle 1932 to MDT 8.33 until 10.33
	39-40/37-8	RA 3869-72	T-Stevens B10B	Strachan & Brown B31F		r/n 19/21,14/16 c 1930-1. 19/21 to Stratford Blue 6.31
	41-2	RA 3958-9	T-Stevens B10B	Strachan & Brown B31F		to Cheltenham & District 2.28 - 1.29? r/n 37/46 to Stratford Blue 6.31
	45/43-4/46	RA4002-5	T-Stevens B10B	Davidson B31F		to Leamington & Warwick 2.28 - 1.30, r/n 98/97/54/59
1928	56-61	RA 6238-9/ 6322-5	T-Stevens B10B	Strachan & Brown B31F		r/n 47/62/2/80/79/74 1930. A suffix added to 62/79 1937. 62 rebodied by Beadle 1932
	47	RR 1801	REO Speedwagon	?B14-	1925	ex L Mellows, Sutton in Ashfield 4.28 subsidary until .29
	48	RR 2348	REO Speedwagon	?B14-	1925	ex L Mellows, Sutton in Ashfield 4.28 subsidary until .29
	49-50	NU 8554/9464	REO Speedwagon	?B14-	1926	ex L Mellows, Sutton in Ashfield 4.28 subsidary until .29
	51	RA 1207	REO Pullman	?B20-	1926	ex L Mellows, Sutton in Ashfield 4.28 subsidary until .29
	52	RR 5756	W&G L	?B26-	1927	ex L Mellows, Sutton in Ashfield 4.28 subsidary until .29
	53	RA 2434	REO Pullman	?B20-	1927	ex L Mellows, Sutton in Ashfield 4.28 subsidary until .29
	54-5	RR 6639/7043	W&G L	?B26	1927	ex L Mellows, Sutton in Ashfield, 4.28 subsidary until .29
	62	RR 7505	W&G L	?B30	1927	ex G H Hayton, Mansfield, 6.28 to Mellows fleet.
		RA 4201	Guy B	?B26-	1927	dtto but to Cheltenham & District by 7.28
		NU 3935	Karrier	?B20-	1924	ex B Hatton, Selston 1.28 to MGO lorry
	65	RR 5325	Thornycroft A1	Challands Ross? B20-	1926	ex B Hatton, Selston 1.28 to MGO lorry
	64	RR 5726	Thornycroft A1	Challands Ross? B20-	1926	ex B Hatton, Selston 1.28 to MGO lorry
	63/66	RR 6377/6521	Dennis 30cwt	?B14-	1927	ex B Hatton, Selston 1.28, loaned to MDT 1.29 until 8.33
1929	67	RR 873	Leyland A9	Leyland B20-	1925	ex Davis & Hope, Mansfield subsidary until 7.31
	68	RR 5439	Leyland C7	?B32-	1926	ex Davis & Hope, Mansfield subsidary until 7.31
	69	RR 7563	Leyland PLSC	Leyland B32-	1927	ex ditto to B31 and renumbered 48 by 1931, A suffix added 1937

Year	Fleet No.	Reg.No.	Chassis	Body and Layout	New	Notes
	70	DT 601	T-Stevens B10B	?B31-	1927	ex ditto r/n 46 by 1931 loaned to MDT 8 until 10 33
	71	RR 8642	Chevrolet LO	Willowbrook B14-	1928	ex dittto
	72	RR 7339	Leyland PLC1	Leyland B26-	1927	ex H Booth, Blidworth 1.29 r/n 52 by .30 A suffix 1937
	73	RR 7606	T-Stevens B10B	Dixon B30F	1927	ex H Booth, Blidworth 1.29 r/n 92 by .30 A suffix 1937
	74	RA 922	Minerva	Wilton? B26F	1926	ex Inglis & Beardsley, Ilkeston 5.29
	75	RA 3494	Minerva	Wilton? B26F	1927	ex Inglis & Beardsley, Ilkeston 5.29
	76	RA 3140	REO	?B14-	1927	ex Inglis & Beardsley, Ilkeston 5.29
	77	RA 3062	Chevrolet LM	?B14-	1927	ex ditto, loaned to MDT 7.29 not returned
	78	RA 8250	Chevrolet LQ	?B14-	1929	ex ditto, loaned to MDT 7.29 not returned
1930	3/34	RB 1153-4	T-Stevens B10A2	Ransome B32F		
	112	FG 5227	Commer F4	Hall Lewis C32F	1929	ex General Motor Carrying Co, on loan to Straford Blue 1.33
	103,1	RB 1341-2	Thornycroft BC	Dodson H28/24R		operated in NDT livery not numbered until 1932
	77	RB 2594	Thornycroft BC	Brush H28/26R		operated in NDT livery not numbered until 1932
	102	RB 2595	Thornycroft BC	Strachan H28/26R		operated in NDT livery not numbered until 1932
1931	27-9/32-3	RB 3844-8	TSM B10A2	Ransomes B32F		29 renumbered 35 in 1944. 31 to WD 9.39 until 2.43
	40/30-1/ 35/38	RB 3849-52/4	TSM B10A2	Strachan B32F		38 to WD 9.39 until 4.41
	41-5	RB 3853/5-8	TSM B10A2	Cowieson B32F		
	22-6	RB 3859-63	Leyland LT2	Leyland B30F		25 to MOS 12.40 23/38 to WD 4.41
		NU 4509	Durant	?B14-	1925	ex J T Boam, Heanor 3.31
	49/58	RA 2061/4116	Leyland PLC1	Leyland B26F	1927	ex J T Boam, Heanor 3.31
	55	RA 5538	Leyland PLC1	Wilton? C26D	1928	ex J T Boam, Heanor 3.31
	51	RA 6612	Leyland PLSC1	Leyland B31F	1928	ex J T Boam, Heanor 3.31, A suffix 1937
	60	RA 7999	Leyland TS2	United C32D	1929	ex J T Boam, Heanor 3.31
	66	RA 9944	Leyland LT1	Leyland B35F	1929	ex ditto, to B32F, A suffix 1937, to snow plough
	63	RB 1616	Leyland TS2	Willowbrook C32D	1930	ex J T Boam, Heanor 3.31, to B32D
	126	RA 6969	ADC 416	Hall Lewis B32F	1928	ex J G Severn & Co, Alfreton 3.31
	56	RA 7597	ADC 426	Hall Lewis B32F	1929	ex J G Severn & Co, Alfreton 3.31
	53	RA 8791	ADC 416	Hall Lewis B32F	1929	ex J G Severn & Co, Alfreton 3.31
	106/111/ 107	RB 1282/1757/ /2309	AEC Regal	Willowbrook B32F	1930	ex J G Severn & Co, Alfreton 3.31
	108	JA 1291	AEC Regent	Short H24/26R	1930	ex J G Severn & Co, Alfreton 3.31
	81	RB 3864	AEC Regal	Willowbrook B32F	1931	ex J G Severn & Co, Alfreton 3.31
		9 buses (Fiat, 2 SPA, AEC 413, Buick, Star, Dennis G, 2 Bean)				ex J G Severn & Co, Alfreton 3.31, not operated
		5 buses (3 Chevrolet, Dennis, Gilford 16-SD)				ex H B Hassall, Mansfield 4.31 leased to MDT part returned.
		10 buses (2 Leyland, 3 GMC, ADC, Chevrolet, Gilford Reo, W&G)				ex Thompson Bros, Stanton Hill 4.31, ditto
1932	86-91	RB 6013-8	TSM B39A7	Beadle B32F		
	116-20	RB 6603-7	TSM B39A7	Beadle B32F		
	121-5	RB 6608-12	TSM D60A6	Weymann H30/26R		
	46	KJ 2917	TSM D40A6	Beadle H30/26R	1931	ex MDT
	129?	RA 225	Leyland LSC1	Leyland B32F	1926	ex Ebor Bus Co. Ltd, Mansfield 10.32
		RR 9983	W&G	Reeve & Kenning C20R	1928	ex Ebor Bus Co. Ltd, Mansfield 10.32
		?	REO	?	?	ex Ebor Bus Co. Ltd, Mansfield 10.32. not operated

Year	Fleet No.	Reg.No.	Chassis	Body and layout	New	Notes
1933	21	RR 7741	Leyland PLC1	Leyland B26F	1927	returned from MDT, ex Thompson
	55 or 43?	TO 8459	ADC 426	Hall Lewis B32F	1928	returned from MDT, ex Thompson
	19	VO 2364	Leyland LT1	Leyland B32F	1929	returned from MDT, ex Thompson, A suffix during 1937
	37	VO 2520	Gilford 16-SD	? B26-	1929	returned from MDT, ex Hassall
		VO 3303/4635	GMC	? B20-	1930	returned from MDT, ex Thompson
	127	UT 34	Leyland PLSC1	Leyland B31F	1927	ex F Porter & Sons, Stonebroom 7.33 to MGO fleet 1.10.33
	85	RA 9628	Leyland LT1	Davidson B32F	1929	ex F Porter & Sons, Stonebroom 7.33 to MGO fleet 1.10.33
	112,69	RB 158-9	Leyland LT1	? B32F	1929	ex F Porter & Sons, Stonebroom 7.33 to MGO fleet 1.10.33
	84	RB 2087	Leyland LT2	? B30F	1930	ex F Porter & Sons, Stonebroom 7.33 to MGO fleet 1.10.33
		6 further Guy buses included, not operated?				ex F Porter & Sons, Stonebroom 7.33
	128	RF 1583	Leyland PLSC1	Leyland B32F	1926	ex E Viggars, Alfreton 7.33 to MGO fleet 1.10.33
		RR 6764/6410	W&G L20	? B20F	1927	ex E Viggars, Alfreton 7.33 to MGO fleet 1.10.33
	130	RB 1778	Dennis EV	? B32F	1930	ex E.Wharton, Morton 7.33 to MGO fleet 1.10.33, A suffix 1937
	132	RB 5155	Morris	? DP24F	1931	ex E.Wharton, Morton 7.33 to MGO fleet 1.10.33
	131/3	RB 4553/5536	Morris Viceroy	? B24F	1931-2	ex Severn Bros, Swanwick 7.33 to MGO fleet 1.10.33
		VO 6336	Crossley Hawk	Farnsworth? B26	1931	ex R Fearn, Alfreton 7.33 to MGO fleet 1.10.33
		VO 7050	Crossley Eagle	? B32-	1932	ex R Fearn, Alfreton 7.33 to ditto, converted to carnival coach
1934	135	VA 8458	Leyland TS1	Alexander B32F	1929	ex J H Booth, Westhouses 3.34 A suffix during 1937
	134	VJ 2628	Leyland LT2	? B31R	1930	ex J H Booth, Westhouses 3.34
	136	RB 4394	Morris Dictator	? B32F	1931	ex J H Booth, Westhouses 3.34
		6 (5 GMC & Albion) buses not operated?				ex J H Booth, Westhouses 3.34
		AG 5172/7	Guy OND	Guy B20F	1930	ex E Topham, Leabrooks 3.34
		RB 5318	Albion	? B26F	1931	ex Topham ditto to Leamington & Warwick 20.3.35 until?
		RA 6630	Dennis G	? B20	1928	ex G.Shaw, Ironville 3.34
		RA 7202	Dennis G	Willowbrook B18	1928	ex G.Shaw, Ironville 3.34
1935	96	TV 2919	Crossley Arrow	Crossley B32F	1930	ex Pinxton Bus Co, Sutton in Ashfield 2.35
	95/94	VO 6333/5	Crossley Eagle	Crossley B32F	1931	ex Pinxton Bus Co, Sutton in Ashfield 2.35
	129	UT 9230	Maudslay	? B32-	1931	ex Pinxton Bus Co, Sutton in Ashfield 2.35
	137	AAL 117	Dennis Lancet	? B32-	1933	ex Pinxton Bus Co, Sutton in Ashfield 2.35
		4? (2 GMC T30, Chevrolet LQ, REO Speedwagon?) not operated.ex Pinxton Bus Co, Sutton in Ashfield 2.35				
		3 Ford AA 20 seat buses not operated				ex Brewin & Hudson Ltd, Ilkeston 8.35
		1 GMC not operated				ex Scott, Huthwaite 10.35
1936	156-65	CRA 655-64	AEC Regal	Weymann C32F		158 body rebuilt by MGO 1954. 157-60/2 to WD 12.39
	153	UO 7470	Leyland PLSC3	Hall Lewis B31F	1928	ex G Swain, Mansfield 4.36, A suffix 1937
	141	FV 69	Leyland TS1	Burlingham C29F	1929	ex G Swain, Mansfield 4.36, A suffix 1937
	147	VO 1010	Leyland TS2	United C32F	1929	ex G Swain, Mansfield 4.36
	149	VO 2556	Leyland LT1	Leyland B30F	1929	ex G Swain, Mansfield 4.36. 145 to 32 seats 5.36. A suffix 1937
	139	FV 1132	Leyland TS1	? C30F	1930	ex G Swain, Mansfield 4.36, A suffix 1937
	145	VO 5807	Albion PMB28	? B30F	1931	ex G Swain, Mansfield 4.36, A suffix 1937
	151	VO 7006	Leyland KP	? B20	1931	ex G Swain, Mansfield 4.36, to tower wagon 1944
	143	ANN 686	Leyland TS6	Reeve & Kenning C32R	1931	ex G Swain, Mansfield 4.36
	166	RA 6488	Guy B	? C25F	1928	ex Straw & Fletcher. 4.36 A suffix 1937 to tower wagon 1944
	167	RB 1802	Guy ONDL	? C20F	1930	ex Straw & Fletcher, Ilkeston 4.36 A suffix added 1937
	168	RB 6400	Guy Arab FC32	Harrington C32R	1932	ex Straw & Fletcher, Ilkeston 4.36 A suffix added 1937

Year	Fleet No.	Reg.No.	Chassis	Body and layout	New	Notes
1937	4-6/9-10/ 12/14/16/18/ 20-1/36-7/ 48-50/52/54/ 58-9/61/65/ 67-8/72	DNU 953-77	AEC Regent	Weymann H28/24F		Rebuilt by Nudd Bros & Lockyer 1951-2. Reseated 28/26 1953-5
	73/78/82/ 83/92/ 94-98	DRA 160-9	Leyland TS7	Weymann DP35F		
1938	53/55-6/ 99-101/110/113/126-7	ERA 906-15	AEC Regal	Weymann DP35F		113 to 32 seats 6.42 to 35 during 7.49
	128-9/ 131/137/144	ERA 916-20	Leyland TS8	Weymann DP35F		
	151/155 169-73	ERA 921-7	AEC Regal	Weymann C32F		to 35 seats 1955-6
	174-83	FNU 169-78	AEC Regent	Weymann H28/24F		
	184-5	ABX 78-9	AEC Regal	Weymann DP35F	1938	ex Llanelly District Traction Co. 19/23
1939	13/15/17/ 19/39/47/51/62/66/69/74/79-80/85/ 104/12/15/30/2-3	FRA 828-47	AEC Regal	Weymann DP35F		104 reumbered 111 during 3.55
	135-6/8-40 149-50/2-4	FRB 85-9 FRB 714-8	Leyland TS8	Weymann DP35F		
	142/145-6 166-7	FRB 711-3 FRB 719-20	Leyland TS8	Weymann C32F		to 35 seats 1955-6
1942	186	HRA 417	Leyland TD7	Leyland H30/26R		
	187	HRA 682	Guy Arab I	Brush H30/26R		Rebuilt by Bond 1.54
	188	HRA 815	Guy Arab I	MCW/Weymann H30/26R		
1943	189	HRA 924	Guy Arab I	MCW/Weymann H30/26R		
	190	HRB17	Guy Arab I	Weymann H30/26R		
	191-6	HRB417-8/24-7	Guy Arab II	Weymann H30/26R		191-2/4/6 rebuilt by MGO 1956
1944	197-9	HRB 831-3	Guy Arab II	Weymann H30/26R		197 r/b MGO 1954. 198 r/b Nudd 1955. 199 r/b Bond 1954
	1-2	HRB 976-7	Guy Arab II	Weymann H30/26R		1-2 bodies rebuilt by MGO 1955/6
	3/7-8/11/ 22-6/29-30	HRB 979-83/ JNU 59-61/120-1	Guy Arab II	NCME H30/26R		3/7/22/3/6 rebuilt MGO 1954, 8/11/24/5/9 rebuilt Bond 1955
1945	31/34	JNU 373-4	Guy Arab II	NCME H30/26R		34/31 rebuilt by Bond 1954/5
	200-4	JNU 675-9	Guy Arab II	Weymann L27/28R		Renumbered 400-4 in 1947 400/3-4 rebuilt by Bond 1953. 401-2 rebuilt by MGO 1953.
	205-8	JNU 680-3	Guy Arab II	Roe L27/28R		R/no. 405-8 .47 to 102-5. ECW rebody .55 102/4 to 342/4 .66
1946	209-10	JNU 684-5	Guy Arab II	Roe L27/28R		R/no. 409-10 .47 to 106-7 ECW rebody 1955 to 346-7 1966
	211-3	JNU 735-7	Guy Arab II	Strachan L27/28R		R/no. 411-3 1947 Bond rebuilt 411 1953
	214/5	GRR 61-2	Guy Arab II	Weymann L27/28R		Ex MDT 115-6. R/no.414/5. r/b by Willowbrook and Bond .53
	41-2	JRB 127-8	AEC Regal	Duple DP35F		
	60/63-4/ 70-1/75-7	KNU 601-8	AEC Regent III	Weymann H30/26R		

Year	Fleet No.	Reg. No.	Chassis	Body and layout	New	Notes
1947	43-4	JRB 129-30	AEC Regal	Duple DP35F		
	45-6	JRB 131-2	Leyland PS1/1	Duple DP35F		
	103/5/14/ 134/41/8	KRB 65-70	Bedford OB	Duple C29F		141/8 to MDT Nos. 49/50,1950 to 1952
	121-5/157/ 159-60/2/8	KRB 71-80	AEC Regent II	Weymann H30/26R		
	416-20	KRB 81-5	AEC Regent II	Weymann L27/26R		
1948	200/3-5/8/ 211-2/5-6/ 220-I/3-4	KRB 86/9-91/4	Leyland PS1/1	SEAS DP35F		
		KRB 97-8/101-2	Leyland PS1/1	SEAS DP35F		
		KRB 106-7/9-10	Leyland PS1/1	SEAS DP35F		
	201-2/6-7/ 9-10/3-4/ 217-9/22	KRB 87-8/92-3/5-6/9-00/3-5/8	Leyland PS1/1	SEAS C32F		201-2/6/14/8-9 to 35 seats 5.54 207/9-0/3/7/22 to 35 seats 1956
	27-28/ 86-91/108-9 116-20	MRB 29-43	AEC Regent III	Weymann H30/26R		89/119-20 to MDT in 1966
1950	421-30	ONU 630-9	AEC Regent III	Weymann L27/26R		
1953	431/433	ERU587/AFX 756	Bristol K5G	ECW L27/26R	1939	ex Hants & Dorset 1036/59
	432	FLJ 533	Bristol K5G	ECW L27/26R	1940	ex Hants & Dorset 1081
1954	226-31	VRB 557-62	Bristol LS6G	ECW C39F		
	434-5	VRB 520-1	Bristol LD6G	ECW H33/25 RD		
1955	436-48	VRB 522-4/XNU 423-32	Bristol LD6G	ECW H33/25RD		
	232-41	XNU 413-22	Bristol LS6G	ECW DP43F		238 to B43F in 1968
1956	242-53	956-67 ARA	Bristol LS6G	ECW DP43F		242-5/7/8/50-3 to B43F in 1968
	449-58	968-77 ARA	Bristol LD6G	ECW H33/25RD		
1957	459-63	8-12 DRB	Bristol LDSG	ECW H33/25RD		
	4-6	CAL 192/195-6	AEC Regent	Weymann H30/26R	1936	ex MDT 192/5-6
1958	254-63	23-32 DRB	Bristol MW6G	ECW DP43F		258/63 to MDT 12.71
	474-6	259-61 HNU	Bristol LD6G	ECW H33/25RD		
	174-85	KRR 253/255/264-9/271-4	AEC Regal III	Weymann DP35F	1949	ex MDT 7/9/18-23/25-8
1959	264-80	262-71 HNU/508-14 JRA	Bristol MW6G	ECW DP43F		267 to MDT 5.68 to 12.68
	477-89	515-27 JRA	Bristol LD6G	ECW H33/25RD		
1960	490-4	528 JRA/906-9 MRB	Bristol FS6G	ECW H33/27RD		1968 r/no.590-4 .594 to MDT 12.71
1961	495-500	910-5 MRB	Bristol FS6G	ECW H33/27RD		1968 r/no.595-0 to MDT 1969
	501-5	441-5 SNU	Bristol FSF6G	ECW H33/27F		1968 r/no.601-5
1962	506-10	446-50 SNU	Bristol FSF6G	ECW H34/26F		1968 r/no.606-10
	511-5	526-30 VRB	Bristol FLF6B	ECW H38/32F		1968 r/no.611-5. 614 fitted Gardner 6LW engine 1970
1963	516-20	531-5 VRB	Bristol FLF6G	ECW H38/32/F		1968 r/no.616-20
	281-6	1378-83 R	Bristol MW6G	ECW C39F		
	626-9	1387-90 R	Bristol FLF6B	ECW H38/32F		628 fitted Gardner 6LW engine 1969
1964	30-2	1384-6 R	Bristol RELH6G	ECW C51F		1969 r/no.130-2, to 47 seats 1970
	630-4	1391-2 R/ANU 11B/BRB 492-3B	Bristol FLF6B	ECW H38/32F		632 allocated 1393 R.633-4 to NDT 1.65

Year	Fleet No.	Reg. No.	Chassis	Body and layout	New	Notes
1965	291-7	DNU 11-21C	Bristol MW6G	ECW DP43F		295-7 to MDT 4.68
	642-3	FNU 411-4C	Bristol FLF6B	ECW H38/32F		
	644-5	FNU 413-4C	Bristol FLF6G	ECW H38/32F		
	318-22/5-6	JVO 944-48/51-2	AEC Regent III	Weymann H30/26R	1948	Ex NDT 318-26, 323-4 delivered in 1949
	323-4	JVO 949-50	AEC Regent III	Weymann H30/26R	1949	318-9/21-3/5-6 to MDT 1965-6
1966	660-9	JNU 980-9D	Bristol FLF6G	ECW H38/32F		
	101-4	JNU 990-3D	Bristol MW6G	ECW B45F		4.68 to MDT 101-4
1967	219-21	ONU 919-21E	Bedford VAM14	Duple C41F		
	133-4	SRB 66-7F	Bristol RESH6G	ECW DP43F		
	670-82	SRB 66-80F	Bristol FLF6G	ECW H38/32F		676-82 to NDT 6.72
1968	222-4	TRB 565-7F	Bedford VAM70	Duple C41F		
	307-13	TRB 574-8/81F/YNU 350-1G	Bristol FLF6G	ECW H38/32F		312-3 originally allocated TRB579-80F
	211-2	196-7 BRR	Bristol MW6G	ECW DP39F	1960	ex MDT 211-2 to 43 seats 1969
	533-4	569-70 ERR	Bristol FS6G	ECW H33/27RD	1961	ex MDT 533-4
	535-44	51-60 JAL	Bristol FSF6G	ECW H34/32F	1962	ex MDT 535-44
	213-5	BNN 101-3C	Bristol MW6G	ECW DP39F	1965	ex MDT 213-4 to 43 seats 1969
1969	111-6	BNU 673-8G	Bristol LH6L	ECW B45F		
	315-20	BNU 679-81G/DRB 307-9H	Bristol VRTSL6G	ECW H39/31F		
	135-9	DRB 302-6H	Bristol RELL6G	ECW B44D		
1970	230-1	ERB 343-4H	Bedford VAM70	Duple C41F		
	146-7	FRB 208-9H	Bristol RELL6G	ECW B44D		
	321-2	FRB 210-1H	Bristol VRTSL6G	ECW H39/31F		
	117-21	JRB 768-72J	Bristol LH6L	ECWB45F		
1971	232-33	LNU 344-5J	Bedford YRQ	Plaxton C41F		
	148-53	NNU 447-9J/ORB 245-7K	Bristol RELL6G	ECW B44D		
	122-4	ORB 248-50K	Bristol LH6L	ECW R45F		
	287-8	370-1 RNN	Bristol MW6G	ECW C39F	1963	ex MDT 287-8
	216-8	KNN 610-2E	Bedford VAM14	Duple C41F	1967	ex MDT 216-8
	225-7	TRB 582-4F	Bedford VAM70	Duple C41F	1968	ex MDT 225-7 8.71 returned 12.71
	143	DRA 354G	Bristol RELL6G	ECW B44D	1969	ex MDT 143
	228-9	ERB 345-6H	Bedford VAM70	Duple C41F	1970	ex MDT 228-9 8.71 returned 12.71
	144-5	FRB 206-7H	Bristol RELL6G	ECW B44D	1970	ex MDT 144-5
	234-5	LNU 346-7J	Bedford YRQ	Plaxton C41F	1971	ex MDT 234-5
	633-4	BRB 492-3B	Bristol FLF6G	ECW H38/32F	1964	
	635-6/40-1	DNU 15-6/668-9C	Bristol FLF6B	ECW H38/32F	1965	
	637-9	DNU 685-7D	Bristol FLF6G	ECW H38/32F	1965	ex NDT 301-6/633-41/76-82
	676-82	SRB 74-80F	Bristol FLF6G	ECW H38/32F	1967	
	301-6	TRB 568-73F	Bristol FLF6G	ECW H38/32F	1968	
1972	154-8	ORB 251-5K	Bristol RELL6G	ECW B44D		

NOTTS & DERBY - FLEET LIST from Tramways Co. to Traction Co. 9.28

Year	Fleet No.	Type	Body and seats	Truck	Motors	New	Notes
1913	1-12	Open top	UEC 32/24	Peckham P22	BTH GE67-3T 2 x 40hp		1-3 fitted EE top covers 1922. By 1930 9/11-2 to 30/23 seats,1-8/10 to 30/26 seats. Three loaned MDT 1925, one returned 1926, and 5-6 retained?.
	13-24	Balcony	UEC 32/24	Peckham P22	BTH GE67-3T 2 x 40hp		Received with covered tops. Seating to 30/26
1916	1-9	Open top	ER&TCW 26/22	Brill 21E	DK25B 2 x 25hp	1902	ex Ilkeston Corporation. 7-8 to Dunfermline &
	10-13	Open top	Milnes 26/22	Brill 21E	Westinghouse 46M 2 x 25hp	1903	District 44-5 by 9.19. Two ER&TCW and one Milnes to Carlisle 13-5 ,1919-21. Remainder rebuilt as 1-8, new No.7 to one man 30seat single deck

Year	Fleet No.	Reg. No.	Chassis	Body and layout	New	Notes
1920		R 4226	AEC type	AEC/LGOC B27R	?	Lorry- bus ex LGOC?
1932	300-5	RB 5568-73	English Electric	EEC B32F		
	306-15	RB 6613-22	AEC 661T-EEC	EEC B32F		
	316	UK9601	Guy BT32-BTH	Guy B32F	1930	Formerly Guy demonstrator
1933	317-31	RB 8951-65	AEC 661T-EEC	MCCW H31/24R		
1937	300-5/32	DRB 616-22	AEC 661T-EEC	Weymann H30/26R		
1941	333-6	HNU 826-30	AEC 661T-EEC	Weymann H30/26R		
1942	337-42	HNU 970-4	AEC 661T-EEC	Weymann H30/26R		
1949	343-57	NNU 224-38	BUT 9611T-EEC	Weymann H30/26R		
1953	300-14	SRB 528-42	Bristol KW6G	ECW H32/28R		
	315-22/5-6	JVO 941-8/51-2	AEC Regent III	Weymann H30/26R	1948	ex MDT 145-52/5-6/318-22/5-6 to MGO.65 315 rebodied by ECW 1955
	323-4	JVO 949/50	AEC Regent III	Weymann H30/26R	1949	ex MDT 153-4 to MGO 1.65
1957	464	13 DRB	Bristol LDL6G	ECW H37/33R		Platform doors fitted 6.64
1958	465-73	14-17 DRB	Bristol LD6G	ECW H37/25R		Ditto during 1964
1965	635-6/40-	DNU 15-6C/688-9C	Bristol FLF6B	ECW H38/32F		12.71 to MGO 635-6/40-1
	637-9	DNU 685-7C	Bristol FLF6G	ECW H38/32F		Ditto 637-9
	633-4	BRB 492-3B	Bristol FLF6G	ECW H38/32F	1964	ex MGO 633-4 returned .71
1968	301-6	TRB 568-73F	Bristol FLF6G	ECW H38/32F		12.71 to MGO 301-6
1970	676-82	SRB 74-80F	Bristol FLF6G	ECW H38/32F	1967	ex MGO 676-82 returned 12.71

DAWSON'S ENTERPRISE - FLEET LIST from formation to MGO associate company.

Year	Fleet No.	Reg. No.	Chassis	Body and layout	New	Notes
	?	?	REO	? B14-	1922	ex A.E.Dawson 11.27 burnt out .27
	1,3	NU 6704/7955	Thornycroft A1	? B20F	1925	ex A.E.Dawson 11.27
	4	RA 1608	Thornycroft A1	? B20-	1927	ex A.E.Dawson 11.27
	2	RA 2943	Thornycroft A2	? B20F	1927	ex A.E.Dawson 11.27
	6?	RA 3164	Minerva	? B26-	1927	ex Dawson's Super Service 11.27.
	10?/11?	RA 1719-20	Laffly	? B20F	1927	ex Dawson's Super Service 11.27.
	5	RA 2325	Thornycroft A2	? B20F	1927	ex Dawson's Super Service 11.27.
	8	RA 3342	De Dion Bouton	? B20-	1927	ex R.W.Dixon 3.28.
	9?	R 6079	De Dion Bouton JE2	?B20F	1926	ex R.W.Dixon 3.28.
1927	7	RA 4568	Thornycroft A2	? B20F		
1930	70/6	RB 2138-9	T-Stevens B10A2	Ransomes B32F		

No.1 to lorry Stratford Blue 1931, No. 3 to MGO G8 c31, No.4 to MGO lorry G3. Nos.5,2,7 r/no. 94-6. 94 to lorry G7 by 1933, 96 to van by 1933.
From 7.29 vehicles part of Williamson operations but still owned by Dawson. 70/6 owned by Dawson until 1.1.41, but ran in Williamson or MGO livery.

WILLIAMSON'S GARAGE - FLEET LIST of all known vehicles,# not transferred to MGO associate co.

Year	Fleet No.	Reg.No.	Chassis	Body and layout	New	Notes
1923		NU 1755	REO Speedwagon	Hartshorn B14-		Probably all front entrance
1924		NU 2304//3556/4216/4484	REO Speedwagon	Hartshorn B14-		ditto
		NU 4911/20	REO Speedwagon	? B14-		ditto with Eaton or Hartshorn bodies
1925		NU 5169/80	REO Sprinter	? B14-		ditto with ditto
		NU 6419/7283	REO Pullman	Eaton B20F		
		NU 7459	REO Speedwagon	? B14		#
		NU 7460/7969	REO Pullman	Eaton B20F		
1926		NU 8384/444	REO S/W Sprinter	? B20-		ditto with Eaton or Hartshorn body
		NU 8525	REO Speedwagon	Eaton B14F		#
	-/-/84	NU 8528/RA1267/74	REO Pullman	? B24-		ditto with ditto reduced to 23 seats by .32
		NU 9050-1/RA 572-3	REO Pullman	Eaton B24F		Reduced to 23 seats by .32
		RA 1063	REO	? B14-		
1927	-/-/69/-	RA 1463/512/31/638	REO Pullman	? B24		Front entrance? to 23 seats by .32
		RA 2280	REO Pullman	Hartshorn B24F		To 23 seats by .32
		RA 3379	REO Pullman	Eaton B24F		To 23 seats by .32
		NU 8553	REO	Eaton B14F	1926	ex A & W N Henshaw, Ilkeston
		RA 502?	Thornycroft	ChallandsRoss B20F	1927	ex A & W N Henshaw, Ilkeston
		RA 661	Thornycroft AI	ChallandsRoss B20R	1927	ex A & W N Henshaw, Ilkeston
		RA 3470-1/749/81	REO Pullman	? B24-		Front entrance? Eaton or Hartshorn.
	20/61/18/ 36	RA 4516-9	Bristol B	Roe B32F		
1928		RA 4939	REO Pullman	? B26-		ex Tarlton & Brown, Codnor 9.28
		NU 8388	REO Speedwagon	? B14-	1927	ex Tarlton & Brown, Codnor 9.28
		RA 2501-2/3135	REO Major	? B20-	1927	ex Tarlton & Brown, Codnor 9.28
1929	7/11/17/15 8/13	RA 9649-54	T-Stevens B10A	Strachan&Brown B32F		
		RR 4863	REO Speedwagon	? B14-	1926	ex J Saxton or E E Hamilton
		RA 4904	REO Speedwagon	? B14-	1929	ex J Saxton, Heanor 9.29
		TO 5686/6016	REO Pullman	? B23-	1927	ex E E Hamilton?,Heanor 9.29
1930	71/5	RB 2039/40	T-Stevens B10A2	Ransomes B32F		
		R 5055	Guy	Guy ? B20F	1921	ex Prince of Wales Service,Ilkeston
		NU 4575	Guy BA	Guy B20F	1924	ex Prince of Wales Service,Ilkeston
		NU 5315	Guy B	Guy B26F	1925	ex Prince of Wales Service,Ilkeston
		WU 1427	Guy BB	Guy? B26-	1925	ex Prince of Wales Service,Ilkeston †
		NU 7973	Guy BA	Guy B20-	1925	ex Prince of Wales Service,Ilkeston
		RA 1653	Guy BB	Guy B30	1927	ex Prince of Wales Service,Ilkeston †

† WU 1427/RA 1653 loaned to Carlisle & District Transport Co, Ltd.

Although the operations passed to MGO 7.31 the fleet was owned by Williamson but ran in MGO livery. 7-8/13/17/71/75 purchased by MGO 1.1.43
Fleet numbers allocated upon takeover 1.28.

TANSEY & SEVERN - FLEET LIST all known vehicles; § to MGO associate coy. MGO livery afer 7.31

Year	Fleet No.	Reg.No.	Chassis	Body and layout	New	Notes
1921		NN 1758	Leyland	Leyland? B18-		
1922		NN2399	Thornycroft	? B29-		
		?	Leyland RAF (G7)	Leyland? B?		
1923		NN 5582	Crossley	? B14-		
		?	Leyland RAF	Leyland B32-		
1924		NN 6696-7	Leyland Z5	Leyland B20-		
		?	Leyland C3	Leyland B21-		
1925		?	Leyland Z5	Leyland B20		
1926	50/99/82	RR 30256/3814	Leyland LSC1	Leyland B31F		§ 50/99 A suffixes 1937
	72	RR 4909	Leyland PLSC1	Leyland B31F		§ A suffix 1937
1927	100-1/10/3	RR 6902/5927/7716/7836	Leyland PLSC1	Leyland B31F		§
1928	39/104	RR 8604-5	Leyland PLSC3	Leyland B35F		§104 A suffix 1937
	105/-	RA 9948/?	Leyland TD1	Leyland L27/24RO		§ ? to Leyland .29 then Sheffield .29
1929	115,64	VO 1827-8	Leyland LT1	Leyland B35F		
1930	109	VO 3486	Leyland TD1	Leyland L24/24R		
	93/114	VO 4279-80	T-Stevens B10A2	? B32F		May have had Strachan & Brown bodies
		NU 9260	Dennis	? B20-	1926	ex W J Wright South Normanton 4.31
		RA 3732	Dennis	? B20-	1927	ex W J Wright South Normanton 4.31
		RA 5845	Karrier	? B20-	1928	ex W J Wright South Normanton 4.31

RR 3814 had fleet No. 12. Operations to MGO 7.31 with vehicles retained by Tansey & Severn, but ran in MGO livery. Nos.64/93/105/9/13-5 purchased by MGO1.2.43

ALFRETON MOTOR TRANSPORT known vehicles; § to MGO assosciate coy.

Year	Fleet No.	Reg.No.	Chassis	Body and layout	New	Notes
1921?		R 3352	Commer	? B32		
1923?		NU 68??	Crossley	? B12?F		
1925		NU7526/??36	Guy	? B26F		
		?	Leyland A1	Leyland B20		
1926		NU ?/8604	Leyland PLSC1	Leyland B31F		
1927		RA 225	Leyland PLSC1	Leyland B32F		
1927		RA 1735/?	Leyland PLSC1	Leyland B31F/B35F		
		?	Thornycroft	? B20		
1927	154/152	VT 27/RA 4284	Leyland PLSC3	Leyland B35F		§
1928	142/150	RA 5472/5970	Leyland PLSC3	Leyland B35F		§
1929	148	RA 7586	Leyland PLSC3	Leyland B35F		§
	138	RA 8499	Gilford 1660T	Wycombe B32F		§
	140	RA 8699	Gilford 1680T	? C32F		§
	146	RA 9030	Leyland LT1	Leyland B35F		§ fitted with a Beardmore diesel engine.
	144	RA 9512	Karrier JKL	? B32-		§
1930	155	RB 1334	Karrier Chaser 4	Ransomes B32D		§ exhibited 1929 Commercial Motor Show.
		RA 9304	Ford A	Reeve & Kenning B14D		ex J A Barker, Brackenfield ?
		?	Commer	Reeve & Kenning B14D		ditto? § not retained by MGO

A Suffix added142/8/50/2/4 1937. With effect from 1.3.43 the six remaining vehicles (Nos.142/6/8/50/2/4) purchased by MGO.

Acquired Operators

30.9.16 Ilkeston Corporation Tramways.
21.7.25 South Normanton Bus Co., South Normanton.
23.10.25 Midland Bus Co. Kimberley.
5.1.28 Williamsons Garage Ltd., Heanor.
    19.9.28 Tarlton & Brown, Codnor.
    12.7.29 Dawson's Enterprise Omnibus Co Ltd, Cotmanhay.
    25.9.29 J.Saxton & Son, Heanor.
    25.9.29 E.E.Hamilton, Heanor.
    29.1.30 J.Argyle, Codnor.
    26.3.30 Prince of Wales Service (E&J Bramley), Ilkeston.
    (jointly with Trent, MGO, and Dawson's Enterprise)
    operated by Williamsons and Trent
    16.7.31 merged with MGO, (not garage and carriers).
    1.3.33? carriers and garage business ceased operation.
    17.12.46 wound up as an associated company.
3.4.28 L.Mellows (Star Saloon Services), Sutton in Ashfield.
12.6.28 G.H.Hayton, Mansfield, (operated by MDT).
1.12.28 B.Hatton (Hattons Motor Services), Selston.
1.1.29 Davis & Hope, Mansfield.
1.1.29 Dawson's Enterprise Omnibus Co.Ltd, Cotmanhay.
    12.7.29 operations to Williamsons Garage Ltd.
    26.3.30 Prince of Wales Service (see MGO & Williamson).
    17.12.46 wound up as an associated company.
2.1.29 H.Booth (Booths Motor Services), Blidworth,
    (ceased 1.12.36).
6.4.29 Tansey & Severn Ltd, Underwood.
    30.4.30 W.J. Wright, South Normanton.
    16.7.31 operations to MGO
    17.12.46 wound up as an associated company.
17.5.29 Inglis & Beardsley (Reliance Omnibus Co.), Ilkeston.
8.12.29 Webster & Briggs (United Bus Services), Sutton in Ashfield.
26.3.30 E & J Bramley (Prince of Wales Service), Cotmanhay.
    (jointly Dawson's Enterprise, Trent and Williamsons)
5.3.31 H.B.Hassall, Mansfield. (operated by M&DT).
17.3.31 Thompson Brothers, Stanton Hill. (operated by M&DT).
26.3.31 J.T.Boam (The Ray Service), Heanor.
31.3.31 J.G.Severn & Co, (SMA), Alfreton.
4.5.31 Grail & Joiner (Stratford-upon-Avon Blue Motor Services),
    Stratford on Avon. (to Stratford-upon-Avon Blue Motors Ltd)
    18.2.32 Crompton & Longford (Reliance Bus Co.),
    Bidford on Avon.

    14.6.32 management to Leamington & Warwick Transport.
    12.12.35 shares and business to BMMO
20.1.32 Ebor Trading Co.Ltd, York, (Ripley-Mansfield service)
11.4.33 Mansfield & District Tramways Ltd.(Mansfield -Stanton Hill
    and Clay Cross services)
11.4.33 F.U.Charlton, Ilkeston. (Ilkeston-Kimberley service)
27.4.33 Mrs.A.M.Whitworth, Lower Pilsley. (Joint operated by M&DT)
4.7.33 E.Wharton (Morton Bus Co.), Morton.
4.7.33 F. Porter & Son, Stonebroom.
4.7.33 Leah Brothers, Huthwaite.
    (Sutton in Ashfield-Tibshelf and Huthwaite-Tibshelf)
17.7.33 E.Viggars, Alfreton.
17.7.33 R.Fearn, Alfreton. (part of business to Trent 9.32)
17.7.33 Severn Brothers, Swanwick.(part of business to Trent 9.32)
27.3.34 J.H.Booth, Westhouses.(13.6.34 tours and excursions
    licences from Alfreton to Trent)
27.3.34 W.E.Topham, Leabrooks. (part of business to Trent 9.32)
26.4.34 G.Shaw & Sons, Ironville . (part of business to Trent 10.32)
16.10.34 J.Cresswell, Clay Cross. (joint with Chesterfield Corporation)
18.2.35 F.U.Charlton, Ilkeston. (Cotmanhay-Shipley Colliery)
18.2.35 Pinxton Bus Co., Sutton in Ashfield.
1.8.35 Billingham Bros, Ilkeston. (joint with Barton)
21.8.35 Brewin & Hudson, Heanor.
30.10.35 A.Scott, Huthwaite.
11.35 F. W. Chambers, Ilkeston. (joint with Barton)
1.4.36 Alfreton Motor Transport Co.Ltd, Alfreton.
    17.12.46 wound up as an associated company.
23.4.36 G.Swain (Supreme Motor Coach Co.), Mansfield.
    (27.5.36 tours and excurisons licences to MDOC)
24.4.36 Straw & Fletcher (Pride of Ilson Coaches), Ilkeston.
27.5.36 Agreement with MDOC on exchange of licences.
4.11.36 East Midlands Motor Services.(Tupton-Lea Mills)
    ex W.Stoppard & Sons, Clay Cross)
1.3.37 E.Gregory, Ilkeston, (joint with Barton)
1.5.38 Heanor & District Omnibus Co.Ltd., 4 Burr Lane, Ilkeston.
    (joint with Barton and Trent)
15.5.38 C.Kirk (Blidworth Blue), Blidworth.
20.6.39 Exchange of services to MDT and T &E licences to MGO
17.6.40 T.Winfield & Son (Star), Awsworth (joint with Barton).
    tours andexcursion licence not taken up until 5.48.
19.6.40 T.M.Mitchell, Selston.
25.9.41 Blue Services (Grainger Bros) Ltd, Ilkeston (joint with Barton).
    tours and excursion licences not taken up until 7.45
26.2.43 Trent Motor Traction, transfer of Nottingham-Cotmanhay service.

Route Numbering Changes

Route No.				Route
1929	1930	1935	1936	
Tram	Tram			Nottingham (Parliament Street)- Ripley
Tram	Tram			Cotmanhay-Hallam Fields
Tram	Tram			Ilkeston (Station Road)- Ilkeston Junction.
1	1			Ilkeston-Heanor
2	2	1P	B1	Nottingham-Heanor-Ripley via Bobbers Mill.
3	3	4	B4	Nottingham-South Normanton via Watnall
4	4	9	B8	Nottingham-Rainworth via Hucknall
	4	9	B9	Nottingham-Rainworth via Bestwood
5?				Mansfield-Rainworth
6	6	7	B6	Mansfield-Ilkeston
7	5	17	C8	Nottingham-Kimberley-Ilkeston.
8	6A	6A	B6	Mansfield-East Kirkby
9	8	8	B7	Mansfield-Ripley
	7	7		Mansfield-Blidworth
	9	5	B5	Eastwood-Ilkeston
10	10	3	B3	Nottingham-Alfreton via Underwood
	11	2	B2	Nottingham-Cotmanhay
	12	10	C1	Mansfield-Bilsthorpe
		1	A1	Nottingham- Ripley (Trolleybus)
		6	A2	Hallam Fields-Cotmanhay-Loscoe (Trolleybus)
		6	A3	Ilkeston (Manor Rd)-Loscoe (Trolleybus)
		11	C2	Alfreton-Mansfield
		12	C3	Mansfield-Clay Cross via Pilsley
		13	C4	Ripley-Pinxton
		14	C5	Nottingham-Alfreton via Jacksdale
		15	C6	Adercar-Heanor-Waingroves-Ripley.
		16	C7	Alfreton-Sutton in Ashfield
		17	C8	Ilkeston-Kimberley-Nottingham
		20	C9	Heanor-Hucknall
		21	D1	Mansfield-Chesterfield
		22	D2	Alfreton-Clay Cross direct
		23	D3	Mansfield-Teversal
		24	D4	Ripley-Chesterfield
		25	D5	Sutton in Asfield-Chesterfield
		26	D6	Alfreton-Clay Cross via Morton
		27	D7	Alfreton-Heanor
		28	D8	Alfreton-Chesterfield via Temple Normanton
		29	D9	Sutton in Asfield-Tibshelf via Whiteborough
		30	E1	Sutton in Asfield-Stanton Hill
		31	E2	Alfreton-Matlock via Crich
		32	E3	Alfreton-Matlock via Tansley
		33	E4	Alfreton-Brackenfield
		33	E5	Alfreton-Wheatcroft
			u/n	Heanor-Matlock

Notes;-
B1 numbered1 from 1930 then 1P when trolleybuses introduced 10.33
Trolleybus service A3 was originally numbered 13.
u/n:- Un numbered until 1953 when it became F7.
A1- A9/B1-2/6/C6/D9/E1/8/F2/4-5/9 joint with Notts & Derby from 26.4.53.

Services Operated April 1972

Route No.	Route
A1	Nottingham- Basford-Eastwood-Ripley
A2	Cotmanhay Farm-Ilkeston-Kirk Hallam
A3	Cotmanhay Farm-Ilkeston-Hallam Fields
A5	Hallam Fields-Cotmanhay-Heanor-Langley Mill
A6	Hallam Fields-Heanor-New Eastood
A7	Heanor-Marlpool Farm (circular)
A8	Heanor-Langley-New Eastwood
A9	Ilkeston-Heanor-Aldercar-Eastwood
B1	Nottingham-Eastwood-Heanor-Codnor-Ripley
B2	Nottingham-Cotmanhay-Heanor-Codnor Ripley
B3	Nottingham-Alfreton via Eastwood and Underwood
B4	Nottingham-South Normanton via Watnall
B5	New Eastwood-Awsworth-Ilkeston
B6	Mansfield-Ilkeston-Larklands
B7	Mansfield-Ripley
B8	Nottingham-Mansfield via Hucknall and Rainworth
C1	Mansfield-Teversal
42	Alfreton-Mansfield via Pinxton (joint with Trent)
43	Alfreton-Mansfield via Fulwood (joint with Trent)
C3	Mansfield-Clay Cross via Pilsley
C5	Nottingham-Alfreton via Jacksdale
C6	Nottingham-Cotmanhay-Heanor-Waingroves-Ripley.
C7	Alfreton-Skegby (Healdswood Estate)
C8	Ilkeston-Hucknall or Swingate
C9	Alfreton-Hucknall-Beauvale Estate
C9	Hucknall-Papplewick Lane Estate
D1	Mansfield-Chesterfield
D2	Alfreton-Clay Cross direct
44	Chesterfield-Alfreton-Ripley-Derby (joint with Trent and East Midland)
D3	Mansfield -Teversal
D4	Ripley-Chesterfield
D6	Alfreton-Clay Cross via Morton
D8	Alfreton-Chesterfield via Temple Normanton
D9	Nottingham-Wollaton-Ilkeston
E1	Nottingham-Wollaton-Balloon Wood Flats
E2	Alfreton-Matlock via Crich
E3	Alfreton-Matlock via Tansley
E4	Alfreton-Brackenfield
E5	Alfreton-Wheatcroft
E6	Mansfield-Skegby-Sutton-Kirkby (Sycamore Avenue)
E7	Heanor-Codnor via Aldercar?
E8	Wollaton Vale (Kevin Road)- Wollaton-Nottingham
F1	Mansfield-Coxmoor Estate-Kirkby
F2	Nottingham-Kimberley-High Spania-Awsworth-Ilkeston
F3	Nottingham-Rainworth-Mansfield via Redhill
F4	Nottingham-Basford-Hucknall (Beauvale Estate)
F5	Nottingham-Wollaton Vale via Woodbank Drive
F7	Heanor-Matlock
F9	Nottingham-Kirk Hallam
G1	Stanton Hill- Sutton Junction

Works Services-April 1972

Route No.	Route
W3	Underwood-Alfreton
W4	Sutton-Stanton Ironworks
W8	Sutton-Pilsley
W12/14/15	Lea Mills-Clay Cross
W20	Underwood-Spondon
W21	Langley Mill-Marlpool-Heanor Gate School
W23	Heanor-Moorgreen
W30	Teversal/Silverhill Collieries-Huthwaite
W31	Tibshelf-Sutton Junction Factories
W33	Moorgreen Colliery-Hucknall/Pinxton
W35	Clay Cross-Belper Mills
W39	Stanton Ironworks-Alfreton
W42	Lea Mills-Ripley
W43	Teversal-Sutton Junction Factories
W44/45	Alfreton-Glapwell Colliery Services
W46/51	South Normanton-Bentinck Colliery-Mansfield
W52	Stanton Ironworks-Nottingham
W57	Ripley-Peasehill
W58	Edward Revill-New Higham Schools-Clay Cross
W61	Somercotes-Stanton Hill Sutton Colliery
W65	Cotmanhay Farm-Moorgreen Colliery
C3/D3	Mansfield-Teversal/Silverhill Collieries

Express Services- listed for 1972

Route No.	Route
X1	Ripley-Skegness-Sutton on Sea-Mablethorpe
X2	Underwood-Blackpool
X4	Clay Cross-Blackpool
X5	Dronfield-Chesterfield-Mansfield-Norwich-Great Yarmouth (Joint with East Midland)
X6	Eckington-Warsop-Ollerton-Norwich-Great Yarmouth (Joint with East Midland)
X7	Blidworth-Mansfield-Blackpool
X8	Kirk Hallam-Blackpool
X9	Sutton in Ashfield-Eastwood-Norwich-Great Yarmouth
X10	Underwood-Liverpool-Southport (Joint with East Midland)
X11	Mansfield-Wrexham-Rhyl-Abergele-Colwyn Bay-Llandudno (Joint with East Midland)
X12	Kirk Hallam-Bridlington-Filey-Scarborough (Joint with Trent)
X13	Alfreton-Heanor-Ilkeston-Norwich-Great Yarmouth (Joint with Trent)
MX4	Alfreton-Ripley-Heanor-Derby-Leicester-Luton-London (Joint with Trent, United Counties and Yelloway)

No. 282 [1379R] one of six Bristol MW6G's with ECW 39 seat body, with a sister vehicle at Blackpool during 1963. Although on private hire duties the vehicle would have been turned out as smartly for express work. These coaches very quickly had frontal changes as shown on page 110

GARAGES

Alfreton
Angel Yard

MGO rented part of this site from the 1st October 1933, which they shared with Alfreton Motor Transport vehicles until MGO bought them out in April 1936. The premises, including two dwelling houses, remained with Alfreton Motor Transport, which became a subsidiary company until 17th December 1946. Further land, shop and premises were purchased in 1938 and an extension for sixteen vehicles was built. Also the restricted right of way passage to the site was widened by 7ft. 3ins.

During 1957 consideration was given to raising the roof of the single deck garage, but it was decided to provide additional accommodation for thirty nine double deckers. Nos. 34/36/38 and 40 King Street, had been purchased during 1957/8 and demolished the following year with the intention of developing the site. However, the frontage remained fenced off as the local authority refused planning permission for an office block, as this conflicted with the town plan

Land at the rear became available when the Alfreton UDC purchased the Hall and estate, and MGO purchased a plot for future development. The proposed extensions to the rear, however, infringed the Park, and so it was decided to sell the plot to Alfreton UDC.

Following an approach, during 1968, by Trent to garage their buses at Angel Yard, plans were drawn up and work put in hand. This included the replacement of the single deck garage and modernisation of maintenance facilities, fuelling, depot, administrative and enquiry offices, canteen, etc. It was not until just before the transfer to Trent in April 1972 that work had commenced on the new development, which involved the purchase of a dwelling at 32 King Street and a printing works at 42 King Street.

Heanor
Derby Road

Came to MGO when they purchased Williamson's Garage business in January 1928. A steel framed

Alfreton - Angel Yard c 1934. At the time the premises were shared with Alfreton Motor Transport, and looking at the roof it would appear the MGO section had been recently added. All buses visible in the picture are Tilling-Stevens. From the left are:- Nos. 5/35/13/43 and 40 all with Strachan bodies except 43 which is Cowieson.

Alfreton - Angel Yard c 1959. Taken at similar position as the above, but changes are obvious. Seen are Nos. 103 Guy Arab/ECW, 419 AEC Regent III/Weymann, 277 Bristol MW6G/ECW and 217 Leyland PS1/1 SEAS.

Alfreton
Angel Yard c 1959. Following demolition of premises on King Street, the garage was opened up considerably, as this view from King Street shows. Seen with a Lodekka and a Leyland Ps1/1 with SEAS body are a Vauxhall

Ilkeston - Park Road. It was possible to see the position of the tramtracks in the cobble paviors, in this c1933 view of the entrance. Visible from the left are:- Trolleybus No. 303 and Tilling-Stevens No.11/71/75.

building with brick infill and corrugated roof was erected or adapted around 1926.

It was closed during 1932, but negotiations for a sale were not completed. Interestingly Trent had made an approach to rent the premises, but required a seven years lease, which was longer than MGO were prepared to give. During 1952 ACV Sales Ltd., took over the tenancy of the property. It was sold to Heanor UDC on the 15th March 1960.

Heanor
Ray Street

This was the original Williamson's headquarters, and following the takeover became the branch garage. The yard which may have been partially covered was triangular in shape, and catered for approximately six to eight vehicles It is assumed this was leased from the Williamson family, and appears to have been surrended around 1931.

Ilkeston
Bath Street

The Ilkeston railway station site was purchased for £11.000, in 1958 by NDT after some eight years of negotiations. Opened in September 1961, the main building was built with light weight framing, sheeting and a single span roof, to house fifty buses under cover. There was the usual maintenance bay and offices. The site, which included hardstanding for a dozen or so buses, was landscaped with grass, roses shrubs and small trees.

During Spring of 1965 a vehicle parking area was laid, being accessible from Rutland Street.

An enquiry office facing directly on to Bath Street, was opened on the 1st December 1966.

Transferred to Trent in April 1972.

Ilkeston
Cotmanhay Road

Continued to be used by Dawson's when it became a MGO subsidiary company. The land and garage was sold during October 1937 to the Derbyshire & Notts Electric Power Co, for £720.

Ilkeston
Granby Street

For a short period during 1924/5 leased premises to provide a waiting room for tram and bus passengers and interchange facilities.

Ilkeston
Park Road

NDT acquired the tram depot in 1916, which had a very impressive brick and a stone office frontage, Access was from the side for the five tram tracks. Trolleybuses took up two bays, reversing into the yard upon departure. In 1937 it was extended at both ends, almost doubling the capacity of twenty vehicles, and included an additional bay for trolleybuses. By covering the yard area access was made from the front

Sold to the East Midlands Electricity Board in 1960.

Kimberley-
Regent Street

Continued to garage buses at the side of the Regent Cinema following the purchase of the Midland Bus Co. Lease surrendered on the 29th September 1930.

Ilkeston - Bath Street. 1960. The line includes Bristol MW6Gs Nos.260/254, an unidentified Regent III, Bristol KSW6G No.314, ex MDT AEC Regent III No.175 and former MDT AEC Regal III No.315 both with Weymann bodywork.

Langley Mill
Station Road

NDT built the tram shed parallel to Station Road, with six tracks to accommodate 24 cars. Eventually this became part of the Workshop area. A small bus garage was attached to this in 1922. Following the purchase of additional land at the rear of depot for £300 from the Butterley Co, a new mess room was built Also new offices, and extensions to the garage were completed during 1930. Heating was installed in the workshops and garage during 1936. The main garage was extended in !938, to provide accommodation for twelve double deckers

Mining subsidence in the area was a major problem and in 1944 mining was now affecting the depot.

The anthracite store was converted to a workshop during March 1946. Additional wooden buildings were erected opposite the main office block in 1949.They housed the company secretary and his staff, following the transfer of the company headquarters.

On the 5th May 1969, the offices gave way to a new head office on the adjacent Mansfield Road, Heanor site. They were officially opened on the 8th May. Rent was apportioned to MGO and MDT for use of workshops and the Heanor office. However, the old offices continued in use for many more years housing the canteen and other depot functions transferred from outbuildings to the rear of the site, which were demolished

The former Ormonde Colliery line which ran between the new office block and the original site, covering an area of 4.000 sq.yds, was purchased in 1971. Phase 2 of the redevelopment; a new depot maintenance facilities, washing and refuelling bays) was authorised to be constructed, but not completed until after the takeover in 1972. Phase 3 (new workshops, depot offices, and canteen) was rescinded.

Mansfield
Oxford Street/Woodhouse Road

The premises were acquired with the G Swain Supreme Motor Coach Co, business on the 23rd April 1936. Due shortage of space at their other premises they were only occupied for a short period,

Langley Mill - Station Road. The new office block opened in summer of 1930, was situated between the entrance and fuelling bay on the left and the garage block just visible on the right.

Langley Mill - Station Road. An aerial view of the site taken c1950, clearly shows to the right the Ormonde Colliery line and the triangular wedge upon which the new office block was erected in 1969. To the left is the entrance, with the office block and maintenance units butting up to the garage.

and were sold by the 1st July 1936.

Mansfield
Southwell Road.

Freehold garage obtained with purchase of Davis & Hope. Vehicles transferred upon the opening of Sutton Road in 1933, and premises sold in June 1934.

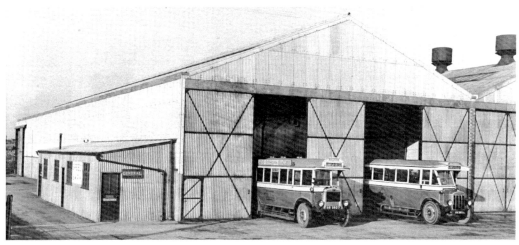

Mansfield - Sutton Road. Again typical MGO construction of lightweight steel frame and corrugated sheeting. Just poking their noses out of the building are Leyland PLSC1 No. 101 and Tilling-Stevens B10A2 No. 30.

A period interior view of the Mansfield garage. In the foreground are three Leyland bodied buses, from the left No. 58 ex Boam PLC1, No.99 Tansey & Severn LSC1 and No.52 ex Booth PLC1. Also identifiable in front of No. 52 is No.57 a Tilling-Stevens B10A with Strachan & Brown body complete with rear destination display.

Mansfield - Sutton Road c1952. The first three openings denote the new eighty vehicle garage extension. The original bay, the first of three gables from the right, can be seen behind the new facade.

Mansfield

Sutton Road

2329 square yards of land adjoining the MDT garage on Sutton Road, Mansfield was purchased from J B Hole during the early part of 1933. Plans were drawn up for a twenty bus garage on the front half of the site, with the provision for extending on the remaining half later. However, with the major acquisition of operators, the transfer of the MDT services, plus the closure of Sutton in Ashfield and Southwell Road garages, it was built to the increased capacity.

Heating was installed, including the MDT premises on a shared cost basis. The lease of the toilets was signed over to MGO from the MDOC during 1934.

Further land was purchased fronting Sutton Road, and also a plot to the rear for the provision of a recreation room, during 1937. Two years later it was run jointly with MDT as a social club.

The depot was requisitioned for military purposes as from the 14th October 1940, and garaging of vehicles was transferred immediately to the adjoining MDT depot.

The completion of a new garage, to hold eighty vehicles at Sutton Road, Mansfield, which included alterations to the facade of the existing, was reported at the 18th June 1952 Board meeting. A new toilet block built on the adjoining MDT land was sold to them. MDT was charged for part occupation of the new garage.

During 1958 the garage was sold to MDT for £53.779 and MGO paid them rent for part use, which continued until the transfer to Trent in 1972.

South Normanton

Taken over from South Normanton Bus Co Ltd, on 8th July 1925. Closed in February 1931 and sold in June 1934

Sutton in Ashfield

Russell Street

Formerly the garage premises of L Mellows (Star Saloon Services), which was occupied by MGO from April 1928 (albeit the Mellows business continued as a subsidiary until October 1929). Although

Underwood - (Upper) Mansfield Road garage, acquired by MGO with the Tansey & Severn business, provided covered accommodation for 5 buses. Seen on the picture are Leylands:-TS2 No.63 ex Boam with Willowbrook body and converted cab (see page 85), Nos.22/3 LT2 with Leyland bodies, and one of the two ex Tansey & Severn TD1s. The steel frame and cladded Alfreton Road garage can be seen in the background (Left). Inside Alfreton Road garage showing the rears of Nos. 108/84/63 and the offside of 105. (Right) Alfreton Road garage [can be seen in the background of the top picture] 12th May 1968 shows the rear of Bristols Nos.402/602 [renumbered from 502 a little earlier]. The quaint fuel pumps were still in use at this stage.

an offer was accepted for the premises in October 1932, they were not sold until June 1934. The original had been accepted, as it was possible to provide suitable alternative accommodation in Mansfield, but may have been delayed until Sutton Road was completed.

Underwood
When MGO acquired the Tansey & Severn business

it became a subsidiary company, who continued to own the premises on Mansfield Road and Alfreton Road until December 1946.
The front entrance to one of the Alfreton Road garage buildings was raised to allow the accommodation of a further five double deckers, in 1938.
During 1941 an agreement was reached with Basford RDC, to use part of the single deck garage on Mansfield Road as a fire station for the period the

war.
In 1958, a further single deck section was heightened, and alterations were made to the office, canteen and social room, during 1964.
Subsidence was affecting the garage and water was entering the new inspection pit. A little later in 1965 it was also found to be affecting the offices.
Became a Trent garage in 1972.

Acknowledgements

It is always a great pleasure to acknowledge the assistance that I been given in compiling a book, and again there is no exception with sincere thanks to Philip Groves and Alan Mills, who not only read and corrected the manuscript but provided additional information and made helpful suggestions.

Roy Marshall and Geoff Atkins have again allowed me access to their extensive and impressive collection of photographs. Other photographers who have provided photographs include Alan B Cross, Richard J Butler, Peter Badgery and Lawson Little for the full colour front cover picture of the Guy Arab. .

Rosie Thacker, the National Tramway Museum Librarian at Crich and Mike Bennett, the former Librarian at Eastwood Library gave me access to various documents, which was particularly helpful when researching the earlier years.

Fellow enthusiasts John Bennett, Paul Chambers, John Clark, the late Eddie Harrison, Eric and Les Tuxford, are always a source of information which is readily given from their own researches. Trent employees David Fletcher and Ken Rowe have volunteered information and photographs

The original sources of my research included the various minute books of The Midland General Omnibus Co Ltd, and Notts & Derby Traction, records offices at Angel Row and Wilford Lane, Nottingham, Ilkeston, Mansfield and the University of Nottingham.

I have referred to the following books and magazines:;
Blue Triangle-AA Townsin.
BP book of Industrial Archaeology- Neil Cossons.
Butterley Brick-Roy Christian.
Forgotten Railways of the East Midland-P Howard Anderson.
Great British tramway Networks-W H Bett and J C Gillham.
Heanor & District Local History Society publication-Two Centuries of Transport in the Heanor Area.
Leyland Bus-Douglas Jack
National Bus Company-John Birks and others.
The origins of Stratford Blue-Chris Taylor.
Trent part one-David Bean.
Tramways of the East Midlands-W H Bett and J C Gillham and the the earlier edition; Tramways of the North Midlands.
Various editions of Buses, Buses Illustrated, Classic Bus, Tramway Review and the Eastwood & Kimberley Advertiser.

The Omnibus Society and The PSV Circle are the enthusiasts organisations who between them provide a great deal information, in particular the various fleet histories which they publish and the library of The Omnibus Society at Ironbridge. Two fleet histories; PE3 and PM13, were invaluable to me. I can recommend these organisations to anyone with an interest in bus operation.

Finally, I would particularly thank Brian King, the Managing Director of the Wellglade group of companies, for writing the Foreword and his encouragement by allowing access to various avenues of research.

Photo Credits

G H F Atkins 3, 42, 44, 45, 48, 64, 66 upper, 67 upper, 68 both lower, 67 top right, lower left, 70 lower, 74 top, 76 top, 77 except bottom right, 82 except top left, 83 both left, 84 both right, 85 lower, 88 top,centre, 89 both lower, 90, 91, 92 not centre, 93, 94, 95, 97 both top, 98 except lower right, 99, 100 top and centre, 101 top and centre, 102 top left and lower right, 104, 105 top and bottom, 106 top left and lower right, 111 lower, 112 ,115 top left, 114 all left, 116 top right.
P Badgery 53, 54, 57, 61, 62, 63, 100 lower, 107 top and lower left, 108 top left, 116 lower left.
D Bean Collection 17, 73 lower, 76 centre,7 8 top left and lower right, 80 lower, 83 right, 87 lower,
P Chambers Collection 71 bottom left, 73 top right and bottom, 88 lower.
R J Butler 56, 106 top right, 108 lower, 110 both top.
J Clarke 96 top right,
J Clarke Collection 4, 24, 35, 41 lower, 65 lower, 67 lower, 68 upper, 69 top right, 72 lower, 76 lower ,85 centre 86 lower right.
A B Cross 103 top right, 106 lower left, 109 top, centre, 117 top left.
W J Haynes 77 bottom right, 86 top.
D. Hudson 28.
A Knighton 71 lower right.
L Little front cover
R Marshall 92 centre, 96 except top right, 97 both lower, 98 lower right, 101 lower left, 103 top left and lower, 108 top right, 110 lower, 111 except lower, 115 top right and lower, 109 lower, 115, 117 lower left, 129.
R Marshall Collection 9 lower, 12, 16, 27, 31, 33, 34, 66 lower, 69 lower right, 70 both top, 74 centre and lower, 75 , 80 centre, 87 centre and lower, 89 top right.
Omnibus Society 84 left, 89 top left.
A F Oxley Collection 9 upper, 10, 11, 14, 15, 18, 19, 20, 25, 30, 38, 39, 41upper, 47, 49, 51, 52, 58, 65 both upper, 71 both top, 72 top left and centre, 73 both top, 78 top right and lower left, 79, 80 top, 81, 82 top left, 85 top right, 86 lower left, 102, 105 centre, 107 lower left, 114 top left 116 top left and lower right, 117 lower right, 130, 131, 132, 133, 134, 136..
R F Mack 102 lower left.

Final note

Anyone retracing the old tram route from Nottingham to Ripley will find very little evidence of its existence, except for the only two places known to the Author; At the playing field on the junction with Stockhill lane and Nuthall Road, Basford, a small embankment follows the line of the track on the old Dark Lane right of way. The last remnant of street furniture is the stub of a tram pole on the east side of the A610 Nottingham Road, Ripley.

The entrance to the Langley Mill premises from Station Road, was the most easterly point of the site, it provided direct access for the trolleybuses on the right, and two petrol pumps refuelled the vehicles upon entry to the site. Photographed are TSM B10A2 No. 45 [RB 3858] with Cowieson coachwork and No. 121 a TSM D60A6 with Weymannn 56 seat highbridge body. No. 121 is possibly still carrying the Notts & Derby fleet name.